WEALTH, POVERTY AND POLITICS

An International Perspective

THOMAS SOWELL

BASIC BOOKS
A Member of the Perseus Books Group
New York

Books published by Basic Books are available at special discounts for bulk
purchases in the United States by corporations, institutions, and other
organizations. For more information, please contact the
Special Markets Department at the Perseus Books Group,
2300 Chestnut Street, Suite 200, Philadelphia, PA 19103,
or call (800) 810-4145, ext. 5000, or e-mail
special.markets@perseusbooks.com.

Library of Congress Control Number: 2015934248

A CIP catalog record for this book is available from the Library of Congress.

ISBN: 978-0-465-08293-3 (hardcover)
ISBN: 978-0-465-07348-1 (e-book)

10 9 8 7 6 5 4 3 2

CONTENTS

I S S U E S

Shocked as we may be today by drastic contrasts between the standards of living in modern industrial nations and the standards of living in Third World countries, such disparities have been common for thousands of years of recorded history. These disparities have extended beyond wealth to the things that create wealth— including the knowledge, skills, habits and discipline that have developed unequally in different geographic, cultural and political settings.

The ancient Greeks had geometry, philosophy, architecture and literature at a time when Britain was a land of illiterate tribal peoples, living at a primitive level. Athens had the Acropolis— whose ruins are still impressive today, thousands of years later— at a time when there was not a single building in all of Britain. The ancient Greeks had Plato, Aristotle, Euclid and other landmark figures who helped lay the intellectual foundations of Western civilization, at a time when there was not a single Briton whose name had entered the pages of history.

Scholars have estimated that there were parts of Europe in ancient times that were living at a level that Greece had transcended thousands of years earlier.[1] There were other complex civilizations in the ancient world— not just in Greece but also in Egypt and China, for example— at a time when peoples in various parts of Europe and elsewhere were just beginning to learn the rudiments of agriculture.[2]

Vast disparities in wealth, and in wealth-creating capacity, have been common for millennia. But while large economic inequalities have persisted throughout the recorded history of the human race, the particular *pattern* of those inequalities has changed drastically over the centuries. While Greeks were far more advanced than Britons in ancient times, Britons were far more advanced than Greeks in the nineteenth century, when Britain led the world into the industrial age.

The Chinese were for centuries more advanced than any of the Europeans, including among their discoveries and inventions the compass, printing, paper, rudders and the porcelain plates that the West called "chinaware" or simply "china." Cast iron was produced in China a thousand years before it was produced in Europe.[3] A Chinese admiral made a voyage of discovery longer than Columbus' voyage, generations before Columbus' voyage, and in ships larger and more advanced than Columbus' ships.[4] But the relative positions of China and Europe also reversed over the centuries. Various other peoples, living in various other parts of the world, have had their own eras of leadership in particular fields or in advances across many specialties.

Agriculture, perhaps the most life-changing advance in the evolution of human societies, came to Europe from the Middle East in ancient times. Agriculture made cities possible, while hunter-gatherers required far too much land to provide themselves with food for them to settle permanently in such compact and densely populated communities. Moreover, for centuries cities around the world have produced a wholly disproportionate share of all the advances in the arts, sciences and technology, compared to the achievements of a similar number of people scattered in the hinterlands.[5]

Because Greeks were located nearer to the Middle East than the peoples of Northern Europe or Western Europe, agriculture spread to the Greeks earlier and they could become urbanized earlier— by centuries— and advanced in many ways far beyond peoples elsewhere who had not yet received the many benefits made possible by urban living. The accident of geographic location could not create genius, but it made possible a setting in which many people could develop their own mental potential far beyond what was possible among bands of hunter-gatherers roaming over vast territory, preoccupied with the pressing need to search for food.

Geography is just one of the influences behind vast economic differences among peoples and places. Moreover, these differences are not simply differences in standards of living, important as such differences are. Different geographic settings also expand or restrict the development of people's own mental potential into what economists call their human capital by presenting different peoples with access to a wider or narrower cultural universe. These geographic settings differ not only horizontally— as between Europe, Asia and Africa, for example— but also vertically, as between peoples of the plains versus peoples living up in the mountains. As one geographic study put it:

> Mountain regions discourage the budding of genius because they are areas of isolation, confinement, remote from the great currents of men and ideas that move along the river valleys.[6]

Many mountain regions around the world— whether the Appalachian Mountains in the United States, the Rif Mountains of Morocco, the Pindus Mountains of Greece, the Himalayas or other mountains elsewhere— show very similar patterns of poverty and backwardness. As distinguished French historian Fernand Braudel put it, "Mountain life persistently lagged behind the plain."[7] This was especially so during the millennia before the transportation and communications revolutions of the past two centuries, which belatedly brought more of the progress of the outside world to isolated mountain villages. What these technological revolutions could not bring to the mountains, however, were the previous centuries of cultural development that other people had in more favorable environments. Peoples living in mountains could try to catch up, but of course the rest of the world would not be standing still while they were doing so.

Mountains are just one geographic feature, and geography is just one influence on human development. But whether considering geography or culture, *isolation* is a recurring factor in poverty and backwardness around the world, whether that is physical isolation or cultural isolation, for any number of particular reasons that will be explored in the chapters ahead.

Whatever the reasons for economic disparities among peoples and nations, such disparities have been as common in modern times as in ancient times. In the twenty-first century, Switzerland, Denmark and Germany have each had more than three times the per capita Gross Domestic Product (GDP) of Albania, Serbia or Ukraine, and Norway has had more than five times the per capita GDP of these latter countries.[8] Such economic disparities are not peculiar to Europe. In Asia as well, Japan has more than three times the per capita GDP of China and more than nine times the per capita GDP of India.[9] Sub-Saharan Africa has less than one-tenth the per capita GDP of the countries of the Euro zone.[10]

Within nations, as well as between nations, income disparities abound, whether between classes, races or other subdivisions of the human species. Reactions to these economic disparities have ranged from resignation to revolution. Because many people regard these disparities in their own country as strange, if not sinister, it is necessary to note that such disparities are not peculiar to any particular time or place. Therefore explanations of economic differences cannot be confined to factors peculiar to a particular time or place, such as modern capitalism or the industrial revolution,* much less to factors that are politically convenient or emotionally satisfying.

Factors which raise morally momentous issues, such as conquest and enslavement, cannot automatically be assumed to be equally

---

* According to the authors of *Why Nations Fail,* "World inequality today exists because during the nineteenth and twentieth centuries some nations were able to take advantage of the Industrial Revolution and the technologies and methods of organization that it brought while others were unable to do so." Daron Acemoglu and James A. Robinson, *Why Nations Fail: The Origins of Power, Prosperity, and Poverty* (New York: Crown Business, 2012), p. 271. But economic inequalities among nations did not begin with the industrial revolution, and the international inequalities of ancient times were by no means necessarily less than the inequalities of today.

momentous as *causal* explanations of current economic disparities. They may be or they may not, in particular cases. Peoples or nations may be rich or poor because (1) they *produced* more or produced less than others or (2) they seized more of what others had produced or had what they produced seized from them. What anyone might prefer to believe at a given place or time has nothing to do with what the hard facts are.

There is no question that the Spaniards' conquests in the Western Hemisphere, for example, not only brutalized the conquered peoples and destroyed viable civilizations, but also drained vast amounts of existing wealth in gold and silver from the Western Hemisphere to Spain— 200 tons of gold and more than 18,000 tons of silver[11]— the result of the looting of existing treasures from the indigenous peoples and the forced labor of that same population in gold and silver mines. Nor was Spain unique in such behavior. But the question here, however, is: To what extent can transfers of wealth explain economic differences between peoples and nations in the world today?

Spain is today one of the poorer countries in Western Europe, surpassed economically by countries like Switzerland and Norway, which have never had comparable empires. The vast wealth that poured into Spain in its "golden age" could have been invested in its economy or in its people. But it was not. It was spent. Spaniards themselves spoke of gold as pouring down on Spain like rain on a roof, flowing on away immediately.[12] Nor has it been uncommon in history for a vast amount of human suffering— whether by conquered or enslaved people— to produce nothing more than a transient enrichment of a ruling elite.

The monumental moral depredations of Spain in the Western Hemisphere had very little causal effect on the long-run prosperity of the Spanish economy. As late as 1900, more than half the people in Spain were still illiterate,[13] while most blacks in the United States were literate, despite having been free for less than 50 years.[14] A century later, in the year 2000, the real per capita income in Spain was slightly lower than the real per capita income of black Americans.[15]

Moral questions and causal questions are both important. But confusing one with the other, or imagining that they can simply be combined into one politically or ideologically attractive package, is not a very promising approach to an explanation of economic differences.

Economic disparities among nations are just part of the story of economic inequalities. Large economic disparities within nations also need to be addressed. When considering economic differences among the people of a given country, there is a tendency to see these differences as issues about what is called "income distribution."[16] But real income— that is, money income adjusted for inflation— consists of the goods and services produced in the nation. To look at this output solely from the viewpoint of those receiving money for having produced those goods and services risks needless misconceptions, and serious social problems growing out of misconceptions.

The standard of living of a nation depends more on its output per capita than on the money received as income for producing that output. Otherwise, government could make us all rich, simply by printing more money. By focusing on what is called "income distribution," many people proceed as if the government can rearrange these flows of money, so as to have incomes become more "fair"— however defined— disregarding what the repercussions of such a policy might be on the more fundamental process of producing goods and services, on which a country's standard of living depends. But in the vision presented in the media, and often even in academia, it is as if output or wealth just exist *somehow*, and the really interesting question is how it is distributed.

Sometimes this preoccupation with the receipt of incomes, to the neglect of attention to the production of the output behind that receipt of incomes, can lead to attempts to explain the receipt of very large incomes by "greed"— as if an insatiable desire for vast amounts of money will somehow cause others to pay those vast amounts for the purchase of one's goods or services.

Among the many possible causes of differences in income and wealth, whether among peoples, regions or nations, one of the most obvious is often ignored. As economist Henry Hazlitt put it:

> The real problem of poverty is not a problem of "distribution" but of production. The poor are poor not because something is being withheld from them but because, for whatever reason, they are not producing enough.[17]

What seemed obvious to Henry Hazlitt was not obvious to many others, who have had alternative visions, with alternative agendas as corollaries of those visions. The difference between seeing economic disparities as due to differences in the *production* of wealth and seeing those disparities as due to the *transfer* of wealth from some people to other people is fundamental.

History shows that either cause of economic disparities can prevail at particular times and places. The approach here will be to seek explanations of disparities in the *production* of wealth, though the transfer of wealth— whether through conquest or enslavement in the past or through the welfare state domestically or foreign aid internationally today— will also be dealt with.

When exploring the influences of geographic, cultural and other factors affecting the production of wealth, a sharp distinction must be made between influence and determinism. At one time, some people based their explanations of economic disparities among peoples and nations on geographic determinism. Places with rich natural resources, for example, were supposed to be more prosperous than places lacking such resources. It was easy enough for critics to show that this was by no means always the case, nor necessarily true in most cases, since there are poverty-stricken countries like Venezuela and Nigeria with rich natural resources and prosperous countries like Japan and Switzerland with very few natural resources. Such results have led to a dismissal, not only of geographic determinism, but also of geography as a major influence in other senses.

Geography, however, influences economic outcomes in other, very different ways. Moreover, this influence is not necessarily due to particular geographic features considered in isolation, but is often due to *interactions* among particular geographic features with other geographic features— as well as interactions with other, *non*-geographic factors such as cultural, demographic, political or other influences.

Even such a simple and undisputed geographic fact as places located nearer the poles having lower temperatures, on average, than places located nearer the equator, does not always hold up when interactions with other geographic factors are taken into account. Thus London, which is hundreds of miles farther north than Boston, has average winter temperatures warmer than those in Boston, and very similar to winter temperatures in American cities hundreds of miles *south* of Boston.[18] The average December daily high temperature in London is the same as the average December daily high temperature in Washington, D.C., which is more than 850 miles farther south than London. The average daily low temperature in Washington is slightly lower than in London for every month from December through March.[19] Latitude matters, but so too does the varying warmth of different ocean currents,* and the interaction of the two can create very different outcomes from what either would produce by itself.

When particular geographic factors interact with other, *non*-geographic factors as well, the outcomes can likewise be very different from what they would be if considering particular geographic, cultural, demographic or political factors in isolation. That is why *influence* is not the same as *determinism*. Since many, if not most, economic outcomes depend on more than one factor, the likelihood of all the various factors coming together in such a way as to produce equal levels of prosperity and progress among peoples and

---

* The Gulf Stream, originating in the subtropical waters of the Gulf of Mexico, flows northeastward through the Atlantic Ocean past the British Isles, creating milder winters in Western Europe than at the same latitudes in Eastern Europe, Asia or North America.

nations around the world seems very remote. Radically different geographic settings are just one of the factors making equal economic outcomes unlikely.

Cultures are another factor that differs greatly among peoples and nations, as well as among individuals and groups within a given nation. Like critics of geographic influences, critics of cultural influences have likewise sometimes resorted to an oversimplified picture of these influences. For example, an attempt to discredit the influence of cultural factors in economic outcomes by a well-known study— *Why Nations Fail*— rejected the idea that the culture inherited from England explained why former colonies of England like the United States, Canada and Australia were prosperous:

> Canada and the United States were English colonies, but so were Sierra Leone and Nigeria. The variation in prosperity within former English colonies is as great as that in the entire world. The English legacy is not the reason for the success of North America.[20]

While it is true that all these countries are former colonies of England, and thus might be described as having been influenced by the culture of England, it is also true that the people who founded Canada and the United States were Englishmen, descendants of people steeped in the culture of England as it unfolded over the centuries— while people in Sierra Leone and Nigeria were descendants of people steeped in the very different cultures of a region of sub-Saharan Africa for many centuries, and exposed to the culture of England for less than one century, during which their own indigenous cultures were by no means extinguished during the historically brief period when they were part of the British Empire.

Many former English colonies populated by non-English peoples continued to observe some aspect of the culture of England after becoming independent— lawyers wearing wigs in court, for example— but these outward observances of English traditions did not prevent these former colonies from having a fundamentally very different cultural legacy from that of England and a very different economic and political experience going forward after independence.

Believers in genetic determinism likewise seek to discredit cultural factors, which compete with their view that it is innate differences in intelligence among individuals and groups which explain differences in economic disparities among races, nations and civilizations. But genetic determinism, based on undeniable contemporary differences in various kinds of achievements and mental test scores,[21] cannot explain equally undeniable radical changes in which particular races, nations or civilizations have been far ahead and which have been far behind in different periods of history— the British and the Greeks being just one example of role reversals out of many.

Nations which went from being poor and backward to reaching the front ranks of human achievement in a century— Scotland, beginning in the eighteenth century and Japan, beginning in the nineteenth century, for example— have changed faster than genetic makeup seems likely to change, and in fact with no indication of any genetic changes at all, though there are many indications of cultural changes in both these cases. Researchers may be frustrated by the fact that the origins of particular cultures may be lost in the mists of time, though their contemporary manifestations are visible. Culture also does not readily lend itself to quantification, as a contemporary genetic determinist has pointed out,[22] or to statistical analysis that can show such things as correlations between IQ and Gross Domestic Product, lending an air of scientific precision. But, as statisticians have often pointed out, correlation is not causation. And, as was said long ago, "It is better to be roughly right than precisely wrong."[23]

Whether considering cultural, geographic, political or other factors, *interactions* of these factors are part of the reason why understanding influences is very different from claiming determinism.

Chapter 2

GEOGRAPHIC FACTORS

The world has never been a level playing field, and everything costs.

David S. Landes[1]

It is obvious that peoples around the world have lived and developed over the millennia in different geographic settings. What is not so obvious is how much those settings have differed from one another, and the economic and social consequences of those differences. *Geography is not egalitarian.*

Geographic features are not even approximately equal in different regions of the world. The disparities in geographic settings, and in the phenomena which arise from those settings, are at least as great as the income disparities that many people find so surprising. For example, far more tornadoes occur in the middle of the United States than in any other country, or in all of the other countries of the world combined.[2] Most of the geysers in the world are in Yellowstone National Park.[3] Earthquakes are as common around the rim of the Pacific— in both Asia and the Western Hemisphere— as they are rare around the rim of the Atlantic.[4]

These natural phenomena are simply illustrations of disparities in the physical effects of great variations in geographic conditions. But there are also major economic and social effects of other disparities in geographically based phenomena. The very land that people stand on is not the same in different places. Highly fertile soils that scientists call mollisols are neither evenly nor randomly distributed around the world. Such soils are found almost exclusively in the temperate zones of the Northern and Southern Hemispheres, and are scattered very unevenly there, but are virtually non-existent in the tropics.[5]

This was especially important during the ages when agriculture was the most prevalent and most important of human economic activities— which is to say, for thousands of years, except for some more fortunate regions within the most recent centuries. The economies and cultures that evolved during those millennia did so within very different economic limits in different geographic settings.

The economic effects of geographic differences are both direct, affecting standards of living, and indirect, affecting the development of peoples themselves, depending on whether a given geographic setting facilitates or impedes their communication and interactions with the rest of the human race. No society has had a monopoly on the discoveries and inventions that have advanced human beings, so for a given set of people— whether a class, a race or a nation— to be in touch with what other peoples around the world are doing has been a major advantage.

A larger cultural universe is important not simply because of the products, technologies and knowledge that are transferred— important as these are— but also, and perhaps equally or more important, because people seeing repeatedly how things have been done differently by others in different places can break through the normal human inertia that keeps people doing the same things in the same familiar ways, for generations or even centuries, as happens in many geographically isolated societies. It has been said that "intellectual force" is something that "feeds upon the nutritious food of wide comparisons."[6]

Conversely, isolation tends to have the opposite effect. When the Spaniards discovered the isolated Canary Islands in the fifteenth century, they found the people there living much as people had lived in the stone age.[7] Similarly when the British discovered the isolated Australian aborigines in the eighteenth century.[8] In other isolated settings as well, whether in distant mountain villages or deep in tropical jungles, peoples have been found living as others had lived in earlier centuries or millennia.[9]

Deserts are another geographic factor isolating peoples. The largest of the world's deserts by far is the Sahara Desert, which is a negative factor for the peoples of North Africa but a devastating handicap for the peoples to the south, black Africans in tropical, sub-Saharan Africa. This incomparably vast desert— slightly larger than the 48 contiguous states of the United States[10]— has been for centuries the largest single factor isolating the peoples of sub-Saharan Africa from the rest of the world. The dearth of good harbors in tropical Africa also limited contacts with overseas cultures. As Fernand Braudel put it, "external influence filtered only very slowly, drop by drop, into the vast African continent South of the Sahara."[11]

Despite geographic influences, there can be no geographic *determinism* because, where peoples are in touch with other peoples, even an unchanging geographic setting interacts with changing human knowledge and differing human cultures that have different values and aspirations, producing very different outcomes at different times and places. Most of what are natural resources for us today were not natural resources for the cave man, who had not yet acquired the knowledge of how these things could be used for his own purposes. There have been vast deposits of petroleum in the Middle East from time immemorial. But it was only after science and technology had advanced to a level that created industrial nations elsewhere that the Middle East's oil became a valuable asset, profoundly changing life in both the Middle East and in the industrial countries.

Individual geographic influences cannot be considered in isolation, since their *interactions* crucially affect outcomes. The relationship between rainfall and soil is just one example of these interactions. Not only does rainfall vary greatly from one place to another, so does the ability of the soil to hold the water that rains down on it. This crucial ability to hold water is much less in the limestone soils of the Balkans than in the loess soils of northern China. Since climate and soil affect how well different crops can be grown in different places, that has virtually precluded equal prosperity in all regions of the world during the millennia when agriculture was the most important economic activity around the world, and the basis for the urban development of different societies and peoples.

As with many other things, the ability of land to hold water is a benefit only within some given range of variation. Back in Roman times, the very flat lands of northwestern Europe, located in an area of plentiful rainfall, resulted in many swamps and swampy places, which were major impediments to agriculture. Only after centuries of development and application of drainage techniques did much of this land become fertile.[12] Fertility is not always something inherent and immutable. The development of drainage and irrigation techniques, or of plows that can be harnessed to horses or oxen to plow heavy soils, greatly affects their fertility. It was the *interaction* of the soil, rainfall and changing human knowledge and technology over time that made the lands of northwestern Europe *become* very fertile.

What this means more generally is that the possible combinations and permutations of geographic factors greatly exceed the number of factors considered separately, especially when combined with changing human knowledge over time. Therefore the large number of possible economic and other outcomes in differing geographic settings makes equal outcomes for different regions and peoples around the world even less likely than a separate enumeration of geographic differences might suggest. There has been nothing resembling equal opportunities to become equally productive among the tribal, racial or national groups that developed for thousands of years in different parts of the world and evolved their respective cultures in different geographic settings.

Not only have equal economic outcomes been rare to non-existent, the particular patterns of inequality in one era have differed greatly from the particular patterns of inequality in another era.

The vast superiority of ancient Greek society to that in ancient Britain reflected Greece's geographic advantage in being located near the Middle East, where agriculture developed and spread into nearby southeastern Europe, centuries before it spread to all of Europe and beyond. Without agriculture, it is difficult, if not virtually impossible, to have densely populated urban societies, as distinguished from societies of wandering hunters and gatherers, or herders— all of whom require vast amounts of land on which to roam, in order to get enough food to sustain a given number of people.

To the present day, cities have remained the sources of much, if not most, of the advancements in civilization. Far more of these advances, and especially of landmark scientific and technological achievements, have occurred among the populations of cities than among a similar number of people living in other settings.[13] Peoples without the geographic prerequisites for cities have long lagged behind peoples in settings that facilitated urbanization. Cities developed relatively late in the existence of the human species— and so did most of the advances in what we today recognize as civilization. By making cities possible, agriculture made possible the great industrial, medical and other advances that flourished in urban environments.

Modern advances in transportation and communication can break through the isolation of many peoples, just as other technological advances can mitigate, or sometimes even eliminate, the handicaps of various other kinds of geographic impediments to economic and social development. But what these historically recent advances cannot do is retroactively erase the effects of thousands of years of different cultural development that took place where there were serious geographic restrictions, as compared to places inhabited by peoples with millennia of experiences enriched by wider exposures to the achievements and ideas of other peoples around the world.

How we define the concept of environment is crucial. One distinguished geographer's definition was, "Environment is the total physical setting amid which people live."[14] But another geographer said, "environment means something more than local geographic conditions," and called for a "larger conception of environment,"[15] pointing out how the past experiences of forebears "have left their mark on the present race in the form of inherited aptitudes and traditional customs acquired in those remote ancestral habitats."[16] Whether an environment is described geographically or socioeconomically, the most fundamental distinction is between defining environment as what is *around* a given people and defining environment to include also what is *within* those people.

We cannot understand what is happening today without understanding past conditions that shaped both the physical and mental worlds of people living today, which are a legacy of the past, for better or worse. As one cultural historian put it, "men are not blank tablets upon which the environment inscribes a culture which can readily be erased to make way for a new inscription."[17] As another noted historian put it: "We do not live in the past, but the past in us."[18]

Against this general background, we can now examine in more detail the influences of such geographic factors as waterways, mountains and flora and fauna. Geographic location, as such, is also a factor whose influence is worth noting, quite aside from the particular geographic features of a particular location.

WATERWAYS

Waterways play many vital roles— as drinking water for humans and animals, as sources of food such as fish and other aquatic creatures, as sources of irrigation for crops and as arteries of transportation for cargo and people. In all these roles, waterways differ from one another, in ways that can make them more valuable or less valuable to humans.

Waterways obviously differ in kind— from rivers to lakes, harbors and seas— and each kind in turn has its own internal differences, in navigability for example. Rivers flowing gently across wide level plains, as in Western Europe, are far more usable, for both commerce and the transportation of people, than rivers plunging down from great heights through rapids, cascades and waterfalls, as in most of sub-Saharan Africa. Indeed, the same stream of water can differ at different places along its route to the sea:

> A torrent that issues from its source in the mountains is not the river which reaches the sea. On its long journey from highland to lowland it receives now the milky waters of a glacier-fed stream, now a muddy tributary from agricultural lands, now the clear waters from a limestone plateau, while all the time its racing current bears a burden of soil torn from its own banks.[19]

Although the most indispensable role of waterways has been to provide drinking water for humans and animals, without which they cannot survive, one of the most important roles of waterways for economic development has been their role as transportation arteries. The crucial fact about the role of waterways as transportation arteries for cargo and people is the vast difference in cost between land transport and water transport, which was even greater in the millennia before the advent of motorized land transport, less than two centuries ago.

In 1830, for example, it cost more than 30 dollars to move a ton of cargo 300 miles on land but only 10 dollars to ship it 3,000 miles across the Atlantic Ocean.[20] One consequence of such transportation cost differentials was that people living in the city of Tiflis in the Caucasus, 341 miles from the Baku oil fields by land, bought oil imported from America, 8,000 miles away by water.[21] Similarly in mid-nineteenth century America, before the transcontinental railroad was built, San Francisco could be reached both faster and cheaper across the Pacific Ocean from a port in China than it could be reached over land from the banks of the Missouri River.[22]

Given the vast amounts of food, fuel and other necessities of life that must be transported into cities, and the vast amounts of a city's output that must be transported out to sell, there is no mystery why so many cities around the world have been located on navigable waterways, especially before the transportation revolutions within the past 200 years that produced motorized transport on land.

Even in the twentieth century, the differential cost of land transport and water transport did not disappear. In twentieth century

Africa, the estimated cost of shipping an automobile by land from Djibouti to Addis Ababa (342 miles) was the same as the cost of shipping it by water from Detroit to Djibouti (7,386 miles).[23]

Looked at differently, where there has been a lack of navigable waterways, accessibility to the outside world has often been severely limited, shrinking the cultural universe drastically— and with it shrinking the opportunities of peoples to connect with other peoples and cultures far away. In some cases, a dearth of waterways and the presence of geographic barriers meant that people living only 10 or 20 miles from each other often had very little contact. This was especially so in places lacking horses, camels or other beasts of burden, during the many centuries before modern transportation and communications developed.

One of the remarkable facts about the continent of Africa is that, although Africa is more than twice the size of Europe, the African coastline is shorter than the European coastline.[24] This is possible only because the European coastline twists and turns, creating many harbors where ships can dock, sheltered from the rough waters of the open seas. Moreover, the coastline of Europe is increased by the many islands and peninsulas that make up more than one-third of that continent's total land area.

By contrast, the African coastline is smooth, with few substantial indentations, few good natural harbors, and fewer islands and peninsulas— which make up only 2 percent of Africa's land area. Moreover, coastal waters around sub-Saharan Africa are often too shallow for ocean-going ships to dock.[25] In such places, large ocean-going ships must anchor offshore, and have their cargoes unloaded onto smaller vessels that can operate in shallow waters. But this time-consuming process, and the greater amount of labor and equipment required, is more costly— often prohibitively costly. For centuries, seaborne commerce between Europe and Asia sailed around Africa, and seldom stopped.

Even in those few places where large ships can enter Africa on deep rivers, tropical Africa's coasts have narrow coastal plains that often end abruptly against escarpments.[26] One important consequence of this shape of the land is that, even in places where ships can enter the continent on African rivers, they can seldom get very far inland before being confronted with cascades and waterfalls. For the same reason, boats coming from the vast interior of the continent are seldom able to continue out to the open sea, as boats— and even large ships— can do in various places on the Eurasian landmass or in parts of the Western Hemisphere.

By contrast with Africa, China has had a huge network of navigable waterways, described as "unique in the world," formed by the Yangtze River and its tributaries, as well as an indented coastline, full of harbors.[27] What was also unique were the centuries during which China was the most advanced nation in the world, on into what were called the Middle Ages in Europe.

It was not just in harbors, but also in rivers, that China's waterways have contrasted with those in Africa. Africa is a dry continent, with many of its rivers not deep enough to carry the large ships with heavy loads that are carried on the rivers of China, Western Europe or the United States. Even the Nile was unable to carry the largest ships in the days of the Roman Empire,[28] much less the even larger ships of today.

The *average* depth of a river is not as important as its *minimum* depth on the route of a given vessel's journey, which is what determines how far a boat or ship of a given size and weight can go. The same word— "navigable"— may be applied to many very different waterways, but with very different meanings in specific, concrete circumstances. Although the St. Lawrence Seaway is navigable by ocean-going ships, all the way into the Great Lakes, that does not mean that it is navigable by *all* ocean-going ships. When major, man-made improvements were made to the Seaway in 1959, and for many years thereafter, it was navigable by most of the ocean-going ships in the world but, as such ships grew larger and larger over the years, today it is no longer navigable by most ocean-going ships, though it is still navigable by many.[29]

The Zambezi River in Africa has highly variable depths from place to place and from rainy season to dry season. In some times and places the Zambezi is barely navigable by boats requiring just 3 feet of water, though at other times and places the water level is 20 feet deeper.[30] Some rivers in Angola can support boats requiring no more than 8 feet of water.[31] During the dry season, even a major West African river like the Niger can carry barges weighing no more than 12 tons.[32] But, in China, ships weighing 10,000 tons have been able to go hundreds of miles up the Yangtze River, and smaller vessels another thousand miles beyond that.[33]

Rivers in tropical Africa are seldom continuously navigable for any such distances, even when these rivers have ample water. In terms of the contours of the land, sub-Saharan Africa has been characterized as "cursed with a mesa form which converts nearly every river into a plunging torrent on its approach to the sea."[34]

Most of tropical Africa is more than 1,000 feet above sea level and much of it is more than 2,000 feet above sea level. Thus the Zaire River begins at an altitude of 4,700 feet and so must come down that vertical distance before flowing out into the Atlantic Ocean, creating rapids, cascades and waterfalls on the way. Although the Zaire has more water than the Mississippi, the Yangtze or the Rhine, that does not make it the equivalent of these and other major commercial waterways elsewhere, because the Zaire's many plunges interrupt its navigability, though it may carry extensive inland traffic for various distances on level stretches. This pattern is common among the rivers of sub-Saharan Africa.

Another pattern that is common in tropical Africa is a wide fluctuation in the water level of its rivers, due to highly varying rainfall amounts in different seasons. Unlike Western Europe, where the rain falls more or less evenly throughout the year,[35] rainfall patterns in sub-Saharan Africa include long periods when there is no rain at all, followed by torrential downpours during rainy seasons.[36] Because of such seasonal rainfall patterns, the Niger River's chief tributary, the Benue River, has in places been navigable only two months of the year. This has led to a hectic shipping pattern:

If they let the craft stay up the Benue a day too long, the vessels will be stuck on sandbanks for ten months! Yet if through caution or misinformation they withdraw the fleet too soon, much valuable merchandise is left behind and can only be evacuated by land at much greater cost. . . The first boats to go in are the commercial canoes, then follow the larger craft, and finally, when there is sufficient water at Lokoja, the largest power-craft and their barges sail up the river as fast as possible. Towards the end of the short season, the large craft have to come out first because of the fall in the level of the water; the medium-sized craft follow, and the small canoes may continue for some time evacuating small quantities of produce.[37]

Statistics on how many miles of navigable rivers there are in Africa can be very misleading when these are not *continuous* miles that a vessel of a given size and weight can travel before encountering water too shallow to support it, or encountering cascades or waterfalls that stop all vessels. Sometimes a canoe can go ashore and be emptied of its cargo before reaching a waterfall, with both the canoe and the cargo then being carried around the waterfall, so that the reloaded canoe can proceed on another level stretch of water. However, this is both a time-consuming— and therefore expensive— process, and one that limits the size of both the canoe and its cargo. The net result is that only a cargo that is very valuable in proportion to its size and weight is economically feasible to transport in such places.

By contrast, in other parts of the world, where rivers are continuously navigable for hundreds of miles across level plains, as in various places on the Eurasian landmass or in the Western Hemisphere, bulky cargoes with relatively low value in proportion to their size and weight— wood, coal or wheat, for example— may be economically viable to transport long distances by water.

Even within the same continent, Western Europe's rivers have been very different from the rivers in Eastern Europe or Southern Europe, as well as radically different from the rivers of sub-Saharan Africa. A broad coastal plain, where the land nowhere reaches 1,000 feet above sea level, means that Western Europe has had slow-flowing rivers, which were especially valuable in the long ages before power boats could readily go against the flow of swift-moving currents. In many places during that era, logs for example could be floated down a river, even when the only way for people in charge of those logs to return home was by land.*

Western Europe's rivers often lead out into the open seas, providing access to seaports around the world. But most rivers in Eastern Europe and Southern Europe are quite different, in ways that affect both economic activity and the size of the cultural universe available to the peoples living in the regions through which these rivers flow. Because the warming effect of the Gulf Stream on the climate of Western Europe is lessened the farther east one goes, the waterways of Eastern Europe are frozen more often, and longer, in the winters.

Even when the rivers of Eastern Europe are flowing, often they are flowing into lakes or inland seas, rather than out into the open seas that connect with the rest of the world. The waters of the Danube, the Don and the Dnieper flow into the Black Sea, for example, and the waters of the Volga flow into the Caspian Sea. But most of the water in Russian rivers flows into the Arctic Ocean, which is hardly as accessible to the rest of the world as are the Atlantic or the Pacific. These differences in waterways are among the many reasons why Eastern Europe has lagged economically behind Western Europe for centuries.

The rivers of Southern Europe have contributed even less to the economic development of that region, partly because there are fewer major rivers than in Western Europe or Eastern Europe, and partly because the climate in the lands of Mediterranean Europe is one with torrential downpours in winter and very little rain in the summer, when rivers almost dry up. In the mountainous Balkans, rivers often flow too steeply to be navigable, except for some that are locally navigable by small boats and rafts.[38]

In the Western Hemisphere, the United States has had huge geographic advantages in its waterways, as in other ways— "a well-

---

* In the United States as well, "the steamboat changed the Mississippi from a one-way artery of traffic" to one in which, after 1815, a steamboat could go back up the river from New Orleans to Louisville. Rupert B. Vance, *Human Geography of the South*, p. 264.

indented coastline punctuated by superb harbors," in the words of distinguished economic historian David S. Landes,[39] and large rivers, of which the Mississippi is the most impressive. In contrast to the plunging waters of many African rivers— more than thirty cataracts, falling a total of nearly a thousand feet in a distance of 150 miles on the Zaire River[40]— the riverbed of the Mississippi slopes downward at a rate of 4 inches per mile.[41] Although the Nile is the longest river in the world, the Mississippi pours many times as much water into the Gulf of Mexico as the Nile pours into the Mediterranean.[42] Water is what rivers are all about, and the Mississippi has far more of it than the Nile, even though the smaller amount of water in the Nile is stretched out over a longer distance.

In contrast to the limited ability of the Nile to carry large ships, the Hudson River and the harbors at San Francisco and San Diego are all deep enough for aircraft carriers to dock right up against the land. The Great Lakes are a vast system of connected waterways, of which Lake Michigan alone is larger than the nation of Israel, and Lake Superior is larger than Lake Michigan. These lakes are also deep enough to handle many ocean-going ships, as they have since 1959, when man-made improvements to the St. Lawrence River allowed such ships to extend their journeys from the Atlantic Ocean all the way to Chicago and other midwestern cities on the Great Lakes.

As a noted geographer put it:

> No other equally large area of the earth is so generously equipped by nature for the production and distribution of the articles of commerce as southern Canada and that part of the United States lying east of the Rocky Mountains. The simple build of the North American continent, consisting of a broad central trough between distant mountain ranges, and characterized by gentle slopes to the Atlantic Ocean and the Gulf of Mexico, has generated great and small rivers with easy-going currents, that everywhere opened up the land to explorer, trader and settler.[43]

Waterways differ not only physically from place to place but also in their human significance from one time period to another. The Mediterranean Sea, for example, was for centuries a more inviting waterway than the Atlantic Ocean before there were later advances in knowledge, because of the ease of navigating around the Mediterranean:

> The long summer of cloudless days and starry nights, of steady winds and fogless atmosphere provided a favorable season for sailing, when the strong diurnal breezes favored the out-going and home-coming ships, and the countless promontories and mountainous islands, visible in the lucid air, furnished points to steer by before the invention of the compass.[44]

Oceans changed from being transportation barriers to being transportation avenues only after humans learned how to navigate where there were no landmarks to follow, but simply water to be seen in all directions, all the way out to the horizon. Navigation on the oceans became possible only after science, mathematics and technology had developed sufficiently to overcome this fundamental handicap— first through various ways of using the position of the sun in the sky during the day and the positions of stars at night, providing as it were "landmarks" in the sky by which to determine directions on the ocean— and, eventually and decisively, developing the magnetic compass, which could be used more readily, and even when clouds obscured the sky.

Seaports around the gentle waters of the Mediterranean were for centuries more busy than seaports on the more turbulent Atlantic coast of Europe, before Europeans discovered the Western Hemisphere. This changed the main direction of Europe's international trade. Because different kinds of ships were required to handle the very different rough waters of the Atlantic, the leading commercial and naval powers of the Mediterranean were eclipsed by the leading commercial and naval powers of the Atlantic, who had ships better adapted for the new transatlantic commerce. The seas had not changed, but their economic and other significance had, with the advance of knowledge and technology.

Despite the crucial importance of agriculture as a source of a dependable food supply for a concentrated and sedentary population, fishing has been another source, and one available in regions where agriculture has not been sufficiently productive to sustain human life by itself. This has been especially important in very cold climates.[45]

In other climates as well, fishing can be a major economic activity. It was said at one time that Amsterdam was built on herring,[46] and fishing has also been important to the economy of Japan, among other places. However, agriculture may not be as productive in tropical lands where the fertility of the soil is often poor, as in the Amazon jungles, where there are many fishing villages.

Fishing villages represent a step upward from a hunter-gathering society to a sedentary life, even though these villages may not represent the same degree of population concentration as cities fed by agriculture. However, commercial fishing, supplying a market reaching far beyond the local area, can be a major contributor to the development of cities.[47] In some of the lands around the Mediterranean, the soil yields so little in agriculture that many people have had to piece together a livelihood by combining the products of both the land and the sea, as others in that region have by combining agriculture and herding animals.[48]

Fishing opportunities, however, are no more evenly distributed around the world than other opportunities. A long continental shelf reaching out into the Atlantic Ocean creates an underwater environment where fish and other marine life can flourish.[49] But the land is shaped differently around and under the Mediterranean Sea,[50] which lacks the shallow shelves of the Atlantic.[51]

As a result, while there has long been fishing in the Mediterranean, it has not been comparable to the rich fishing regions that attract commercial fishing vessels great distances to the Atlantic waters near Newfoundland and Iceland, or into the North Sea fishing grounds.[52] The net result in the early twentieth century was that an Italian fisherman's earnings averaged about one-fourth the earnings of a French fisherman and one-eighth those of an English fisherman. Nor was this due to differences in the price of fish, which was no higher in France or England than in Italy.[53]

While waterways have played major roles in the economic and social development of many regions of the world, these roles have often been due to *interactions* of waterways with other geographic and non-geographic factors, rather than being based on the nature of the waterways alone. South America's Amazon River, for example, is by far the most physically impressive of the world's rivers, in terms of its volume of water— the largest of any river in the world— its navigability* and its length, which is nearly as long as that of the Nile, while the Amazon empties dozens of times more water into the Atlantic than the Nile empties into the Mediterranean.[54] It also empties several times as much water as the Mississippi empties into the Gulf of Mexico.

Nevertheless, the region through which the Amazon flows, with its jungles and poor quality soils, has had no such economic development as would make the Amazon at all comparable, as an artery of commerce, to the Mississippi, the Rhine, the Danube or other rivers that, put together, do not have as much water as the Amazon. Conversely, a very modest-sized river like the Thames, less than 10 percent as long as the Amazon, plays a major economic role as the shipping outlet for a land of thriving industry and commerce. In Russia, the Yenisey and the Lena rivers each have more than twice as much water as the Volga, but it is the Volga that carries more shipping tonnage than any other Russian river, because it flows through regions containing most of the nation's population and most of its industry and farmland.

What these differences between waterways, and within a given kind of waterway, mean for their human consequences is that the possible combinations and permutations of the factors that make them useful to humans are so numerous as to make equal values of waterways to human beings located in different parts of the world very unlikely, quite aside from the fact that waterways are more available in some regions of the world than in others, and are virtually non-existent in deserts.

---

* "If the Amazon flowed through North America, an ocean freighter could sail from Boston to Denver." Jonathan B. Tourtellot, "The Amazon: Sailing a Jungle Sea," *Great Rivers of the World*, edited by Margaret Sedeen, p. 299.

LAND AND CLIMATE

Land has many aspects. The simple fact of the shape of the land determines how water will flow, and that in turn has major implications for the fate of people living in a given region. The physical and chemical composition of the soil is crucial for agriculture, as is climate. Special features of the land, such as mountains, deserts and rift valleys, can fragment a population and isolate the fragments from each other. This has been the fate of much of the Balkans, of sub-Saharan Africa and of mountain communities in many countries around the world.

Mountains

Mountains affect both the lives of people living in those mountains and the lives of people living on the land below— and it affects these two sets of people very differently.

About 10 to 12 percent of the world's population lives in mountains, about half in Asia, and about 90 percent live no higher in the mountains than 2,500 meters or 8,200 feet. Population density in mountains is usually relatively low.[55] Certain common patterns have appeared in the lives of people living in various mountain communities around the world, whether the Appalachian Mountains in the United States, the Rif Mountains of Morocco, the Pindus Mountains of Greece, or the Himalayas in Asia. The most common of these patterns have included poverty, isolation and backwardness.[56] Nor is it hard to see why. The very nature of mountains long denied the people living there many of the things that promote prosperity and connection with the general progress in the rest of the world.

Fertile land can seldom be found on mountainsides, where soil is readily washed away by rain, though some of this soil collects down in mountain valleys, while the rest of it is washed away down into the lowlands. People tend to gather in the flat areas of land in the valleys amid the mountains, since this is where crops can be grown most readily. But mountain valleys are often isolated from each other, with "the population being as scattered as the flat lands they occupy," as was said of mountain communities in the Southern mountains in the United States,[57] though the same pattern has existed elsewhere around the world. The amount of usable soil in each valley tends to limit the number of people who can be fed there, so that small villages have often been the norm. These villages may be isolated from each other, as well as being isolated from the outside world, even when these villages are not far from each other as the crow flies, but are not very accessible to each other across rough mountain terrain.[58]

These historic handicaps were especially severe during the millennia before modern transportation and communications technologies were created. However, these technological advances have almost invariably originated outside the mountains themselves, and the extent to which they have been adopted has varied with local geographic and economic conditions. Moreover, even where these advances have been adopted extensively, that cannot undo the effects of previous centuries of cultural isolation.

Navigable waterways are often lacking in mountain terrain, where the steepness of the land makes for rapids, cascades and waterfalls, so this means of transportation and communication has often been denied to people in many mountain communities, such as in the Balkans.[59] Land transportation is also likely to be difficult, especially where the rugged terrain is inhospitable to wheeled vehicles, so that travel on foot is the only feasible way to get around in many places. Distinguished historian Fernand Braudel pointed out that "in 1881 the wheeled vehicle was still unknown in Morocco."[60] As another scholar said of people in the Rif Mountains of Morocco, "The Rifians are great walkers and they have to be."[61]

Although such patterns may be general, there are also exceptions. Parts of the Himalayas and the Andes, for example, have fertile and well-watered land.[62] The Alps have numerous mountain passes[63] broad enough to accommodate much commercial traffic and, in ancient times, Hannibal's army with its elephants.

Building roads— not to mention water systems, sewage systems, or electric power systems— can be extremely expensive where isolated and thinly populated mountain communities mean very high costs per capita for creating such infrastructure. In Italy's Apennines Mountains, as late as 1860, there were no roads whatever in 91 out of 123 Lucanian villages.[64] Even in the twentieth century, there were places in the Pindus Mountains of Greece more accessible to mules and to people on foot than to wheeled vehicles, and one village acquired electricity as late as 1956.[65]

As a study of mountains around the Mediterranean in the late twentieth century noted, "Only a few roads penetrate the Pindus today, and most of those are of recent construction. The great majority are unpaved."[66] Substandard infrastructure remains common in mountains around the world, even in the twenty-first century.[67] However, modern transportation and communications technologies are making inroads into the isolation of many mountain communities,[68] though with great differences among different regions of the world. Switzerland, for example, has more than 20 times as many miles of road per capita as in Ethiopia.[69]

Distinguished American scholar Edward C. Banfield's classic account of an Italian mountain village where he lived in 1954 and 1955, *The Moral Basis of a Backward Society*, noted that there was only one telephone in town. In this community of 3,400 people, to which he gave the pseudonym "Montegrano," there were five automobiles for hire but no one owned a private car. Most of the people were poor farmers and laborers. One-third of the men and two-thirds of the women could neither read nor write, and some peasants had never gone beyond the next village, just four miles away.[70] When they traveled, they seldom used a cart, much less a car, to transport the belongings they took with them. As Professor Banfield noted:

> When the farm people of Montegrano travel, it is on foot leading a donkey to the sides of which large baskets are fixed . . .The range of travel, then, is limited to nearby towns. Many people have never travelled beyond these neighboring towns and some women have never left Montegrano.[71]

It was not only infrastructure and technological advances that reached mountain communities belatedly. So did cultures prevailing on the plains below. Although Islam has for centuries been the prevailing religion and culture of the Middle East and North Africa, a different religion and culture continued to prevail in the neighboring mountainous regions of Armenia and Abyssinia. And though people in the Rif Mountains of Morocco eventually adopted Islam, this was centuries after the people on the land below had already become Muslims.[72]

Language likewise moved slowly up from the lowlands to the highlands. Gaelic continued to survive in the Scottish highlands long after the Scottish lowlanders were speaking English, and the Vlach language survived in the Pindus Mountains of Greece centuries after people on the land below were speaking Greek.[73] Language differences have added to the sources of isolation in the mountains, especially when the languages or dialects spoken in the mountains were unknown in most of the outside world. Of the more than one thousand languages in New Guinea, more than 70 percent originate in the mountainous regions, which cover only one-third of the island.[74] A multiplicity of languages and dialects has been common in isolated mountain communities around the world.[75]

Law and order are yet another part of the social infrastructure that has been harder to establish and maintain in many mountain regions. Even mountains nominally under the control of a nation or empire have not always or in all places been effectively under such control. Examples include the mountains of Montenegro under the Ottoman Empire, the Rif Mountains under Moroccan sultans, and the uplands of India under the Mughal rulers.[76] Both the Scottish highlands and the highlands of colonial Ceylon remained independent for many years after their respective nearby lowlands were conquered and incorporated into another cultural universe. In centuries past, it was common in many mountain regions around the world for the highland people to raid and plunder the more prosperous people in the lowlands.[77]

Poverty in many mountain communities long exceeded anything known as poverty in most other settings. As Professor Banfield said of the Italian mountain village in which he lived in 1954 and 1955:

> Most people in Montegrano are desperately poor. Many have nothing to eat but bread, and not enough of that. Even the well-to-do are poor by American standards. Such a town cannot support a newspaper or the kinds of activity which a newspaper would report.[78]

Such poverty in the mountains was not unique to this Italian village. A twentieth century Oxford scholar in Greece said, "I have met a Greek, brought up in this century in a mountain village, who had never seen an olive (or a fish or an orange) until he was 12 years old."[79]

In various mountains in countries around the Mediterranean, it was long common in the past for peasants to rarely eat meat, and even cheese was largely confined to a few fortunately situated villages.[80] Bread was the common food for peasants in all three meals of the day. In earlier times, women made clothes for their families, and mountain people with animals brought those animals inside in cold weather. As a landmark history of Western civilization put it: "Only the most prosperous had wooden dividers separating the human from animal quarters."[81] A traveler through the Bulgarian mountains in 1574 said that he preferred to sleep outdoors, under a tree, rather than in mountain peasants' huts, where animals and people lived together "in such filth that we could not bear the stench."[82]

These broad generalizations do not, of course, apply to every mountain community everywhere. But the general pattern has been all too true in all too many mountains and highlands around the world, especially in centuries past. A twentieth century study of a village in the Himalayas found that 20 percent of newborn babies died before they were a year old.[83] Even in prosperous America, in the early twentieth century a sample of farmers in North Carolina showed that those located in the coastal plains earned three to five times the income of farmers in mountain counties.[84]

An Appalachian county in Kentucky was called a "pauper county" in the 1890s, and was still in 2010 one of the poorest counties in the United States.[85] The life expectancy of a man in that county was less than the life expectancy of a man in Fairfax County, Virginia *by more than a decade*. Women's life expectancy in that same Kentucky county had actually declined slightly over a period of 20 years. The population of this county, incidentally, was 98.5 percent white.[86]

Even in the early twenty-first century, most of the mountain people in the world still practiced subsistence agriculture.[87] The negative economic consequences of mountain life have been accompanied by broader negative human consequences. In many mountain communities around the world, especially in times past, the struggle for existence caused children to have to work at an early age, curtailing their education,[88] and thus isolating them from even second-hand knowledge of the wider world beyond the mountains. Illiteracy was common among people in mountain communities around the Mediterranean on into the nineteenth and early twentieth centuries.[89]

Few people from the lands below moved up into the mountains to live, especially in times past, and those mountain people who moved down to the lower elevations encountered a different world, one which they often found difficult to adjust to, and a world in which they were often not accepted, except perhaps as sojourners for seasonal work. This pattern persisted for centuries. In medieval times, the Adriatic port of Dubrovnik "traded and maintained good relations with the people of the hinterland"— the Vlach shepherds from the mountains— "but the latter were not allowed to winter on the territory of the Republic nor to remain within the city."[90] Such negative reactions to mountain people in the lowlands were not peculiar to medieval Europe. Similar negative reactions to mountain peoples were common in nineteenth century France and Morocco, and in modern Nepal, India and Thailand.[91]

There was much the same resistant attitude toward mountain folk in twentieth century America, as shown by press reactions when large numbers of mountain people moved into urban communities, exemplified by the reactions of the *Chicago Tribune*, as noted in a scholarly study of migrations from the mountains:

> The "hillbillies" were described as a degenerate population "with the lowest standard of living and moral code (if any). . . and the most savage tactics when drunk, which is most of the time." National publicity followed, with stories in *Time, Look,* and *Harper's,* the latter under the headline "The Hillbillies Invade Chicago." That article's subhead gave away the racial slippage: "The city's toughest integration problem has nothing to do with Negroes. . . . It involves a small army of white Protestant, Early American migrants from the South— who are usually proud, poor, primitive, and fast with a knife." The message was clear and intentional: these people are "worse than the colored."[92]

The parallels with blacks go beyond the opinions of others. A 1932 study of white children from small communities in the Blue Ridge Mountains found that these white children not only had IQ scores somewhat lower than the national average of 85 for black children, but also had IQ *patterns* similar to those of black children— such as doing their worst on abstract questions and having IQs closer to the U.S. national average of 100 in their early years, with a widening gap as they grew older.[93]

Another study of mountain children, in East Tennessee schools in 1930, found similar patterns. These children had a median IQ of 82 on one test and 78 on another. On the test where they did better, their median IQ was 95 at age six and declined to 74 by age sixteen. A decade later, after social, economic and educational improvements in these East Tennessee communities, the median IQ in the same schools rose to 87.6.[94]

Among those young people from the mountains in the early twentieth century who sought higher education at Berea College in Kentucky, only half returned to their home communities, usually those who failed to graduate.[95] The tendency of more able or ambitious young people to move down from the mountains, while the less able or less ambitious remained, or moved farther up into the mountains, was expressed by a local paradoxical saying that "cream sinks and the skim milk rises" in the mountains.[96] In Spain, there was a similar Catalan saying— "always go down, never go up."[97] This pattern of an out-migration of young people from mountain communities has been a common pattern, whether in the United States or in India or other places around the world.[98]

There have also long been seasonal migrants from the mountains, whether the mountainous regions of Spain, Nepal, South America or South Africa.[99] Remittances from both seasonal and longer term migrants have played a significant role in supporting families remaining behind in the mountains.[100] Longer lasting migrations have included many mountain men who became mercenaries in various armies[101]— the Swiss and Scottish highlanders in Europe and the Gurkhas and Montagnards in Asia, for example. Rifs from North Africa were part of General Francisco Franco's army that won the Spanish civil war and made Spain a fascist country in the 1930s. Over the centuries, it has been estimated that perhaps as many as a million Swiss soldiers died fighting in other countries' wars.[102]

Despite the largely negative influence of mountains on those who live in them, mountains are often a boon to those on the lands below. As moisture-laden winds collide with mountain slopes, these winds are forced upward, where the colder air reduces their moisture-carrying capacity, leading to rain and snow. It is not uncommon for rainfall on the windward side of a mountain range to be several times as much as the rainfall on the other side, in what is called the "rain shadow" of the mountains. As rain water flows down the mountainsides, creating trickles of water that join together to form streams, these streams in turn join together to create rivers. Thus water collected from a wide area of mountain territory is concentrated and delivered as rivers with many uses to people on the land below. All the major rivers of the world have their beginnings in mountains.[103]

Where precipitation in the mountains takes the form of snow, the water is not released all at once, but much of it is released later and gradually, when this snow melts during warmer weather. This means that rivers are not solely dependent on the immediate rainfall to keep flowing, because melting snow from the mountains provides water to sustain the rivers during dry periods.

As with many other things, we can see its importance by seeing what happens in its absence. Although tropical Africa has Mount Kilimanjaro, it has no major mountain ranges comparable to those found in Asia, Europe or the Western Hemisphere. Therefore, during the dry season in sub-Saharan Africa, rivers and streams shrink drastically, in the absence of melting snows in the mountains to keep these waterways supplied with water.

Meanwhile, the Sierra Nevada Mountains in Spain and the Taurus Mountains in Turkey both supply the water that makes a flourishing irrigated agriculture possible in the lowlands,[104] where rainfall alone would not be sufficient during the Mediterranean summer, when the sun evaporates more water than falls as rain in that region of the world.[105]

Soil and Climate

It is hard to think of any innovation in the long history of the human race that has had a greater impact than agriculture. It was some time within roughly the last 5 percent of the existence of human beings that people moved beyond gathering their food from the spontaneous produce of nature, or fishing or herding domesticated animals, and began instead to plant the foods they wanted. Virtually everything that we today recognize as civilization dates from the beginning of agriculture, and with it the beginning of cities.

Exactly how agriculture itself arose is one of those questions whose answer is lost in the mists of ancient times. But how agriculture came to the Western world is known. It came from the Middle East, thousands of years ago, and apparently originated somewhere between the Tigris and Euphrates rivers, in what is today Iraq. This was a geographic setting in which agriculture could not only exist but thrive, at the existing level of knowledge at that time.

The first farmers are unlikely to have known from the outset that crops use up nutrients in the soil, which have to be replenished if the soil is to continue to yield crops of the same magnitude. But, in the land between the Tigris and Euphrates rivers, farmers did not have to know that. Annual floods washed new nutrients over the lands, as annual floods would also do on the lands along the Nile, where another great ancient civilization arose in Egypt.

In Asia, agriculture began on the Indian subcontinent, in the valley of the Indus river, in what is today Pakistan. Despite the arid climate, melting snows from the vast Himalayan mountain range provided the annual flooding which fertilized the land for agriculture. Here too, some of the earliest cities were built, and some of the earliest civilizations developed. It was much the same story as regards the beginning of agriculture and civilization in China:

> Agriculture seems to have started in North China in the region of the great bend of the Yellow River. . . In fact, this center of early Chinese civilization resembled in some ways the homes of other ancient civilizations— the flood plains of the Nile in Egypt, the Tigris and Euphrates in Mesopotamia, and the Indus in modern Pakistan.[106]

Elsewhere, the earliest farmers had to move on after farming a given land a number of years and seeing the successive annual crops grow successively smaller as the nutrients in the soil were used up, threatening the food supply on which human survival depended. Some peoples simply waited for nature to restore the fertility of the soil after they left for other lands to farm, while some other peoples burned the vegetation before moving on, thereby providing the new nutrients that would gradually restore fertility as these nutrients were absorbed into the soil. But between the Tigris and Euphrates rivers, and along the Nile, annual floods could keep the land fertile, long before human beings figured out what was happening. But most other places in the world did not have this windfall gain.

Here again, we see a profound geographic inequality affecting the fates of different peoples very differently. That inequality of fertility in the land has continued on to the present day. As already noted, the most fertile soils are neither evenly nor randomly distributed around the world. A huge swath of these unusually fertile soils spreads across the vast Eurasian landmass, beginning in Eastern Europe and extending into northeastern China.

In the Western Hemisphere, there is a large concentration of these rich soils in the American upper midwestern and plains states, extending into parts of Canada. In the temperate zone of South America there is another concentration of such soils across Uruguay and in the southern part of Argentina.[107] But the natural processes by which such soils are generated or sustained seem not to be found in the tropics, where soil fertility is seldom comparable.

The crop yields per acre in tropical Africa are a fraction of the crop yields in China or the United States.[108] Among the many deficiencies of the soil in sub-Saharan Africa is that the topsoil is often shallow, allowing little space for plant roots to reach deep into the ground for nutrients and water.[109] Moreover, the dryness of much of Africa inhibits the use of fertilizers to supply the nutrients missing in the soil. Fertilizers used without adequate water can inhibit, rather than enhance, the growth of crops.

Even in places where there are wetlands in central Africa, these wetlands have not been as often cultivated as wetlands in temperate climates, because dangerous tropical diseases like malaria and river blindness flourish in tropical Africa's wetlands.[110] Here again, it is the *interactions* of different geographic features— in this case, climate, soil and disease— that can make outcomes very different from what they might seem from a comparison of individual gross features such as wetlands that occur in different regions of the world.

Differences in rainfall patterns also interact with the soil to make agriculture more successful in some regions of the world than in others. The rainfall pattern in sub-Saharan Africa— long dry spells followed by torrential downpours— is a major handicap for growing crops, in part because the land is baked hard and dry before the massive downpours wash away part of the topsoil. This whole pattern contrasts sharply with the interaction of climate and soil in Western Europe or in the eastern and central parts of the United States, where rain falls more of less evenly throughout the year, largely on fertile soils.

We have noted in Chapter 1 how the interaction between latitude and the varying warmth of ocean currents makes winter temperatures in London warmer than in American cities hundreds of miles farther south than London. Other interactions involving other geographic factors elsewhere likewise make temperatures very different from what they would be if determined by latitude alone or by any other factor alone. The highest temperature ever recorded in Asia, Africa, North America or South America has in each case been recorded *outside* the tropics.[111] Even though the heat of sunlight is greatest in the tropics, nevertheless the sun shines more hours per day during the summer in the temperate zones than in the tropics,[112] allowing a longer daily buildup of heat. Thus cities in the temperate zone, such as Athens and Seville in Europe or Las Vegas and Phoenix in the United States, have had higher record temperatures than many cities located in the tropics, including some located virtually on the Equator, such as Singapore in Asia or Quito, Ecuador in South America.[113]

Clouds are another interaction with latitude, because clouds intercept sunlight and reflect it back into outer space. Thus the many cloudless summer days along the Mediterranean coast of Africa have produced higher temperature records in cities located in the temperate zone there, such as Algiers, Tripoli and Alexandria, than in many cities in tropical Africa, even cities very near the equator, such as Nairobi or Libreville.[114] Altitude also affects heat, so that the highest temperatures recorded in the city of Cuzco, located in tropical latitudes in the Andes Mountains of South America, are much lower than in cities like Paris or New York in the temperate zone.[115]

Mountain ranges can also affect the climate of nearby regions, by blocking either warm or cold air from those regions. In southeastern Europe, for example, winter temperatures in Sarajevo may be nearly 50 degrees colder than temperatures on the Dalmatian coast, little more than a hundred miles away, because the Balkan mountains block off the warm air of the Mediterranean from reaching far inland.[116] In Asia, the

Himalayas block warm air from reaching Central Asia and block cold air from reaching India.[117]

While we may legitimately speak in general terms about tropical climates, temperate climates or arctic climates, more specific questions about climates in specific places, such as cities, must take into account the *interactions* of particular combinations of factors peculiar to particular locales. More generally, interactions within and between geographic, cultural, political and other factors are necessary to understand economic and social outcomes.

Many have tried to explain the fact that countries in the temperate zones are generally far more advanced economically than countries in the tropics by the energy-draining heat in the tropics or by the many diseases that flourish there, whose microorganisms are killed off by cold winters in the temperate zones. We have also seen that the most fertile soils are seldom found in the tropics. Nevertheless, many people from outside the tropics have gone to live in the tropics and prospered there, often far more so than the indigenous populations. The overseas Chinese minority in Southeast Asia and the Lebanese minority in West Africa are striking examples.

The British who settled in Australia are perhaps an even more striking example, since they became the majority population of the country, and about 40 percent of Australia is in the tropics. People of Japanese, Chinese and European ancestry are a major part of the population of tropical Hawaii, and are prospering there.

Ordinarily, it might be expected that people indigenous to a given geographic setting would be better able to make the most of that setting's opportunities, and better able to cope with its disadvantages, than people from a very different setting. Yet the evidence seems to suggest the opposite. But, as we have seen in other contexts, geographic environments affect people not only by the direct economic benefits or handicaps of those environments but also by the extent to which those environments facilitate or restrict the development of the knowledge, skills, experiences, habits and values— the human capital— of the people themselves.

If the geographic settings of the temperate zones foster the kind of human capital that promotes prosperity in whatever climate people live, then it is not so surprising that peoples transplanted from temperate to tropical climates prosper more in those climates than the people indigenous to the tropics. As a noted geographer observed, particular cultures may thrive "in regions where they could never have originated."[118]

What cultural consequences of life in the temperate zones might be valuable in other regions that were unlikely to produce such cultures?

The most striking social difference between living in the temperate zones and living in the tropics is not simply the difference in average temperatures. The life-threatening challenge that dominated the temperate zones of the world for millennia was growing enough food during the limited spring and summer months to last through the cold winter months. It was an inescapable necessity, for sheer physical survival, to begin plowing or otherwise breaking up the land for planting when the ground thawed in the spring.

This meant that peoples living where seasons changed drastically had to develop a sense of urgency about time, and the discipline to adjust to its requirements— qualities that were not nearly so necessary in places where food could be grown year round, in addition to the availability of much food spontaneously supplied by nature in many tropical lands.

The other inescapable necessity of the temperate zones, where seasons are so different, was saving food to store for the winter. This required not only the discipline of saving, but also the conversion of perishable foods like milk and fruit into storable foods like cheese and jam. Here again, this was not such a pressing necessity in the tropics. Moreover, tropical foods such as bananas and pineapples were not as storable in a hot climate as wheat or potatoes were in a cooler climate.

Modern economic and technological conditions have so freed us from having to consider such things that it is easy to overlook how imperative those things were for physical survival in the millennia before humans were able to transport vast amounts of food over great distances or to have refrigerators and freezers.

Much has been made of the fact that the Incas created a more sophisticated civilization than most of those indigenous to places elsewhere in the tropics. However, the climate in which the Inca civilization developed was not typical of either the tropics or the temperate zones. Not only does the highest daily high temperature for any month average 73 degrees in Cuzco, the former capital of the Incas, the lowest daily high temperature for any month averages 68 degrees. Despite very little change in daily high temperatures during the course of a year, there is a rainy season and a dry season, with variations in precipitation ranging from a monthly average of 5mm in June to 163mm in January. In addition, overnight temperatures range down to freezing levels in winter.[119]

Because of differences in rainfall and differences in overnight temperatures in different times of the year, there were different seasons when particular crops could be grown, even though agriculture in general was a year-round activity. In short, while the climate in which the Inca Empire arose was not typical of either the tropics or the temperate zone, its highly variable growing seasons for different crops[120] did present the same inescapable challenge faced by inhabitants of the temperate zones— namely, the discipline of conforming one's life to a time frame dictated by the seasonally changing conditions in agriculture.

With the high altitudes of the Andes Mountains offsetting the heat of tropical sunshine, the empire of the Incas was tropical only in the narrowest sense of being located between particular lines on a map.

ANIMALS

The geography of the Western Hemisphere is in many ways much like the geography of Western Europe, especially in the generous supply of rivers and harbors in the United States, as well as vast level plains and, in New England, rich fishing regions offshore in the Atlantic. Yet the indigenous cultures of the Western Hemisphere were very different from the cultures of Western Europe.

This might seem to suggest that geography has had little or no influence on the economic fate of peoples. However, we need to recall yet again that it is the *interactions* of various geographic factors that are crucial to economic and social outcomes. What was totally lacking throughout the Western Hemisphere when the Europeans arrived were horses, oxen and other heavy-duty draft animals or heavy-duty beasts of burden.

During the millennia before motorized vehicles were invented, horses were crucial to everything from transportation to farming to warfare in Europe. Without horses or oxen, the evolution of the whole European economy and society would have had to be radically different. And, without such heavy-duty draft animals or heavy-duty beasts of burden as existed in Europe (or the camels, water buffalo or elephants elsewhere), the economies and societies throughout the Western Hemisphere were in fact radically different from those in Europe.

The economic and cultural repercussions reached further: Nowhere in the Western Hemisphere were there wheeled vehicles. Although the wheel has often been regarded as a landmark in the technological progress of the human race, the value of wheeled vehicles depended greatly on the availability of draft animals to pull such vehicles. The Mayans created wheels but they were used on children's toys. The issue is not the intellectual capacity to invent the wheel but the economic value of wheels in the absence of animals to pull vehicles, during the millennia before motorized transport.

The lack of heavy-duty draft animals or heavy-duty beasts of burden on land even affected what was economically feasible in water transportation. At the time of the arrival of Europeans in the Western Hemisphere, nowhere in North America or South America were there boats as large as the ships of Europeans, much less the even larger ships that the Chinese had developed earlier. The economic viability of large ships depends on the availability of means of efficiently collecting large enough cargoes on land— both from the immediate ports and from the hinterlands— to fill such ships before a voyage, and an ability to efficiently disperse large cargoes at the destination port and into its hinterlands.

A complete absence of animals capable of carrying out such tasks limits the size of vessels that are economically viable. Waterborne commerce in the Western Hemisphere, as of the time of the arrival of Europeans, was conducted in smaller vessels, such as canoes.

What this meant was that the indigenous populations of North America and South America had both a smaller economic universe and a smaller cultural universe than that of peoples in Europe, Asia or North Africa. Not only could exotic goods travel thousands of miles across the Eurasian landmass, they could also travel thousands of miles across water in large ships.

These imports included many things that originated in Asia— paper, printing, gunpowder, the compass, rudders, stirrups, spaghetti, chess, and a numbering system that Europeans called Arabic numerals (because they first saw these numerals in use among the Arabs, even though the numerals actually originated in India). All these things created in Asia became part of the cultural universe of Europeans. Much knowledge from the Middle East and North Africa also found its way into Europe, including the agricultural and architectural advances that the North African Moors brought with them when they invaded and conquered Spain.

When the British confronted the Iroquois on the east coast of North America, the mental and material resources at the disposal of these two races were by no means confined to what they had each developed themselves. The British had been able to navigate across the Atlantic, in the first place, by using the compass invented in China, doing mathematical calculations with a numbering system from India, steering with rudders invented in China, writing on paper invented in China, using letters created by the Romans, and ultimately prevailing in combat using gunpowder, also invented in China.

The cultural universe matters, and animals have been among the reasons for large disparities in the size of the cultural universe in different geographic settings. The relative cultural handicaps of the indigenous peoples of the Western Hemisphere were not unique. Similar handicaps, among others, restricted the cultural universe of the peoples of sub-Saharan Africa, and still more so the cultural universe of the aboriginal population of Australia.

A common handicap of lagging groups around the world has been *isolation*, whether in mountain valleys, on islands far from the nearest mainland, or living where deserts obstruct access to the rest of the world. A dearth of animals also contributes to the isolation of peoples living in the same environment, often physically not very far from each other, who nevertheless may have relatively little communication.

In addition to having impediments to communication with the outside world, the peoples of sub-Saharan Africa have had major impediments to communication with each other. The dearth of navigable waterways was just one of those impediments. The presence of rift valleys and jungles also fragmented many of the indigenous peoples. The dearth of beasts of burden, due to the tsetse fly that flourishes in much of tropical Africa, and carries a disease deadly to animals, completes the impediments to local transportation and communication. The colorful African custom of people carrying bundles on their heads is a painful sign of a grim reality where there are few beasts of burden like horses or camels, which can carry much more freight much more efficiently.

Another of the cultural factors fragmenting the peoples in tropical Africa is a multiplicity of languages, out of all proportion to the size of the population. Although Africans are only about 50 percent more numerous than Europeans, they have nine times as many languages as Europeans. Africans have about 90 percent as many languages as Asians, who outnumber them nearly four to one.[121] Linguistic diversity is not only a sign of cultural isolation and fragmentation, it contributes to the barriers separating African peoples from each other, as well as from the outside world.

Isolation has not been absolute, either in the Western Hemisphere or in sub-Saharan Africa, but cultural universes have not been at all comparable in size to those in much of Europe, Asia or North Africa. An even more severe isolation, in an even more geographically unpromising environment, was the fate of the aboriginal population of Australia before the Europeans arrived there in the eighteenth century.

Beasts of burden were even more completely lacking in Australia than in sub-Saharan Africa or in the Western Hemisphere before Europeans arrived there. Such animals were totally non-existent in Australia when the British arrived in the eighteenth century, just as they were non-existent in most of the Western Hemisphere when Europeans arrived there in the fifteenth century, though there were at least llamas in the Andes, where they were used as pack animals.[122] However, llamas were not large enough to be ridden like horses. Their biggest advantage was their ability to function in the rarefied mountain air where they originated.

Australia had other severe geographic handicaps. In the ages before modern transportation, this vast island continent was isolated in the Southern Hemisphere, far from the mainland of Asia and even more distant from other inhabited continents. Much of the soil of Australia was of low fertility and much of the interior was a desert. Rainfall was even less reliable in the interior of Australia than in sub-Saharan Africa, with its long months without rain, followed by torrential downpours. In the vast interior desert of Australia, there were *years* without rain, followed by summer downpours.[123] This was not an environment favoring either agriculture or spontaneous vegetation.

Back in times when it was common to speak more frankly about different levels of achievements by different peoples, a scholarly study of world geography said that blacks in Africa, "taken as a whole, occupy a higher economic and cultural rank than the black races of Australia and Melanesia."[124] When the Europeans arrived in Australia in the eighteenth century, they found the aborigines lacking iron, even though iron was used by indigenous peoples in sub-Saharan Africa more than a thousand years earlier— and even though Australia had some of the world's largest iron ore deposits. Again, the role of geography has not been simply as a direct supplier of natural wealth, but also and more importantly as a facilitator or impediment to a larger cultural universe, from which to gain the knowledge to turn natural resources into wealth.

The Australian aborigines likewise lacked a knowledge of animal husbandry and many kinds of agriculture known to the peoples of sub-Saharan Africa, among other peoples in geographic settings with the physical prerequisites for acquiring or developing such knowledge. But even during the era of genetic determinism in the early twentieth century, not everyone attributed the lags of the Australian aborigines to genes.

The aborigines' lack of knowledge of things known to others, according to a geographic study published in 1911, "must be attributed to their insularity," such as was also the case among "the native Canary Islanders"[125]— who are classified as Caucasian by some.[126] The fundamental problem of the Australian aborigines was seen as the geography of Australia— "the classic ground of retardation,"[127] shielding the interior tribes especially from "external influences" and leaving them with "the most primitive customs and beliefs."[128]

This isolation applied to animals as well as human beings. None of the animals of Asia— the next nearest continent— was present in Australia when the British arrived in the eighteenth century.[129] Animals that were common in other parts of the world, such as bears, monkeys, hoofed animals and the various kinds of cats— from house cats to lions and tigers— were also non-existent in Australia,[130] like the cattle, sheep and goats already mentioned.

Nor were such Australian animals as kangaroos or koalas indigenous elsewhere. Most of the trees in Australia were of the Eucalyptus family, which is indigenous nowhere else. Many kinds of plants, birds and freshwater fish were also unique to Australia. To a remarkable extent, Australia was for millennia its own separate world biologically.

The isolation of the island continent's flora and fauna gives some idea of the isolation of its human beings. But the same conclusion is reinforced by genetic studies of the aborigines which indicate that, unlike most other races, they had little or no racial intermixture until historically recent times.[131] Multiple evidences point toward an isolated land and an isolated people. There was similar evidence of prolonged isolation in the Canary Islands, where there were hundreds of plants unique to those islands,[132] and a backwardness similar to that of the Australian aborigines, though the two groups are racially different and located thousands of miles apart.

In Australia, as in the Western Hemisphere, the arrival of Europeans led to the transplanting of European animals— and, even more important, the transplanting of European knowledge, gathered from vastly larger geographic regions, forming a far larger cultural universe than that available to the indigenous population of Australia.

Europeans largely avoided the huge interior desert of Australia and settled primarily around the coastal fringes of the continent, concentrated in cities that could be supplied with food from advanced agricultural practices developed elsewhere, and from domesticated animals brought from Europe— cities that would not have been viable for hunter-gatherers, such as the aborigines.

The low fertility of much Australian soil was compensated by the presence of rich natural resources, including not only iron ore but also titanium ore, of which Australia became the world's leading exporter.[133] But what were natural resources for the Europeans were not natural resources for the Australian aborigines, lacking exposure to the scientific knowledge developed over the centuries in a cultural universe extending across the vast Eurasian landmass and including the Middle East and North Africa.

DISEASES

Europeans knew of the existence of Africa thousands of years before they learned of the existence of the Western Hemisphere. Yet European empires were established in the Western Hemisphere hundreds of years before the "scramble for Africa" began in the late nineteenth century and led to European colonial empires that extended throughout the continent. Diseases had much to do with the differing fates of these different regions of the world. Microorganisms that most of the humans involved knew nothing about at the time were on the side of the Europeans during their conquests in the Western Hemisphere. But those microorganisms were on the side of the indigenous peoples in tropical Africa.

The much larger cultural universe of the Europeans, compared to that of the peoples of the Western Hemisphere, meant a much larger disease universe as well. Diseases endemic in Asia repeatedly made their way to Europe along with the goods traded across thousands of miles on the Eurasian landmass, and by seaborne trade as well. This international commerce transmitted diseases from Asia, creating epidemics in Europe that, from time to time, wiped out significant fractions of the European population— from a third to a half of the population in parts of Europe during the bubonic plague of the fourteenth century.[134] But the survivors of these devastating incursions of diseases from Asia developed biological resistance to these diseases, in addition to having biological resistance to diseases originating in Europe.

When European and indigenous races confronted each other in the Western Hemisphere, whether in battle or in peace, the microorganisms that neither of them knew about decimated the indigenous peoples, while the Europeans were not nearly as vulnerable to the diseases of the Western Hemisphere.

Once European diseases took root in the indigenous populations, these diseases spread through whole native societies, to people who had no direct contact with Europeans. When Pizzaro's army was marching toward the capital of the Incas, people who had never seen a European were dying of European diseases inside that capital.[135] It was said of a kindly Spanish priest, who went among the native peoples of the Western Hemisphere in friendship, as a missionary, that he was probably responsible for more deaths among them than even the most brutal conquistador.[136] It was not uncommon in parts of the Western Hemisphere for half or more of a given tribe of indigenous people to be wiped out by European diseases to which they had no biological resistance.

In sub-Saharan Africa, the tropical diseases were so deadly to outsiders that, at one time, the average life expectancy of a white man in tropical Africa was said to be less than one year. Only after medical science reached the point where it could cope with deadly tropical diseases— by either curing them or preventing them by public health measures— was it feasible for Europeans to establish empires in sub-Saharan Africa. The swiftness with which these conquests were accomplished suggests that the human defenders in tropical Africa were not nearly as formidable as the unseen microorganisms that had held European conquerors at bay for centuries. Yet again, a given environment does not determine a fixed outcome because of its interactions with changing human knowledge— in this case, medical knowledge.

North and south of the tropics, the situation was very different in Africa. Europeans began settling in what is now the Republic of South Africa— the great majority of which is in the temperate zone of the Southern Hemisphere— in the middle of the seventeenth century. In ancient times, the Romans incorporated much of North Africa, in the temperate zone of the Northern Hemisphere, within their empire. There being no decisive disease barrier between Europeans and North Africans around the Mediterranean, conquests went each way in different periods of history. The North African Moors invaded and conquered Spain during what were the Middle Ages in Europe, and retained control of Spain for centuries, leaving behind both physical and cultural remains of the society they created during their reign. Centuries later Napoleon said, "Africa begins at the Pyrenees," the mountain boundary between Spain and France.

Among the peoples of tropical Africa, diseases contributed to their isolation from each other by their devastating effects on animals that might otherwise have become beasts of burden or draft animals that could have helped connect different peoples, as well as playing useful roles in agriculture.

LOCATION

Location is a significant geographic factor, even aside from the particular characteristics of the location itself. For the ancient Greeks to be located near where agriculture developed in the Middle East gave them historic opportunities that they used to make historic intellectual contributions to Western civilization and the world.

For the islands of Japan to be located where China was readily accessible across water meant that the Japanese had access to a civilization that for centuries was in the forefront of human advances— and thus Japan could, for example, adapt Chinese writing to make their own language a written language. This meant that the Japanese had an opportunity to become literate, centuries before other peoples in Asia or elsewhere who were not located near a more advanced civilization. Nor did small, isolated communities have the same incentives for developing writing themselves as larger, more widespread societies with numerous commercial and other interactions taking place at distances too great for verbal communication alone.

The advantages of coastal peoples over inland peoples, or the advantages of peoples on the plains over peoples living in mountains, are advantages conferred by the simple fact of location, and are advantages common around the world. During the era of mass immigration from Europe to the United States, Polish immigrants from Russia or from Austria— Poland itself having been absorbed into these empires— were almost always unskilled workers, but those relatively few Polish immigrants who did have specialized work skills as weavers, tailors or cabinet makers were predominantly from Prussia,[137] where they acquired such skills from being located in a German culture.

During the era of European colonialism, location near Western institutions like schools gave those segments of the conquered people in such locations major advantages over their compatriots. In colonial Ceylon, for example, British missionaries set up schools in more favored portions of the island nation, while the British authorities assigned American missionaries to the less favored northern tip of the island, where the Tamil minority was concentrated. But, because the American missionary schools concentrated more in science and mathematics, the Tamils became more proficient in these fields and better represented in occupations requiring such training. A study found that members of the Tamil minority received a majority of the A's on university entry exams.[138]

In Nigeria, the Ibos lived in the poorly endowed southern part of the country, and had once been slaves, but they seized upon opportunities provided by Western missionary schools, while the Muslim peoples of the north rejected schools run by Christian missionaries. The Ibos rose to such professional, administrative and business occupations as were open to Africans, far more so than the peoples in northern Nigeria— and dominated such occupations, even in northern Nigeria.

The location of the United States, insulated by two oceans from the wars that ravaged Europe and Asia, enabled the American people to develop their own way of life in relative peace, using the culture that had developed in Europe without having to suffer the devastating wars that their European ancestors and contemporaries had to endure. By contrast, Mediterranean islands like Sicily and Malta were located in the path of contending nations and empires that, for centuries, fought each other over, and on, the territory of these islands, leaving behind a legacy of destruction, conquest and both culturally and genetically altered populations.

While Britain is an island even closer to the nearest continent than various islands in the Mediterranean, it has not been located in the crossfire between contending empires. Moreover, the rough waters of the English Channel have been more of an obstacle to conquering invaders than the calm waters of the Mediterranean.

Nothing provides absolute protection, of course. After all, Britain was invaded and conquered by the Romans in ancient times and by the Normans nearly a thousand years later. But, after eventually becoming a unified and advanced nation in the wake of the Norman conquest of 1066, Britain has not been invaded in nearly another thousand years since then. What the English Channel has also done during that time has been to make it unnecessary for Britain to maintain a large standing army, like those of nations on the continent of Europe, sparing the British both the expense and the political dangers of large standing armies.

Location has mattered, not only for Britain as a whole, but also for its internal constituents. Being located near enough to continental Europe to have ready access to the trade and technology of its European neighbors allowed the British to gain the benefits of those continental nations that were for centuries more advanced than the British. These advantages were most beneficial to England, the closest part of Britain to the European coast. These advantages passed, with a lag, to other parts of the British Isles— Scotland, Wales and Ireland— as did the further advantages when England began to surpass its continental neighbors and lead the world into the industrial revolution.

Like other geographic features, location is *not* egalitarian. The fate of whole races, nations and civilizations can depend on whether they happen to be located in the right place at the right time or in the wrong place at the wrong time. Moreover, what was the right place or the wrong place has varied greatly over the centuries.

Chapter 3

CULTURAL FACTORS

> *If we learn anything from the history of economic development, it is that culture makes almost all the difference. Witness the enterprise of expatriate minorities— the Chinese in East and Southeast Asia, Indians in East Africa, Lebanese in West Africa, Jews and Calvinists throughout much of Europe, and on and on. Yet culture, in the sense of the inner values and attitudes that guide a population, frightens scholars.*

> *David S. Landes*[1]

Geography is an influence but not predestination. Much of the influence of geography on income and wealth derives from its effects on the size of the cultural universe available to different peoples in different physical settings. An enumeration of places with rich concentrations of natural resources, such as oil in Saudi Arabia or gold in South Africa, would be a very poor guide to places with high incomes per capita. As *The Economist* magazine said of Nigeria in 2014, it is "rich in oil reserves but otherwise desperately poor."[2]

Without the cultural prerequisites for developing natural resources into real wealth, the raw physical resources themselves are of little or no value. The natural resources we use today were even more abundant in the era of the cave man, but the people of that prehistoric era were culturally not yet able to make use of most of those resources.

Even physical capital is of little or no use without the cultural prerequisites to operate it, maintain it, repair and replace it as it wears out. Conversely, the mass destruction of physical capital, as in Western Europe during World War II, was followed by an economic recovery in a relatively few years. This recovery has often been credited to aid from the United States under the Marshall Plan. But subsequent efforts to promote similar economic development in the Third World with transfers of both financial and physical capital to the governments of these countries, over a long period of decades, have failed repeatedly to produce anything comparable.

The difference is that the cultural prerequisites— the human capital— which produced the physical capital in Western Europe before the war, survived the war and could produce it again. But that particular human capital, which developed over the centuries in Western Europe, did not exist on the same scale in the Third World, and could not be created overnight, or even over several decades, in societies with a very different set of cultures.

Third World countries were not being asked to re-create their own societies after some calamity. They were being asked to create a *Western* economy without the centuries of the particular cultural evolution that led up to those economies in the West.

CULTURE AND ENVIRONMENT

When we try to explain differences in economic and other achievements between nations, races or civilizations, some argue that these differences are due to innate genetic differences in mental potential[3] and others argue that differences are due to the environments in which people live. Both seem to assume that all the causes of differences in achievements fall into just two categories, heredity and environment. In fact, these terms are often simply *defined* that way, so that whatever is not hereditary is called environmental. But does this mean that, for those who reject genetic determinism, a group's position in American society is determined by factors peculiar to American society, for which American society can therefore be praised or blamed, as the case may be?

A vast amount of evidence from around the world suggests otherwise. There are many groups with a particular culture of their own, who take that culture with them wherever they go to live, in culturally very different kinds of societies. Germans, for example, have for centuries had both a very specific set of skills and a very specific way of life, whether they lived in Germany, Australia, Brazil, Russia or the United States. Cultures include not only customs, values and attitudes, but also skills and talents that more directly affect economic outcomes, and which economists call human capital.

Among the skills in which Germans have excelled has been the building of pianos. The first pianos in colonial America were built by Germans, who also led the way in building pianos in Australia, France, Russia and England.[4] The world's leading optical firms designing camera lenses in the first half of the twentieth century were German, including Zeiss, Schneider and Voigtländer— and the leading optical firm in the United States was created by two German immigrants named Bausch and Lomb.

Germans have likewise excelled in military skills, literally for millennia. There were German generals in the Roman legions, as well as German generals in czarist Russia[5] and in South America.[6] The United States had German generals in the Revolutionary War of 1776, and American armies fighting in Europe in both World War I and World War II were commanded by generals of German ancestry— Pershing and Eisenhower, respectively.

Other top commanders of American military forces in World War II who were of German ancestry included Admiral Chester Nimitz, who commanded the Pacific fleet, and General Carl Spaatz, whose bombers reduced much of Germany to rubble. During the Middle Ages, the Teutonic Knights conquered Prussia, which became the heartland of German military prowess for centuries to come. In both

World Wars, the armies of Germany inflicted far more casualties on opposing forces than the Germans sustained themselves.[7]

Social patterns among Germans likewise appeared not only in Germany but also in other countries around the world, in cultural environments that differed radically from one another. An emphasis on education was a cultural pattern found in Germany itself, where kindergartens originated and where research universities were developed that were later imitated in the United States. Nineteenth century Germany was one of the first European nations to have free and compulsory education, as well as more teachers per capita than in many other European countries, and with a higher proportion of the national output being devoted to education.[8]

This emphasis on education was also part of the culture of Germans living in other countries, including countries where the culture of the majority population had no such commitment to education. The great majority of Germans living in nineteenth century Russia, for example, were literate at a time when the great majority of Russians were illiterate.[9] In German farming communities pioneering in the wilderness in nineteenth century Brazil, schools appeared in the first clearings in the woods,[10] while most native-born Brazilians remained illiterate on into the early twentieth century.[11] In the Austrian Empire in 1900, the illiteracy rate among German males over the age of ten was 5 percent, while it was 45 percent among Polish males, 67 percent among Serbo-Croatian males and 71 percent among Romanian males in that empire.[12]

When Czernowitz University was established in nineteenth century Romania, there were more German students than Romanian students, and most of the professors were German.[13] In Estonia, a university established in 1802 by the czarist government of the Russian Empire had a majority of Germans among its students and faculty for most of the nineteenth century.[14] In the city of Riga in adjoining Latvia, most of the education was conducted in the German language, even though Germans were no more than one-fourth of the city's population.[15]

Germans are just one of the groups who have taken their own particular culture with them when they immigrated to other societies, so that the general *environments* of those various other societies were not the controlling factor in these groups' economic or other outcomes in those societies. How we define "environment" is crucial. It is not simply a matter of semantic preferences. If we define environment as simply the surrounding circumstances, then we are left unable to account for different cultural groups having very different outcomes in the same environment, creating among other things disparities in income and wealth.

To account for radical differences in income and wealth among groups living in the same society, environment can be defined as what is going on *around* a group, while culture means what is going on *within* each group. If we choose instead to define environment as all non-genetic factors, then the various cultures of different groups in a given society are included in the environment of that society. But what we cannot do is go back and forth between different conceptions of what environment means— not if we expect to reach consistent or rational conclusions.

Many other groups besides Germans have had their own respective cultures, which they take with them into very different settings around the world. These would include the overseas Chinese in various Southeast Asian countries and in the Western Hemisphere;[16] the Lebanese in West Africa, Australia, and North and South America;[17] Jews in Europe, the Middle East, the Western Hemisphere and Australia;[18] and the various peoples of India on every inhabited continent.[19]

Given the cultural differences that these groups take with them wherever they go, there is no reason whatever to expect them to have the same incomes or wealth, either compared to each other or compared to the existing populations of the countries to which they immigrate. Nor do the empirical data show any such equality. That this is a matter of culture, rather than a matter of initial wealth upon arriving in a given country, is shown by how many groups have arrived in various countries far poorer than the existing population of the host country and have nevertheless eventually risen above the economic level of those who were there before them.

The histories of the overseas Chinese in the countries of Southeast Asia—as well as in the United States— are classic examples of immigrants whose first wave arrived with little more than the clothes on their backs and a willingness to work as hard as it took for them to get ahead. Often, in centuries past, these poverty-stricken emigrants from China had little or no education and knew little of the language or customs of the countries they went to.

Seldom did the laws or practices of the Southeast Asian countries in which the Chinese settled offer them equal rights with either members of the colonial ruling race or with the indigenous population. In colonial Malaya, for example, the British provided schools for the children of the Malays but the Chinese had to provide their own.[20] In nineteenth century America, a long and painfully tragic story can be summarized by saying that the Chinese were treated even worse than in Southeast Asia.[21] In Peru, guards were posted on an island where Chinese contract laborers were assigned the task of shovelling bird manure into sacks for export as fertilizer, working under stifling heat and stench. The guards were not there to prevent escape from the island, but to prevent the ultimate escape of suicide.[22]

The desperate situation of the Chinese in various other countries in the nineteenth century also led to high rates of suicide among them. These suicides sometimes began in the Portuguese port of Macao on the coast of China,[23] where many Chinese had been lured or trapped into holding pens for the semi-slave trade of indentured laborers to be shipped to other countries around the world— including hundreds of thousands to the Western Hemisphere. Despite being mostly young men in the prime of life, a majority of those sent to Cuba died under the brutal working conditions there before completing the eight years of their labor contracts.[24] In nineteenth century Cuba, there were years when more than a hundred Chinese committed suicide,[25] but thousands more were simply worked to death.

Although most Chinese immigrants to the United States in the nineteenth century did not come through the Macao indentured labor trade, circumstances in the United States were sufficiently dire that the suicide rate of the Chinese in San Francisco, as late as the mid-twentieth century, was nearly three times the national average.[26]

Over the years and generations, Chinese in the United States have become prosperous, overcoming many obstacles, of which those created by others have not been the only ones. The initial poverty and lack of education of Chinese immigrants to nineteenth century America was another problem they had to overcome, and did. But poverty has also been a problem for hundreds of thousands of new Chinese immigrants arriving as late as the twenty-first century, whether legally or illegally, from Fujian province in China.

Like other immigrants in other times and places, the Chinese from Fujian have not scattered randomly across the United States but have concentrated in their own communities, located in this case in Brooklyn, New York. These Fujianese have been described as "really poor, as in four-people-to-a-single-room, all-rice-diet, soda-can-collecting poor." They have "crammed themselves into dorm-like quarters, working brutally long hours waiting tables, washing dishes, and cleaning hotel rooms— and sending their Chinese-speaking children to the city's elite public schools and on to various universities."[27]

It has been suggested facetiously that the first word of English these Fujianese learn is "Harvard" and the second word is "Stuyvesant," one of New York's elite and highly selective public high schools. While most of the students admitted to the city's elite public high schools come from middle class or higher income neighborhoods, a significant number come from lower income neighborhoods where the Fujianese live. Fujianese parents often get their children tutored, in order that they can do well on tests for admission to elite public high schools, as gateways to good colleges and a better life.[28]

Jews have been classic examples of a very similar pattern, and nowhere more so than in the United States, where most arrived *en masse* from Eastern Europe in the late nineteenth century, among the poorest of the immigrant groups, settling in grossly overcrowded, squalid and unsanitary tenements on New York's Lower East Side. Their men usually began working as lowly peddlers on the streets, and their women and children worked at home in "sweatshop" conditions, with sewing machines whirring for long hours in the tenements, doing piecework on garments.[29]

Despite the Jews' long tradition of reverence for learning, and the spectacular proliferation of world-class Jewish intellectuals in the nineteenth and twentieth centuries, the initial rise of Eastern European Jews in America was *not* through education. Although most Jews who arrived in the United States in the early twentieth century were literate in *some* language, that did not mean that they were literate in English. As a detailed study of these immigrants pointed out, their literacy in Yiddish or Hebrew might serve as "an index of participation in Jewish culture" but it was not "a language tool widely applicable within the context of economic adjustment" in the United States.[30]

A 1911 study showed that two-thirds of the children of Polish Jews were behind the grade level they were supposed to be in, according to age.[31] During the First World War, so many American soldiers of Polish and Russian ancestry— most of them Jews— scored so low on the U.S. Army's mental tests that testing pioneer Carl Brigham (creator of the Scholastic Aptitude Test), declared that the Army test results tended to "disprove the popular belief that the Jew is highly intelligent."[32]

Years later, after more Jews in America acquired more knowledge of English and their mental test scores rose above the national average,[33] Brigham recanted his earlier conclusions. He pointed out, belatedly, that many of the Jewish soldiers tested in the First World War came from homes where English was not the language spoken. He characterized his earlier conclusions as— in his own words— "without foundation."[34]

Although it was not through education that Jews first rose in American society, nevertheless having risen in business— whether to a modest or a greater extent— the Jewish immigrants then pushed their children on to educational achievements, which set the stage for their rise in the professions as physicians, attorneys and the like.

It should also be noted that, neither in the medical nor the legal profession did Jews find all the doors of opportunity open to them. Jewish doctors and lawyers could go into private practice, whether in Jewish or Gentile communities, but they were kept out of many hospitals and leading law firms. In the academic world, there were quota limits on how many Jewish students would be admitted to various colleges and universities, and Jewish professors were a rarity until after the Second World War. Nevertheless, when the barriers began coming down over the years, the Jewish population had a backlog of fully qualified people ready to enter those institutions, and even become disproportionately represented in them.

Lebanese immigrants have had a history in some ways very similar to that of the Jews. Like Jewish immigrants from Eastern Europe who settled in the United States, the earliest Lebanese immigrants to Australia, Brazil, Mexico and West Africa were not very educated, and their initial economic rise came from success in business, typically beginning at the lowest level, as peddlers.

Lebanese immigrants to Brazil in the early twentieth century had a 29 percent illiteracy rate.[35] Most of the Lebanese who first settled in Mexico during the same era had not even completed elementary school. Illiterate Lebanese immigrants in Mexico would often keep letters that they received from Lebanon for months until they could find someone who could read these letters to them and then write their replies for them.[36] Most of the earliest Lebanese immigrants to Australia were illiterate.[37] So were most of the early Lebanese immigrants to West Africa.[38]

In the African nation of Sierra Leone the Creoles looked down on the Lebanese immigrants because they were uneducated and poor. But the Lebanese did not remain that way long— and then the Creoles' contempt turned to resentment and hostility, when the Lebanese became successful in business.[39]

Like other immigrants in other countries around the world, the Lebanese did not emigrate from random locations in their homeland nor settle randomly in the nations to which they moved. The vast majority of the early Lebanese immigrants who arrived in Sierra Leone after the First World War came not from cities like Beirut but from villages where they had been peasants or similarly low level workers.[40] In short, they came from very narrowly specific geographic locations within Lebanon and settled in very narrowly specific locations in Sierra Leone— the Shi'ite Muslims in one area, the Orthodox Christians concentrated in a different location, the Maronite Christians from one part of Lebanon in another location and the Maronites from another part of Lebanon in still a different location.[41] People's behavior is no more random than geographic features, despite how often intellectuals and others regard non-random outcomes as strange, if not suspicious.

Whether in West Africa, North America, South America or Australia, Lebanese immigrants typically began as peddlers,[42] sometimes following in the footsteps of Jewish peddlers, as in Brazil,[43] where successful peddlers moved up to other work, often as owners of small shops, with newer immigrants from the same or other groups replacing them as peddlers. Even such huge and well-known enterprises as Macy's, Bloomingdale's and Levi Strauss among the Jews, and Haggar and Farah among the Lebanese, began at the level of the lowly peddler. Here, as among other groups that rose from poverty to prosperity, dogged perseverance over the years was the key.

In the United States, where large-scale immigration from Lebanon began in the late nineteenth century, most of the early immigrants— including women and children— began as itinerant peddlers, with Lebanese peddler networks spreading literally across the country.[44] After a Lebanese peddler became financially able to settle down with his own store, it was usually a family enterprise, open 16 to 18 hours a day, with children stocking the shelves and making deliveries, and with wives sometimes relieving their husbands in the store, in addition to their other tasks in the home. Home was often next door to the store or upstairs.[45]

This pattern was very similar to that among Lebanese in Sierra Leone,[46] as well as among the Chinese in Southeast Asia or Jews in the United States. Milton Friedman was raised in living quarters over his family's store, a pattern that he described as common among the immigrants to America in that era.[47] Lebanese children were inducted into the family business and its requirements at an early age:

> School-age children, when not in school, were at their parents' elbows, waiting on customers, making change, stocking shelves, and imbibing the shrewdness of operating an independent business on meagre resources. They were inculcated with the parents' work and thrift ethics and the lesson that family unity and self-denial was essential to the family's goals.[48]

In country after country, successive generations of Lebanese moved up, step by step. Commerce was the occupation of most of the early Lebanese immigrants, whether in Argentina,[49] Australia,[50] Sierra Leone,[51] various Caribbean islands,[52] or the United States,[53] among other places. But Lebanese success in business later allowed them to give their children more education, including education at colleges and universities. This too happened in a number of countries in which the Lebanese settled,[54] and increasing numbers of new immigrants from Lebanon in later years also arrived already well-educated.

With the Lebanese, as with the overseas Chinese and the Jews, what mattered was not that they first arrived in various countries as immigrants with very little education, but that they came from a culture which valued education highly— so that, once they became financially able to do so, they saw to it that their children acquired higher education, and thus could expand their horizons from commerce to the professions such as medicine, law and science, as many did.

The patterns of upward mobility seen among the overseas Chinese, the Jews and the Lebanese are of course not the only patterns of upward mobility. Many Cubans who had been professional and business people in their homeland, before Fidel Castro seized control and imposed Communism in Cuba, fled to the United States, where they were concentrated in nearby Florida. Unable to take much of their physical wealth with them to America, and usually unable to resume the same professions they had back in Cuba, since their educational or occupational credentials carried no weight in the United States, these refugees found themselves suddenly at the bottom, economically. As one account put it, "they crammed into small apartments and became dishwashers, janitors, and tomato pickers."[55]

> For the overwhelming majority, the story of their success was one of arduous toil, swallowed pride, and sacrifice for their children. Former executives parked cars; judges washed dishes; doctors delivered newspapers. Women who had never held jobs before worked as seamstresses, hotel maids, or shrimp sorters at warehouses by the Miami River— work so painful they called it *la Siberia*. As one émigré put it, "I was determined that my children would be middle class even if I had to have two jobs— which I did for fourteen years."[56]

Yet these Cuban refugees who found themselves at the bottom, when their exodus began in 1959, had children who, by 1990, earned more than $50,000 a year twice as often as white Americans. Forty years after these Cuban refugees arrived in the United States, the total revenue of Cuban American businesses was greater than the total revenue of the entire nation of Cuba.[57] Similarly, as late as 1994, the 57 million overseas Chinese produced as much wealth as the one billion people in China.[58]

Yet again, all this takes us back to the question: What do we mean by "environment"? If we mean simply the immediate surroundings, then it is hard to see why other groups, living in the same immediate surroundings as the Fujian Chinese in New York— and on the whole living at higher economic levels— do not get their children into the city's elite public high schools as often as the Fujianese do. Nor is it obvious why native-born white Americans do not have high incomes as often as Cuban Americans do.

If instead we see "environment" as including the cultural values that led the Fujianese to make extraordinary sacrifices for the education of their children, or Cuban American refugees to make similarly extraordinary efforts to lift their families up from the bottom, then this situation is less puzzling because it is obvious that not all groups have these same cultural imperatives. But while this makes the problem of understanding the success of these extraordinary groups less puzzling, it also makes the task of trying to get other groups to do the same far more daunting.

CULTURAL DIFFUSION

The history of outsiders' attempts to change the culture of others has largely been a history of failure. The centuries-long attempts of Christian Europe to force Jews to change their religion is just one example. The Czars' "Russification" program likewise created more resentment than results. Yet cultural diffusion has taken place on a massive scale by particular groups, races, nations and civilizations borrowing particular cultural features from others for their own benefit, by their own choices and at their own paces.

Western civilization's replacement of Roman numerals by Arabic numerals, even in countries that were once part of the Roman Empire, and which retained many other features inherited from Rome, was a result of voluntary decisions made throughout Western societies, without any campaigns of persuasion by Arabs or by the people of India, where such numbers originated. Arabic numerals were simply *better*— not merely *different*, as multiculturalists might say— when it came to mathematical operations. Just writing the year of Columbus' voyage to the Western Hemisphere in Roman numerals— MCCCCXCII— shows the cumbersomeness of these numbers, and mathematicians have other objections.

The point here is that cultural borrowing has long taken place on a large scale for largely practical reasons. We have already noted the many cultural features of Asia that spread to Europe over the centuries. A similar process of cultural diffusion occurred between different regions within Europe. Among the cultural advances that spread, over the centuries, from Western Europe to Eastern Europe were coins, castles, crossbows, paved streets, printing presses, power looms, vaccinations, railroads and automobiles.[59] But, just as outsiders' attempts to force changes in other people's cultures have largely failed, outsiders' attempts to artificially prolong the longevity of a particular group's cultural features, preserving them as if they were museum pieces, can be a serious disservice, especially to groups lagging behind, economically or otherwise.

Not all groups, races, nations or civilizations have been equally receptive to absorbing cultural advances from others. Differences in receptivity are among the many cultural differences among groups. In some cases, however, geographic or other handicaps impeding the progress of a group or a nation have been overcome by absorbing advances made by more fortunate peoples elsewhere, and then using and improving those advances for their own economic or other benefit.

Japan was a classic example of a country lacking the geographic advantages of more fortunate nations that had pioneered historic advances. By contrast with ancient China's many outstanding natural harbors and extensive network of navigable rivers, along with unusually fertile land across its northern region, Japan was a much smaller country, with smaller and steeper drainage areas, making its rivers less navigable because their waters flow more steeply and swiftly down to the sea.[60] Much of Japan is mountainous, with only a fraction of the country's land being level enough for agriculture.[61] Japan's largest level plain is only 120 miles long.[62] In addition, there is a dearth of natural resources in Japan.

Given these geographic handicaps, it is not surprising that Japan lagged for centuries behind the economic level of China, during the era of Chinese world leadership in many fields. One of Japan's few geographic advantages has been its accessibility to the sea, so that its coastal areas have been in communication with the outside world. Moreover, these coastal areas are a substantial proportion of the total land area of Japan, where no part of the country is more than 70 miles from the sea.[63]

Among other things, this meant that the more advanced culture of China was physically accessible to Japan for more than a thousand years. More important, Japan was culturally *receptive* to aspects of the Chinese culture. In addition to adapting Chinese writing to create a written version of the Japanese language, Japan also adopted some Chinese philosophical ideas, as well as such mundane things as the cultivation of cotton and the technology for spinning and weaving it into cloth.[64]

For more than two centuries, however, the government of Japan cut the country off from much of the outside world. From 1638 to 1868, emigration from Japan was forbidden, on pain of death, and Japanese who happened to be abroad at the time of this decree were forbidden to return. According to leading scholars of East Asian history, "The Japanese, who had been technologically and institutionally abreast of the Europeans in many respects and ahead in some at the start of the seventeenth century, fell drastically behind."[65] Isolation took its toll in Japan, as it has elsewhere.

The historic shattering of Japan's barriers against the outside world came abruptly in 1853, with the intrusion of Commodore Matthew Perry's American warships into Japan. That Perry could sail into Japanese waters with impunity was one indication of Japan's weakness and backwardness at that time. The country's backwardness was further revealed by the reaction of the Japanese people to a train that Perry presented as a gift:

> At first the Japanese watched the train fearfully from a safe distance, and when the engine began to move they uttered cries of astonishment and drew in their breath.
> Before long they were inspecting it closely, stroking it, and riding on it, and they kept this up throughout the day.[66]

In the years following Commodore Perry's mission, Japanese receptivity to Western culture became extraordinary, approaching adulation. The United States was singled out for special praise and depicted as an "earthly paradise."[67] Euphoric depictions of the United States were part of a general depiction of Western peoples and nations as enviable and great.*

As an indication of the economic level of nineteenth century Japan, its per capita purchasing power in 1886 was one-fortieth of that in the United Kingdom, though by 1898 this had risen to one-sixth.[68] Japan's rise to an economic parity with the leading Western nations over the next century was achieved by a mass importation of Western technology and Western experts to begin teaching that technology in Japan, while Japanese students were sent overseas to study in Western universities. While fewer than half of Japanese children were going to school in 1886, by 1905 that had risen to 95 percent, and continued rising.[69]

By the beginning of the twentieth century, Japan's own people had advanced to the point where most foreign experts were no longer needed and were gone.[70] During the first half of the twentieth century, Japan was producing many industrial products, though much of what it produced during that era were cheaper imitations of Western products, and not of the highest quality. However, the second half of the twentieth century saw the Japanese become pace-setters in both

---

* There were later reversals of these attitudes in Japan during the early twentieth century, as fanatical nationalism arose. Those Japanese emigrants who went to the United States during the earlier, pro-American period largely remained loyal to the United States during the Second World War, despite having been discriminated against before the war and despite being interned during the war. But Japanese emigrants who went to Brazil, during the later, nationalistic and anti-Western period, remained loyal to Japan throughout the war and refused to believe the news that Japan had surrendered. That Japanese Americans were loyal to the United States, despite being discriminated against and interned, while Japanese in Brazil were loyal to Japan, despite being treated better in Brazil than Japanese in the United States and not being interned, suggests again that "environment" must be defined to include the culture originating within the group. See Yasuo Wakatsuki, "Japanese Emigration to the United States, 1866–1924: A Monograph," *Perspectives in American History*, Vol. XII (1979), pp. 465–466; William Petersen, *Japanese Americans: Oppression and Success* (New York: Random House, 1971), pp. 86–87; James Lawrence Tigner, "Shindo Remmei: Japanese Nationalism in Brazil," *Hispanic American Historical Review*, November 1961, pp. 515–532; Yukio Fujii and T. Lynn Smith, *The Acculturation of the Japanese Immigrants in Brazil* (Gainesville: University of Florida Press, 1959), pp. 49–51.

technology and quality, in fields ranging from cameras to automobiles to electronics.

This evolution was especially striking in photography. However, the first Nikon camera was an obvious imitation of a German camera called the Contax, and the first Canon camera was a copy of Germany's world-renowned Leica. But, as time went on, Japan's Nikon and Canon cameras were developed into standard-setters in their field, and their sales eclipsed the sales of the cameras they had initially imitated. Japan also produced high-speed trains that eclipsed anything produced in the United States.

Although Britain and Japan have been culturally quite different in many ways, they were nevertheless similar in being island nations that for centuries lagged behind the progress on the mainland nearest them— that is, continental Western Europe and China, respectively. Britain and Japan were also very much alike in having cultures that were receptive to absorbing the advances of other nations and, eventually, developing these advances further, eventually surpassing their erstwhile superiors.

Within Britain, the Scots likewise absorbed much from the English, beginning with the English language, and eventually rose to surpass the English in engineering and medical science.[71] From the late eighteenth century through the first half of the nineteenth century, a disproportionate share of the leading British intellectuals, in a variety of fields, were of Scottish ancestry. These included David Hume in philosophy, Adam Smith in economics, Joseph Black in chemistry, James Watt in engineering, Robert Burns and Sir Walter Scott in literature, James Mill and John Stuart Mill in economics and politics, and Robert Adam, who was internationally renowned for his designs of everything from palaces to book bindings.[72] As a noted historian put it, "in every branch of knowledge this once poor and ignorant people produced original and successful thinkers."[73]

During the Middle Ages, Europe as a whole learned much from the Islamic world of the Middle East and North Africa, especially in mathematics and philosophy, but also in agriculture and architecture.

Militarily as well, the Islamic world was more advanced at that time. The Ottoman Empire invaded and conquered much of Southeastern Europe, while North African Moors invaded and conquered Spain. As the distinguished British magazine *The Economist* put it in 2014:

> A thousand years ago, the great cities of Baghdad, Damascus and Cairo took turns to race ahead of the Western world. Islam and innovation were twins. The various Arab caliphates were dynamic superpowers— beacons of learning, tolerance and trade. Yet today the Arabs are in a wretched state.[74]

Anyone who doubts the cultural and technological level achieved by the Islamic world a thousand years ago need only visit the great mosque in Cordoba, built when the Moors were the ruling conquerors of Spain. As for tolerance, when in 1492 Christian Spain finally freed itself and drove out the last of the Moors, it also expelled Jews *en masse*— more of whom fled to the Islamic world than to Christian Europe, which was at that time less tolerant than Islamic North Africa and the Ottoman Empire. That world was obviously quite different from the world of today. Part of the difference reflects a difference in receptivity to other cultures.

Eventually, the Western world would overtake the Middle Eastern and North African countries, both militarily and in terms of science and technology. But now the Islamic countries were by no means as receptive to the cultural advances made in the Western countries as the West had once been when the countries of the Middle East and North Africa were ascendant.

One revealing sign of this lack of cultural receptivity is that in today's Arab world— about 300 million people in more than 20 countries[75]— the number of books translated from other languages has been just one-fifth of the number translated by Greece alone, for a population of 11 million people. Over a five-year period, a United Nations study showed that the number of books translated in the Arab world was less than one book for every million Arabs, while in Hungary there were 519 books translated for every million people, and in Spain 920 books per million people.[76] Put differently, Spain translates more books into Spanish annually than the Arabs have translated into Arabic in a thousand years.[77]

Cultural isolation can have effects very similar to the effects of geographic isolation, making it harder for individuals, groups, nations or whole civilizations to keep up with the advances of others. China's decline from world leadership in many fields was likewise marked by resistance to learning from others.

Early in the fifteenth century, the government of China imposed severe restrictions on contacts with the outside world, destroying the large ships in which a Chinese admiral had made voyages of exploration covering longer distances than Columbus' much smaller ships. Such voyages were now not only forbidden but the building of ships capable of making such voyages was banned, and records of earlier voyages to what were regarded as the lands of foreign barbarians were destroyed. A twenty-first century American scientist assessed China's position as of the time this fateful decision was made:

> Before the decision, China had a fleet of ocean-going ships bigger and more capable than any European ships. China was roughly level with Europe in scientific knowledge and far ahead in the technologies of printing, navigation, and rocketry. As a consequence of the decision, China fell disastrously behind in science and technology, and is only catching up now after six hundred years.[78]

In the eighteenth century, when England's King George III sent gifts to the emperor of China that included various devices showing technological advances in the West, the emperor of China replied that there was nothing China lacked. He said: "We have never set much store on strange or ingenious objects, nor do we need any more of your country's manufactures."[79] A rejection of advances from another culture could hardly have been more explicit— or more catastrophic, as China became ever more vulnerable to Western imperialism as the technological gap between the two civilizations widened.

Since no given culture is better in all things, much less for all time, a lack of receptivity to the cultural advances made by others is a self-imposed isolation that can be as damaging as isolation imposed by geography.

Another major factor in cultural isolation among countries around the world is language. It has been said that "Knowledge travels in the baggage of languages."[80] But not all languages contain the same amount or range of written knowledge. The languages of Western Europe developed written versions centuries before the languages of Eastern Europe, because Western Europe was conquered by the Romans and acquired Latin letters as a result. This centuries-long head start in literacy meant that, even after the languages of Eastern Europe developed written versions, they did not instantly acquire the range, volume or variety of knowledge available in the languages of Western Europe.

Even though Estonians, for example, had a written language in the nineteenth century, most of what was written in that language during the first half of that century was confined to religious subjects. But the working language of educated people in Estonia was German, whether a particular individual was of German ancestry or not.[81] Nor was this situation unique to Estonia. Although the Czech language had an earlier and wider literature in Bohemia, this literature had declined by the early nineteenth century and the Czech press at that time was said to be still in its infancy, with a circulation only a fraction of that of the German newspaper in Prague.[82] Elementary schools for Czech children were taught in their native language but, before 1848, there was no high school in Bohemia that taught in Czech. To advance to that level required a child to know German.[83]

For many people in Eastern Europe, becoming educated for careers in science or in various professions meant being educated in the German language. Moreover, given the prevalence of ethnic Germans in many higher occupations in parts of Eastern Europe, entering many elite occupations there often meant acquiring the German culture in general, to fit in with elite colleagues.

Many among the rising generation of educated Czechs and Latvians greatly resented having to change their language and culture, in order to advance in the world. Ethnic Germans of course had no such obstacle to overcome, so no one could claim that this situation was "fair." But the more fundamental question is whether this unfairness was something inherent in the circumstances of the time and place, or something arbitrarily inflicted on non-Germans in Eastern Europe.

While the argument could be made that Germans ruled the Habsburg Empire, and so could be accused of treating other groups unfairly, very similar patterns existed in Romania, ruled by Romanians, and in Latvia and Estonia, then parts of the Russian Empire, ruled by Russians.

The practical question was whether the presence of substantial German minorities in various parts of Eastern Europe, including both the Baltic and the Balkans, increased or decreased the opportunities of the peoples indigenous to that region. From an economic standpoint, it is clear that culturally German educational institutions were open to people who were not Germans and so were available sources of human capital that were not equally available in the languages of the indigenous populations of Eastern Europe.

Similarly, those rural villages in Eastern Europe that were largely populated by German farmers were allowed by Eastern European rulers to live under German law, allowing both Germans and non-Germans living in those villages greater freedom than in most of the rest of Eastern Europe.[84] Moreover, the presence of Germans with higher skills than those in the indigenous population benefitted the whole economy, providing both additional products and additional jobs for the indigenous population. It was precisely the Germans farmers' greater skills and productivity which had prompted Eastern European rulers to welcome them and provide incentives for them to immigrate.

From a political perspective, however, Germans in Eastern Europe were seen by many Eastern European peoples as an alien elite dominating business and the professions, and their culture was seen as a barrier to the indigenous peoples, rather than an opportunity to advance themselves by acquiring the advantages available to them in this foreign culture that was not equally available in their own culture at that time and place. But the Latvian intelligentsia, for example, saw Latvians as a people "consigned by long oppression to lowly stations in life."[85]

The situation of the Germans in Eastern Europe was by no means unique on the world stage. Much the same combination of economic advances and social resentments was created by the presence of the overseas Chinese minority in such Southeast Asian countries as Thailand, Vietnam, the Philippines, Malaysia and Indonesia.[86] Few among the indigenous peoples of these countries sought to acquire the culture of the overseas Chinese, including their willingness to work hard for long hours— certainly not as many as resented Chinese domination in education, industry and commerce.

Much the same pattern appeared in other countries, where either a foreign minority or a different ethnic group within the same country, but with a different culture, outperformed the local majority population in educational institutions and/or in the economy. These would include, at various times and places, Armenians in the Ottoman Empire, Ibos in Nigeria, Tamils in Sri Lanka, Indians and Pakistanis in East Africa, Japanese in Peru, Indians in Fiji, Jews in Eastern Europe and Lebanese in West Africa, among others.

The political incentives in these and other countries have been to demonize whatever minority outperformed the majority population, often accusing these minorities of "taking over" whole industries, even when in fact they created industries that had not existed before. However the political mobilization of resentment turned out— and in some countries, such as Sri Lanka and Nigeria, it produced horrific civil wars— this politicizing of group differences operated against a receptivity to human capital available from more successful cultures.

Often instead, politics promoted a sense of grievance against those with a more successful culture, and a sense of entitlement to some demographically based "fair share" of jobs and incomes. As an ethnic leader in India expressed it, "Are we not entitled to jobs just because we are not as qualified?"[87] An ethnic spokesman in Nigeria similarly decried "the tyranny of skills."[88]

Implicit in this focus on demographically based "fair shares" of economic benefits is an assumption that questions about sharing the wealth can be separated from questions about producing that wealth in the first place. But the damage to national economies after the expulsions of productive minorities suggests otherwise, whether it was the expulsion of the Asians from Uganda in the 1970s,[89] the expulsion of the Germans from Czechoslovakia after the Second World War,[90] the expulsion of the Moriscos from seventeenth century Spain,[91] or the expulsions of Jews from France and various German cities in medieval times.[92]

Similar economic damage has been done in countries where hostile policies by governments, or outright violence by mobs, led productive minorities to flee, as the Huguenots fled from France in 1685[93] or as Jews fled Eastern Europe in the late nineteenth century.[94]

Hostility to more productive minorities, who both increase the national standard of living and provide cultural examples and opportunities for members of the majority population to acquire the human capital of a more advanced culture in order to advance themselves, might seem to be irrational. But it is quite rational, from the standpoint of the self-interest of leaders of lagging groups, to keep the groups they lead resentful of more advanced groups, and to blame those advanced groups for their own group's failure to share more fully in the economic benefits created by skills and knowledge that are not as prevalent in the lagging group's own culture.

Looked at differently, to the extent that individual members of lagging groups acquire the skills and cultures of more advanced groups, they may be absorbed into these groups or, at a minimum, feel less need of their own group leaders. However economically beneficial various aspects of the culture of more advanced groups might be to the lagging group as a whole, the absorption of that culture is a clear threat to group leaders, who see the erosion of the indigenous culture as the erosion of their own role as leaders and the piecemeal loss of their constituency. Indeed, fear of cultural erosion, and ultimately extinction, has been expressed by the leaders and the intelligentsia of many lagging groups, at various times and places around the world.[95]

An eighteenth-century Czech scholar, for example, expressed fears that the increased use of the German language among fellow Czechs meant that, the next generation "will already be German, and in fifty years more German than Czech will be spoken" in the cities of Bohemia.[96]

Nor were such fears groundless. As a later historian said of that era, "Czech-speakers preponderated in Prague only among the lower classes," and though "the Czech language as such was by no means close to death," it had "retreated to the fields, the stables, and the kitchens," where it was spoken by servants and subordinates, and was at this point in history, "a badge not of nationality but of ignorance."[97] Most servants in Prague during this era were Czech, except for an occasional German nurse or governess. Most German households had servants and most Czech households did not.[98]

Halfway around the world, in twentieth century Sri Lanka, with its Sinhalese Buddhist majority speaking Sinhala and its Tamil Hindu minority speaking the Tamil language, the same fear was expressed that the more successful minority would culturally absorb the less successful majority over time. Sinhala language activists in 1956 warned Buddhist priests "that if they didn't do something there would be no more Buddhism and no more Sinhalese."[99]

It was much the same story in Canada's province of Quebec in the 1970s, where the French-speaking majority severely restricted by law the use of English in many institutions, including private businesses. The chief architect of this policy, Cultural Development Minister Camille Laurin, declared that "French must become the common language of all Quebeckers." As elsewhere this was because of a "need for French-speaking Quebeckers to concern themselves constantly with their cultural survival, and their own inferior economic and political positon"[100] in Canada. Similar fears of cultural extinction for similar reasons have been expressed in Fiji, Pakistan, Malaysia, the Philippines and Burma.[101]

Legal restrictions on the use of non-majority languages that seem almost inexplicable in their scope and pettiness, whether in nineteenth century Bohemia or in twentieth century Quebec,[102] are at least comprehensible as part of the drive by group leaders and group intelligentsia to prevent the cultural co-opting of members of lagging groups. These group leaders and intelligentsia have been trying to stave off the assimilation and absorption of fellow group members into economically more advanced groups. Today, in America, black youngsters seeking to speak the standard English of the larger society, often as part of a more general absorption of educational and other components of the larger culture, have been accused of "acting white"— a charge that can bring anything from ridicule to ostracism to harassment or outright violence from fellow blacks.[103]

In short, in many times and places there have been many obstacles to cultural receptivity among lagging groups. The enthusiastic embrace of aspects of a different culture by eighteenth century Scots and nineteenth century Japanese was a rare exception. So too was the spectacular rise of Scotland and Japan to the forefront of world achievements in a remarkably short time, as history is measured.

On a smaller scale, various groups within particular non-Western countries seized upon educational opportunities presented by the presence of Western educational institutions during the era of European colonialism. Like the Scots and the Japanese, these groups often came from regions with geographic handicaps, such as soil too poor for the people in the region to support their growing population. The Ibos in the southern part of Nigeria and the Tamils in the northern part of Sri Lanka were among such groups in various times and places, including Indonesia, Algeria, and the Philippines.[104] Armed with Western education and other Western cultural advantages, the Ibos and the Tamils spread out to other regions of their respective countries, outperforming other groups in businesses, civil service and the professions, bringing benefits to the general population, and at the same time stirring resentments of their striking success.

CULTURE AND PROGRESS

Economic progress depends upon both tangible physical factors like geography, and intangible cultural factors like human capital, including what has been aptly called "the radius of trust" within which individuals and groups cooperate in economic and social endeavors. Attitudes toward work and attitudes toward progress itself are also among the intangibles that combine with tangible factors like geographic features and physical capital to produce economic end results. What is tangible may make a stronger visible impression but it is by no means certain that its economic effect is greater than the intangibles included in the concept of culture.

Among the many ways that cultures differ is in the ability of individuals and groups to trust and cooperate with one another. The radius of trust differs greatly from one group, race, nation and civilization to another— and these differences have major implications for disparities of income and wealth between nations or within nations.

Trust and Honesty

While trust permits many mutually beneficial forms of cooperation, trust without *trustworthiness* is a formula for disaster. The level of honesty in a given society limits the radius of trust in that society, and this can have an economic impact that outweighs many tangible advantages of a given society.

The Soviet Union, for example, was one of the most richly endowed nations on earth, if not *the* most richly endowed, in natural resources. It was one of the few industrial nations with such an abundance of petroleum that it was a major exporter of oil. It contained soil of legendary fertility and the world's largest level plains.[105] The Soviet Union also had the world's largest reserves of iron ore, one-fifth of all the forested land in the world, the world's second-largest deposits of manganese,[106] and one-third of the world's natural gas,[107] in addition to being for many years the world's leading producer of nickel.[108] The Soviet Union was self-sufficient in virtually all natural resources and exported substantial amounts of gold and diamonds. As of 1978, it supplied nearly half of the industrial diamonds in the world.[109]

Yet, despite all these advantages in natural resources, and a well-educated population, the Soviet economy was far less efficient than the economies of Germany, Japan or the United States, according to a study by two of its own economists.[110] The standard of living of the Russian people was significantly lower than that in Western Europe, the United States or Japan— even though Japan is one of the most poorly endowed nations when it comes to natural resources.

How could a country so richly endowed by nature have a standard of living below that of so many other countries with far less in the way of natural resources? The Soviet Union was almost a tailor-made refutation of geographic determinism. The other influences at work that offset the country's many natural advantages were both cultural and political. Back in the nineteenth century, when the country was more candidly called the Russian Empire, John Stuart Mill commented on a cultural handicap that would impede its economic development:

> The universal venality ascribed to Russian functionaries, must be an immense drag on the capabilities of economical improvement possessed so abundantly by the Russian empire: since the emoluments of public officers must depend on the success with which they can multiply vexations, for the purpose of being bought off by bribes.[111]

The cost of corruption in an economy does not consist solely, or even primarily, of the bribes paid, the money stolen or the goods pilfered. The main costs consist of the things that are *not* done— the businesses that are not started, the investments that are not made and the loans that are not granted, because the rate of return on such economic activities would have to be much higher to make such activities worthwhile in a very corrupt economy than in an economy in which the risks of being deprived of the fruits of one's efforts were much lower.

When the czarist government sought to modernize the Russian economy in the late nineteenth century, and invited Western business firms to set up operations in Russia, those firms hired Russian workers and eventually Russians in managerial positions, but they made it a point *not* to hire Russian accountants. Nor were accountants the only problem. A French observer in the early twentieth century referred to "the extraordinary waste— to be polite— that reigns among Russian administrators."[112] "As honest as a German" and "as punctual as a German"[113] were once common expressions in Russia, suggesting the rarity of such qualities among Russians themselves. Why and how these cultural differences came to be what they were may be lost in the mists of time, but the economic importance of such cultural qualities is plain.

Widespread corruption in Russia continued, even under the draconian punishments of the Stalinist dictatorship in the days of the Soviet Union. Despite punishments that included years in slave labor camps, the Soviet economy had whole classes of people known as *tolkachi*, whose sole purpose was to carry out illegal economic activities on behalf of Soviet economic enterprises that could otherwise find it difficult to meet the goals set for them by central planners in Moscow within the severe limitations of what they were officially allowed to do in the government-controlled economy.[114]

The widespread corruption that existed in czarist times persisted in Russia throughout the Soviet era, as well as in Russia after the breakup of the Soviet Union. The stock of a Russian oil company was estimated to sell for about one percent of what the stock of a similar oil company in the United States would sell for, because "the market expects that Russian oil companies will be systematically looted by insiders."[115] Bribes of between $10,000 and $15,000 were required to gain admission to some well-regarded institutions of higher learning in Moscow, according to a Russian newspaper, which estimated that at least $2 billion a year were paid in such outlays by Russian students and their parents.[116]

Russia was not unique, though its great abundance of natural resources and low standard of living provides a dramatic example of how the benefits of tangible factors can be outweighed by the handicaps created by negative intangible factors. Pervasive corruption can make the large investments needed to develop natural resources simply too risky for either local or foreign investors to take a chance.

In other situations, however, the radius of trust can allow particular groups to prosper, not only in prosperous countries, but even in Third World countries with unreliable and corrupt legal systems. Members of such groups as the Marwaris in India or sub-groups of the overseas Chinese in Southeast Asia have been able to engage in financial transactions with one another, without contracts or other recourse to the legal or political institutions of the larger society. That is a special advantage in countries where the formal legal system is either ineffective or corrupt, for this gives members of groups with a wide radius of trust among themselves the advantage of being able to make economic decisions faster and with less risk than can other members of such societies.

A high degree of trust within particular groups can also be an advantage in more advanced economies. Hasidic Jews in New York, for example, can sell consignments of expensive jewelry for one another on the basis of verbal agreements, and share the proceeds later, on the basis of these informal understandings.[117] The Marwaris in India have done the same across international trading networks.[118] In Southeast Asia, the same phenomenon can be found among sub-groups of the overseas Chinese,[119] and a similar pattern can be found among sub-groups of Lebanese immigrants in West Africa and in parts of the Western Hemisphere.[120]

While a whole society can seldom, if ever, develop as strong a sense of trust as that among Marwaris, Hasidic Jews or sub-groups of the overseas Chinese or Lebanese, nevertheless some societies have a strong enough sense of honesty and decency among its people as to enable many useful economic and other activities to take place without the heavy costs and risks that restrict such activities in other societies. Everything from the use of credit cards to the collection of taxes depends on most people being sufficiently trustworthy so that recourse to the forces of the law can be reserved for that segment of the population which lacks the elementary level of trustworthiness required for a viable society on a large scale.

While some theorists may tend to discuss people in the abstract, actual flesh-and-blood human beings differ enormously, not just from individual to individual but from group to group and from one culture to another. Various tests of honesty reveal very striking differences.

When a dozen wallets with money and identification in them were deliberately left in public places in various cities around the world in 2013, the number returned with the money still in them varied from eleven out of twelve in Helsinki to one out of twelve in Lisbon. Moreover, the one that was returned in Lisbon was returned by a visitor from the Netherlands; no Portuguese returned any. In Rio de Janeiro, four were returned.[121] Earlier international tests of wallets with money in them by the *Reader's Digest* found 67 percent of these wallets returned, with the money still there, in the United States, 70 percent in Stockholm, and 100 percent returned in Oslo (Norway) and in Odense (Denmark). In China 30 percent were returned, and in Mexico it was 21 percent.[122]

Similar contrasts among nations were found in a five-year study of which United Nations diplomats paid their parking tickets in New York City, where diplomatic immunity shielded them from prosecution. Egypt, with 24 U.N. diplomats, had thousands of unpaid parking tickets during that five-year period. Meanwhile Canada, with the same number of U.N. diplomats as Egypt, had no unpaid parking tickets at all during the same five-year period. Nor did Britain, with 31 U.N. diplomats or Japan with 47 U.N. diplomats.[123]

More systematic international studies of corruption have found that most of the countries rated as most corrupt were among the poorest countries, even when they had rich natural resources.[124] Honesty is more than a moral issue. It is also an economic factor whose presence or absence can be of major importance. Like other factors that affect income and wealth, it is neither evenly nor randomly distributed among nations or within nations.

Human Capital

Human capital is important, not just in helping a country recover from devastating losses of physical capital, such as after a war. It is also a major factor in economic progress in normal times. Human capital is in fact the biggest difference between ourselves and the cave man.

There is a tendency by some to equate human capital with education. No doubt education is one of the varieties of human capital. While years of education are often used as a rough proxy for human capital in general, not only is much human capital gained outside of educational institutions, some education develops little or no human capital when it produces few, if any, marketable skills— and some education even produces negative human capital, in the form of attitudes, expectations and aversions that negatively impact the economy. Depending on its content, education may sometimes create ideological aversions to working in the private sector or a refusal to do anything that does not seem to qualify as "meaningful work"— that is, work spontaneously agreeable and fulfilling in itself.

The industrial revolution was not created primarily by people with much formal education. It was in fact largely the work of people with practical job skills and experience, rather than a mastery of science or a systematic study of engineering. The industrial revolution was already well underway before formal study of science and engineering became widespread. Even in later times, such industrial pioneers as Thomas Edison and Henry Ford had very little formal education, the Wright brothers were high school dropouts and, in the electronic age, Bill Gates and Michael Dell were dropouts from college. In short, human capital is not synonymous with formal schooling.

Just as human capital takes other forms besides education, so there can be widespread education without equally widespread human capital. Russia in the twenty-first century has been called "a society characterized by high levels of education but low levels of human capital."[125] Among the more directly economic aspects of this is that, while Russia has about 6 percent of the world's college-educated population, it has less than one-fifth of one percent of the world's new patents and patent applications. During the years from 1995 to 2008, Germany produced about 60 times as many patents as Russia, Japan nearly 200 times as many patents and the United States about 500 times as many patents. Even the small city-state of Singapore produced more patents than Russia.[126]

None of this says that education is unimportant. But both its importance as one form of human capital and its distribution require specific scrutiny, rather than general celebration. Here, as elsewhere, few things are equal among individuals, groups or nations. Even among college-educated people in different societies and cultures, disparities are both common and large.

Education As A Cultural Value

The effects of differences between the way different cultures value education do not end with the effect of differences in literacy rates, even though literacy is a fundamental factor in the fate of individuals, groups and nations. Different cultures differ not only in the amount of education people seek, but also in what kinds of education they seek, and in the qualitative levels they achieve in that education. Comparisons of people from different social groups with the "same" education, measured in years of schooling, miss the other dimensions of education— and can therefore often falsely ascribe discrimination when the rewards differ among individuals from different social, racial or other groups with ostensibly the "same" education, as measured by years in school.

It is not uncommon for some culturally distinct minority to have not only more education but also qualitatively better education than the surrounding majority population, either in terms of education in intellectually more challenging specialties or in terms of higher individual achievements in their education. In 1972 most of the A's on university entrance examinations in Sri Lanka went to members of the Tamil minority, rather than members of the Sinhalese majority.[127] During the days of the Ottoman Empire, Armenian students outperformed students from the Turkish majority, and even wrote better in the Ottoman Turkish language than Turkish students did.[128]

Choices of educational specialties can also differ greatly among groups with different cultures in the same society. In Malaysia, during the 1960s, when university admissions were still based on academic qualifications, there were more university students from the Chinese minority than from the Malay majority. The disparity was especially great in mathematical, scientific and technological specialties. During the 1960s, Chinese students received 1,488 Bachelor of Science degrees in Malaysia, while Malay students received just 69. In engineering, Chinese students received 408 Bachelor's degrees during the decade of the 1960s, while Malay students received just four.[129]

In Germany in the late nineteenth and early twentieth centuries, Jewish students were similarly statistically over-represented in German universities,[130] as they were in other times and places, whether in Eastern Europe, Argentina or Australia.[131] Today, in New York City's three elite and highly selective academic public high schools— Stuyvesant, Bronx Science and Brooklyn Tech— Asian students outnumber white students by more than two to one. This is in a city where Asians are only 14 percent of the public school students.[132]

By contrast, majority groups that are lagging economically tend also to lag educationally, both quantitatively and qualitatively. As university students they tend to specialize in easier subjects, rather than in subjects like mathematics, science or engineering. This in turn often leads to less promising careers— or to unemployment. What one study referred to as the "well-educated but underemployed" Czech young men in the nineteenth century[133] had many counterparts in other countries in the twentieth century, when the "educated unemployed" became a common expression, whether in Europe, Asia or elsewhere.[134]

People who have acquired academic degrees, without acquiring many economically meaningful skills, not only face personal disappointment and disaffection with society, but also have often become negative factors in the economy and even sources of danger, especially when they lash out at economically successful minorities and ethnically polarize the whole society they live in.

In various Eastern European countries between the two World Wars, such newly educated young members of lagging majorities provided much of the membership of anti-Semitic movements,[135] which became politically powerful, leading to discrimination and even violence against Jewish students in the universities. Not only were frustrated young graduates from majority populations— many the first generation of their families to reach higher education— among the disaffected who blamed better prepared minorities for their own lags, the intelligentsia of lagging groups have likewise promoted group identity ideology and group identity politics.

This pattern extended far beyond Eastern Europe. In many places and times, soft-subject students and intellectuals have inflamed hostility, and sometimes violence, against many other successful groups, whether in India,[136] Hungary,[137] Nigeria,[138] Kazakhstan,[139] Romania,[140] Sri Lanka,[141] Canada,[142] or Czechoslovakia.[143] In contemporary America, many colleges and universities have whole departments devoted to promoting a sense of racial and ethnic grievances against others, while celebrating the isolation of group identities, epitomized by ethnically separate residences on campus and sometimes even ethnically separate graduation ceremonies.[144]

As in other places and times, whether in Europe, Asia or elsewhere, the intelligentsia of lagging groups have celebrated and/or fabricated past glories of these groups, in the interest of trying to retain individuals who might otherwise be tempted to rise into the larger society. When the author of the celebrated American book and television miniseries *Roots* was challenged on its accuracy by historians, his response was: "I was just trying to give my people a myth to live by."[145]

This approach was by no means unique to blacks or to the United States. An international study of ethnic groups found "cultural revivals" to be a "response" reflecting "an awareness of the danger of a fading group identity."[146] Daniel Patrick Moynihan said of his fellow

Irish Americans: "The cruel part of this history is that by 1916 Irish nationalism in America had little to do with Ireland. It was a hodgepodge of fine feeling and bad history with which the immigrants filled a cultural void."[147] Preoccupation with past glories, even when they are genuine, can be an impediment to receptivity to current advances available from other cultures, as we have seen in the case of China and the Middle East.

The pursuit of accurate knowledge and the pursuit of ideological satisfaction have been conflicting goals, whether in American universities today or in universities in other times and places. A history of East Central Europe between the two World Wars characterized Romanian universities in that era as "numerically swollen, academically rather lax, and politically overheated," serving as "veritable incubators of surplus bureaucrats, politicians, and demagogues."[148] Decades later, universities in Sri Lanka likewise had "a backlog of unemployed graduates" who had specialized in the humanities and the social sciences.[149]

Despite beliefs in some quarters that education makes people more tolerant of other cultures and groups, it has been precisely such newly educated groups, often lacking marketable skills, who have promoted group polarization, whether in Europe, Asia or Africa. As a noted African scholar observed, "the educated Nigerian is the worst peddler of tribalism."[150]

It was much the same story with the nineteenth century Czech intelligentsia, including university students and school teachers, who promoted Czech cultural nationalism.[151] Among their demands were that street signs in Prague, which were in both Czech and German, be exclusively in Czech.[152] In the town of Budweis, Czech cultural nationalists demanded that there be a quota of Czech music to be played by the town orchestra.[153]

There has been a similar insistent pettiness about language, in similar circumstances, in twentieth century Quebec, where laws required that not only street signs be solely in French, but also imposed legal restrictions on the use of English inside private businesses.[154] Quebec authorities even tried to force pilots to communicate in French with air traffic controllers when landing or taking off. Only a threatened international pilot boycott of Quebec forced the local authorities to back down on this dangerous demand that lives be risked by communication in an unfamiliar language.[155]

Even aside from ethnic issues, more years of schooling cannot automatically be equated with increased human capital. Everything depends on whether more years in schools, colleges and universities actually create economically meaningful skills, or whether academic credentials create a sense of entitlement beyond what the holders of those credentials actually produce.

This is not to say that economic benefits are the only benefits of education. But it is to say that expectations, or claims, of entitlement to higher incomes or wealth have no basis unless the specific kinds of education, and the specific qualitative level of that education, actually create sufficient additional output to cover the additional income or wealth expected.

When individuals from lagging groups— whether racial, regional or other social groups— tend to take less challenging courses, especially when these individuals are the first generation of their respective families to reach the college or university level, such individuals are unlikely to create as valuable services as people who study such obviously useful things as medicine, science or technology. In many poorer countries, especially, the "educated unemployed" are often numerous enough to be not only a major disappointment but a social and political danger.

Even many of those with academic credentials, but no economically meaningful skills, who are in fact employed are often employed in government bureaucracies, since they are unlikely to be much in demand in competitive markets, where employers are spending their own money, rather than spending the taxpayers' money. Sometimes jobs in government bureaucracies may be created in order to absorb large numbers of young people who could otherwise be frustrated and embittered enough to be politically troublesome for government officials, or even dangers to the society at large.

In poor countries especially, swollen bureaucracies and the red tape they generate are often an impediment to economic activity by people who do have the human capital to advance the economy and create much needed rises in living standards for the society at large.

Attitudes Toward Work and Progress

Attitudes toward work differ greatly among groups in the same society, as well as between one society and another— and obviously such differences can affect the production of wealth.

Many contemporaries of American antebellum Southern whites commented on the lack of a work ethic among them.[156] These included not only visitors from the North or from other countries, but even such staunch Southerners as General Robert E. Lee.[157] "Many of the whites," according to a leading Southern historian, "were disposed to let good enough alone and put off changes till the morrow."[158]

When German immigrants pioneering in America cut down trees while clearing land for farming, they laboriously dug the stump and the roots out of the ground, so that all the land could be plowed. Southerners usually either cut down the tree, or even simply girdled it and left it to die and rot, but in any case left the stump in the ground and plowed around it.[159]

There were similar contrasts in the production of dairy products. In 1860, the South had 40 percent of the dairy cows in the United States but produced just 20 percent of the butter and only one percent of the cheese.[160] The greater success of the largely German dairy farmers of Wisconsin, compared to the poor showing of dairy production in the South, was explained by a scholar who wrote: "The close attention to duty, the habits of steady, skillful routine accepted by butter fat producers of Wisconsin as a matter of fact, are traits not yet present in southern culture."[161] This was said in 1932. The work attitudes and practices of the South persisted into at least the first half of the twentieth century.

Such differences in work habits have been common in other countries as well, such as among laborers tapping rubber trees in colonial Malaya during the 1940s:

> Many rubber estates kept records of the daily output of each tapper, and distinguished between the output of Chinese and Indian workers. The output of the Chinese was usually more than double that of the Indians, with all of them using the same simple equipment of tapping knife, latex cup and latex bucket. There were similar or even wider differences between Chinese, Indian and Malay smallholders. . .[162]

Some groups avoid work, not necessarily out of laziness, but as a matter of principle. In times past, some European nobility or offspring of affluent classes considered work beneath them. But the British during the reign of the Tudors were not among those with this attitude:

> The younger son of the Tudor gentleman was not permitted to hang idle about the manor-house, a drain on the family income like the impoverished nobles of the Continent who were too proud to work. He was away making money in trade or in law.[163]

Economic outcomes are affected not only by attitudes toward work but attitudes toward progress as well. In modern industrial societies, progress is more or less taken for granted, but this was not always so, even in countries that are today modern societies. As a distinguished history of the rise of Western civilization said of Europe in medieval times, "the very idea of innovation was lacking: men did what custom prescribed, cooperated in the plowing and to some extent in the harvesting, and for many generations did not dream of trying to change."[164]

Here, as in other things, Britain was an exception. Wealthy landowners in Britain were not content to be passive recipients of rents, but actively promoted improvements in farming. By the late eighteenth century, England was one of the leaders in agricultural advances— making farming in Britain very different from farming in the feudal serfdom of Eastern Europe or in the small peasant farming in continental Western Europe.[165] Affluent and educated classes in Britain were also active in commerce and industry, as well as in agriculture, letters, law, and politics.[166]

By contrast, newly educated young people in newly independent countries in sub-Saharan Africa in the twentieth century often disdained the study of agriculture, even in countries where agriculture was a major part of the nation's economy. In Nigeria, more than 40 percent of the jobs for senior agricultural researchers were vacant at one time.[167] In Senegal, it was 1979— nearly three decades after independence— before agriculture was even taught at the university level, though the country's University of Dakar had thousands of liberal arts students.[168]

In parts of the Third World, many people who have gotten an education feel that certain kinds of work are now simply beneath them. This includes working with their hands, even as an engineer, where they "recoil from the prospect of physical contact with machines,"[169] preferring a desk job instead.

The prevalence of such attitudes is another cultural handicap for any group or nation, especially those currently lagging economically. Sometimes the problem is not just an aversion to work, or to certain kinds of work, but also a lack of drive for progress. Here again, America's antebellum South was an example:

> Techniques of Southern agriculture changed slowly, or not at all. So elementary a machine as the plow was adopted only gradually and only in scattered places; as late as 1856, many small farmers in South Carolina were still using the crude colonial hoe. There was little change in the cotton gin, gin house, or baling screw between 1820 and the Civil War.[170]

The cotton gin, a crucial factor in the economy of the antebellum South, was invented by a Northerner. When it came to inventions in general, only 8 percent of the U.S. patents issued in 1851 went to residents of the Southern states, whose white population was approximately one-third of the white population of the country. Even in agriculture, the main economic activity of the region, only 9 out of 62 patents for agricultural implements went to Southerners.[171]

Differences in habits and attitudes are differences in human capital, just as much as differences in knowledge and skills— and such differences create differences in economic outcomes. As of the Civil War era, the North produced 14 times as much textiles as the South, despite the South's virtual monopoly of growing cotton. The North also produced 15 times as much iron as the South, 25 times the merchant ship tonnage and 32 times as many firearms.[172]

Even where the South had natural resource advantages, such as iron ore and coal deposits located much closer together in Birmingham than in such other iron and steel producing centers as Pittsburgh or Gary, Indiana,[173] Southern deficiencies in human capital, among both labor and management, handicapped the development of the steel industry in Birmingham.[174] It was much the same story of rich natural resources and poor human capital in the Southern lumber industry.[175] Similarly, when the Southern textile industry began, with the advantage of being located in one of the world's leading cotton-growing areas, "much of the goods turned out in the South had to be sent to New England for dyeing, bleaching, and finishing."[176]

Fortunately, the South changed over the years, especially in the second half of the twentieth century, partly as a result of a greater influx of people from other parts of the country. However, such cultural changes are not easy to create in all societies or among all groups in a given society.

For outsiders to attempt to change a culture may be resented as well as resisted. As distinguished economic historian David S. Landes put it, "criticisms of culture cut close to the ego," and "injure identity and self-esteem."[177] Outsiders can seldom change a culture, without a receptivity to cultural changes within the lagging group itself.

Chapter 4

SOCIAL FACTORS

Many social factors can affect economic differences between nations and within nations. These include the size and demographic makeup of their populations and the human capital and social mobility in their societies. Like geographic and cultural factors, none of these things is the same between nations or within nations.

POPULATION

One of the reasons sometimes offered for income and wealth disparities among nations is that some nations are said to be "overpopulated" and therefore living in poverty. There are other aspects of populations besides numbers that can also affect economic outcomes for individuals, groups or nations. These include age and mobility, both geographic mobility and social mobility.

Population Size

Over the centuries, a recurrent fear has been that the number of people would grow to exceed the number for which there was adequate food. In times past, this concern has been felt from the individual family to local or national communities, and many have worried that the population of the world would grow to a size exceeding the world's capacity to provide enough food to sustain the people in it.

In times and places where there were families so poor that they were living on the edge of subsistence, it was not uncommon to kill newborn babies. This was especially so when the baby was a girl, because she might not grow strong enough, soon enough, to produce enough food for her own survival, in a family where there was not enough food to keep feeding her without jeopardizing the survival of the family itself. Among the benefits of economic progress was reaching a level of productivity where such desperate and anguished decisions no longer had to be made.

Another benefit of economic progress has been achieving a level of productivity where the growing or gathering of food does not absorb so much of the time and efforts of so many people as to leave too little of both to devote to developing the human capital on which the advancement of civilization depends.

A more favorable geographic environment might allow the people in it to have not only a higher material standard of living but also a more developed culture. However, there is nothing inevitable about such an outcome. A less stressful geographic setting can also lead to a less focused and less disciplined society, able to indulge in more convivial and festive activities, when nature provides food more readily. Geographic opportunities and geographic influences are not geographic determinism.

Concerns over whether the world will produce enough food to sustain the people in it go back even before Thomas R. Malthus' famous *Essay on Population* in 1798. But what Malthus did was to spell out a theory in a stark and dramatic form that made the issue indelible and historic. The Malthusian theory was based on two propositions. The first proposition, according to Malthus, was that "Population, when unchecked, increases in a geometrical ratio," while subsistence "increases only in an arithmetical ratio." The second proposition was: "By that law of our nature which makes food necessary to the life of man, the effects of these two unequal powers must be kept equal."[1]

In other words, if human beings did not restrain their own reproduction, then famine, disease and other disasters would bring population back down to what the food supply could sustain. Such concerns about the sustainability of population have waxed and waned over the centuries since Malthus wrote. But they have never completely died out. In 2014, a *New York Times* writer referred to Malthus' population theory as being based on "an eminently sensible premise: that the earth's carrying capacity has a limit."[2] But to say that there is a limit— on anything— is not to say that we are nearing that limit.

To go from saying that there is a limit to implying that we are nearing that limit is a classic *non-sequitur*, far from being "eminently sensible." Innumerable claims that we were "running out" of oil, coal, iron ore or some other natural resource have proved false, time and again, going back at least as far as the nineteenth century. But the world's known reserves of petroleum at the end of the twentieth century were more than ten times what they were in the middle of that century,[3] when there were dire warnings that we were running out. The world's known reserves of iron ore also increased severalfold, even while the production of steel was rising dramatically. It was much the same story with the known reserves of other natural resources. For economic reasons, it seldom pays to find more than a minute fraction of a natural resource at a given time, even if there is enough in the ground to last for centuries.[4]

However plausible the Malthusian theory might seem, it has consistently failed the test of empirical evidence, even in Malthus' lifetime.[5] There is no consistent correlation between population size or density and real income per capita. Poverty-stricken sub-Saharan Africa has a population density that is only a fraction of that in prosperous Japan.[6] It is possible to find some poverty-stricken countries with greater population densities than some prosperous countries. But there is no consistent relationship between population density and either wealth or poverty. Looking at what happens over time likewise gives no support to the theory that "overpopulation" causes poverty. As one of the leading economic development economists of the twentieth century pointed out:

Between the 1890s and 1930s the sparsely populated area of Malaysia, with hamlets and fishing villages, was transformed into a country with large cities, extensive agricultural and mining operations and extensive commerce. The population rose from about one and a half to about six million; the number of Malays increased from about one to about two and a half million. The much larger population had much higher material standards and lived longer than the small population of the 1890s. Since the 1950s rapid population increase in densely-populated Hong Kong and Singapore has been accompanied by large increases in real income and wages. The population of the Western world has more than quadrupled since the middle of the eighteenth century. Real income per head is estimated to have increased by a factor of five or more.[7]

Although advocates of the "overpopulation" theory argue that rising population threatens to create more poverty, virtually no one seems able to provide examples of countries that had a higher standard of living when their population was half of what it is today.

Famines at various times and places have been taken by some as confirmation of Malthus' theory. But famines ceased in densely populated regions like Western Europe and Japan, while they continued in thinly populated regions like sub-Saharan Africa. Famines have been local phenomena, often caused by local crop failures or by military conflicts or other disasters that interfered with the distribution of food. Even when there is ample food available in the world at large, not all local transportation systems have been capable of moving vast amounts of food into a famine-stricken area quickly enough to avert mass starvation and the diseases to which people weakened by hunger are more vulnerable.

With the development and spread of modern transportation systems, famines have declined. However, particular places at particular times can become susceptible to famine when these places are *politically* isolated for political reasons. Two of the most devastating famines of the twentieth century occurred in the Soviet Union in the 1930s under Stalin, when millions of people died— and, decades later, in China under Mao, when tens of millions died.

Neither of these totalitarian dictators was going to admit to the outside world that there was a famine in his country, much less call on other countries for food, since that would undermine the ideology they were promoting internationally, and perhaps undermine their own regimes. Nor were the people living under these repressive regimes allowed free communication with the outside world. But the long-run capacity to produce enough food to support the people was *not* the issue. In the Soviet Union, the famine was concentrated in the Ukraine, which had been one of the great food-producing regions before the famine, and would be again after the famine.[8] In neither the Soviet Union nor in China had population exceeded the capacity of the land to feed the people, and in both places today an even larger population is being fed. In twenty-first century China, an estimated one-fourth of the population is overweight.[9]

Demographic Composition

The mixture of ages within a given population varies greatly from one society to another, as well as among ethnic or other groups within a given society. The median age in Japan, Germany and Italy is over forty, while the median age in Guatemala, Nigeria and Afghanistan is under twenty.[10] Within the United States, Americans of Japanese ancestry are more than two decades older than Puerto Ricans.[11] If we measure adult work experience from age eighteen on, this means that a forty-year-old worker has more than ten times as much experience as a twenty-year-old worker. How can such a disparity in opportunities to acquire knowledge, skills and maturity not create a disparity in economic outcomes among nations and within nations?

In countries where diseases, poverty and other factors produce shorter life spans, a smaller share of the population reaches the ages where levels of individual productivity are highest and, among those that do, they remain at those levels for less time before dying.

Within a given nation, incomes vary greatly with age, and wealth even more so. Moreover, these disparities among age cohorts have increased over time, as the value of the physical strength and energy of youth counts for less when mechanical sources of power have rendered human strength less important, and more complex technology has made knowledge and analytical skills more valuable. The net result is that the age at which people receive their highest incomes has shifted upward in the United States.

Back in 1951, most Americans reached their peak earnings between 35 and 44 years of age, and people in that age bracket earned 60 percent more than workers in their early twenties. By 1973 people in the same 35-to 44-year-old bracket earned more than double the income of the younger workers. Twenty years later, the peak earnings bracket had moved up to people aged 45 to 54 years, and people in that bracket earned more than three times what workers in their early twenties earned.[12]

None of this should be surprising, because people accumulate human capital as they grow older, whether in the form of specific knowledge and skills or just maturity in dealing with other people and with the responsibilities of their work. What we choose to call "labor" is no longer simply physical exertions in the production process. Many, if not most, workers are supplying not only labor but human capital, and the growing pay differential between experienced workers and entry-level workers suggests that human capital is increasingly in demand in an economy that is growing both technologically and organizationally more complex.

The way children are raised also differs greatly— and consequentially— from group to group and from one income level to another. A study found that American children in families where the parents are in professional occupations hear 2,100 words an hour, on average. Children whose parents are working class hear an average of 1,200 words an hour— and children whose family is on welfare hear 600 words an hour.[13] What this means is that, over the years, a ten-year-old child from a family on welfare will have heard not quite as many words at home as a three-year-old child whose parents are professionals.

It is painful to contemplate what that means cumulatively over the years, as poor children are handicapped from their earliest childhood. It is not just in the quantity of words they hear that they are handicapped. They are also handicapped in both the quantity and the quality of their parents. Only 9 percent of American women with college degrees who gave birth in 2013 were unmarried. But 61 percent of women who were high school dropouts and gave birth that year were unmarried.[14]

It is hard to escape the conclusion reached by *The Economist* magazine: "Nothing the government can do will give the children of Cabin Creek the same life chances as the children of Bethesda."[15] Equal opportunity, in the sense of being judged and rewarded by the same standards as others, cannot possibly mean equal life chances for children born and raised in these very different settings.

Another way of saying the same thing is that the fact that *life* is unfair is not the same as saying that a particular institution, or a particular society, is unfair. *We cannot tell where the unfairness occurred by where the statistics were collected.* If the mix of children raised in welfare families is racially different from the mix of children raised in families with parents who are professionals, then statistics collected at a given employer's business, after these children have grown to adulthood, may well show a racial disparity between which employees are in higher occupations and which are in lower occupations, even if the employer has treated every individual the same when hiring or promoting. Even if these employees were all born into the world with identical brain cells, the prospects of one set of them were enhanced while they were growing up and the prospects of the other set were blighted, years earlier, before either set of people reached the employer.*

Geographic Mobility

One of the ways individuals and groups seek to raise their economic level is by moving from places where prospects seem poor to places where prospects seem more promising. These moves can be

---

* The same implicit assumption that the *cause* of disparities is located where the statistics were collected underlies much fervent denunciation of the fact that "the poor pay more" in low-income neighborhood stores and in interest charges for payday loans. This issue is analyzed in my *Basic Economics*, 5th edition, pp. 66–69, 281–283.

for relatively short distances, as among shepherds leading their flocks from fields where these flocks have eaten most of the vegetation to fields where there is much vegetation still available. Or the moves can be from one country to another or from one continent to another, as people from various parts of Europe immigrated to America and Australia, or people from India immigrated to Fiji, Malaysia and Africa. Like other factors affecting the economic level and progress of peoples, migrations have not been even or random factors, but factors reflecting many inequalities and creating more.

Immigration has not been random, either in the particular places in the home country from which the immigrants leave or in the particular places where they settle in the country to which they relocate. A study of the immigration of southern Europeans to Australia before World War II showed that they "came not as a broad scatter from southern Europe as a whole but in concentrated streams from relatively small and restricted areas" and "the great majority of immigrants settled fairly close together."[16] Nearly nine-tenths of the Italian immigrants to Australia who came from the Mount Etna region of Sicily settled in the northern part of the state of Queensland, while Italian immigrants from the nearby Lipari Islands settled hundreds of miles to the south, in Sydney and Melbourne.[17]

In the United States, such patterns went right down to the neighborhood level. During the era of mass immigration from Europe to America, Italian immigrants from different places in Italy lived clustered together on particular streets within Italian neighborhoods in New York, San Francisco and other American cities.[18] Similar clusters of Italians from particular places in Italy were also common in Buenos Aires and Toronto during that same era.[19]

Such patterns have been common among other immigrants going to and from other countries around the world. As noted in Chapter 3, when immigration from Lebanon to Sierra Leone began after the First World War, most of the immigrants came from particular villages and settled in particular parts of Sierra Leone among people from the same villages and with the same religion. Lebanese immigrants to Colombia likewise came from particular places in the Middle East and settled in clusters together in particular places in Colombia.[20] In the twenty-first century, immigrants from a particular province in China— Fujian— have settled together in a particular Brooklyn neighborhood.[21]

These are long-standing patterns in countries around the world. Frankfort, Kentucky, was founded by immigrants from Frankfurt in Germany,[22] and Grand Island, Nebraska, was first settled by Schleswig-Holsteiners.[23] German farmers who had immigrated to Russia during the eighteenth century, and then emigrated from there to the United States in the nineteenth century, did not settle in existing German American enclaves, much less among the American population at large. These German immigrants from Russia settled in their own separate communities of Volga Germans and Black Sea Germans— separate from each other, as well as from other Germans and from Americans in general.[24]

Such non-random clusters of immigrants from many countries living in many other countries have been the rule, rather than the exception. Moreover, even after the era of mass immigration from Europe was over, if one wished to have Americans of Northern European ancestry and Americans of Southern European ancestry living randomly distributed among one another in the New York metropolitan area in the second half of the twentieth century, one would have had to move just over half of all Americans of Southern European ancestry in the New York area.[25]

The fact that the difference between black and white neighborhoods is visible to the naked eye, in a way that these other differences are not, does not make the black-white difference unique. Moreover, *within* black communities different kinds of people have long clustered in different places. A study of the black community in Chicago during the 1930s showed delinquency rates of more than 40 percent in some black neighborhoods and delinquency rates under 2 percent in other black neighborhoods.[26] Residential separation between different kinds of people within black communities was also found in Harlem and in other black communities as well.[27]

In general, people sort themselves out in all kinds of groups, within races as well as between races, and in all sorts of countries around the world. There are reasons for such non-random residential patterns within groups as well as between groups. Like other patterns in many other kinds of human activities, they are not random because people are not behaving randomly, but *purposefully*— and their purposes, circumstances and values differ. This is too often forgotten by people who react to non-random outcomes as strange, if not sinister, in many contexts.

Social Mobility

Social mobility is often discussed as a matter of individual good fortune, such as that in nineteenth century Horatio Alger novels about plucky lads who overcame adversity and eventually rose to reap their just reward. But social mobility is far more important to the economic fate of nations. Put differently, a nation which creates obstacles to the use of the talents, potentialities and achievements of some of its own people— whether defined by race, religion, sex, caste or whatever— is needlessly depriving itself of a source of greater prosperity. Yet that is precisely what has been done in innumerable times and places, for thousands of years, in countries around the world.

Countries with fewer, or less rigid, barriers have often benefitted from the arrival of productive individuals and groups who were stifled or persecuted in the countries from which they fled. Huguenots who fled religious persecution in seventeenth century France created the watchmaking industry in London and made Switzerland the premier watchmaking nation in the world.[28] Jewish scientists fleeing threats to their personal survival in 1930s Europe played key roles in making the United States the first nuclear superpower.[29] Immigrants and their children also played major roles in creating modern industries in such Latin American countries as Argentina, Brazil and Chile.[30]

Internally, Americans who rose from obscurity, or sometimes even poverty, to create or revolutionize whole industries would include Thomas Edison, Henry Ford, the Wright Brothers, Andrew Carnegie, David Sarnoff and many others whose impacts spread across the country and, in some cases, around the world. Therefore much concern was aroused in the early twenty-first century when claims were made that social mobility had declined greatly in the United States. This concern was often expressed in terms of a setback for "social justice," but a decline in social mobility would also have implications for the economic fate of the country as a whole.

Like so many words and phrases with great emotional and political impact, neither "social mobility" nor "social justice" has been unambiguously defined. A dictionary defines "mobile" as "anything that can be moved." Clearly, by this definition a car with a 500 horsepower engine is mobile, even if it is parked at a given time or even most of the time. Another car, with an engine only half as powerful, would not be said to be more mobile, even if the second car was used as a taxi and was therefore in motion a greater percentage of the time. Mobility exists *ex ante* while movement exists *ex post*.

Similarly as regards social mobility, if we take mobility to mean the freedom or option to move, then we have a different definition from those who measure mobility by how many people have actually moved. These differences in definitions involve far more than semantic preferences. They change the substance of what is being said or insinuated.

To deliberately take an extreme example, even a society with no barriers whatever to upward mobility in its economy may nevertheless have particular groups who do not actually move upward at all. Conversely, a society with many barriers to upward mobility may nevertheless have particular groups who move upward anyway, overcoming or circumventing those barriers.

In short, we cannot determine how much mobility— that is, *opportunity* to move upward— a given society has by how much upward movement actually takes place. That depends also, to a greater or lesser degree, on the behavior of individuals and groups, rather than being solely a question of how much opportunity a given society offers. It is an empirical question as to what the facts are in any particular case, and we cannot allow that question to vanish into thin air by verbal sleight of hand in the definition of words. Personal choices, and personal responsibility for the consequences of those choices, matter. Everything is not solely determined by society, despite how many may prefer to believe that it is.

If native-born Americans in lower income brackets do not move up nearly as often as immigrants who arrived in those same lower income brackets— the Chinese and the Cubans, for example— then the question must be raised whether there are external barriers to mobility blocking the rise of native-born Americans, and which somehow exempt immigrants. Such a hypothesis hardly meets even the test of plausibility. A more realistic explanation might be that low-income immigrants bring a different set of attitudes and values than the attitudes and values of low-income Americans.

In other words, the real question is whether there are external barriers or internal cultures that account for the difference in actual *movement*, even when *mobility* as an opportunity still exists for both. That question has wider implications. If Americans at the bottom do not rise as often as in the past, while immigrants can still rise dramatically from one generation to the next, then the reasons for this retrogression among low-income Americans need to be sought, as will be done in the next chapter, on political factors.

In the meantime, we need to consider those studies which simply measure social mobility by how much movement there is, up and down the economic scale. It is these kinds of studies which have led many to conclude that social mobility as an opportunity has declined in America.

Even within a framework that defines mobility by the amount of movement, there are different questions that can be asked. For example, social mobility might be measured by (1) how much incomes and wealth rise within the lifetime of individuals, (2) how much incomes and wealth rise from one generation to the next, or (3) how much the relative positions of the latest generation differ from the relative positions of their respective parents.

As regards the first question, a number of studies show that the income and wealth of individuals rise substantially over their lifetimes.[31] For example, only 13 percent of American households headed by someone 25 years old have ever been in the top 20 percent in income, while 73 percent of American households headed by someone 60 years old have.[32] This is hardly surprising, since most people begin their careers earning entry-level salaries and then move up over the years, as they acquire more experience, skills and maturity.

When social mobility is defined in terms of how the incomes of one generation compare to the incomes of their parents, that is a fundamentally different question. Fortunately, two of the leading studies of social mobility in recent years— *Getting Ahead or Losing Ground: Economic Mobility in America* (2008) and an update of that study titled *Pursuing the American Dream: Economic Mobility Across Generations* (2012)— were published by the Pew Charitable Trusts, which distinguishes various kinds of social mobility, though some who have quoted from these studies have not. One of the things these Pew studies measure is "whether a person has more or less income, earnings, or wealth than his or her parents did at the same age."[33]

The answer? "The vast majority of Americans have higher family incomes than their parents did." Moreover, "Fifty percent of Americans have greater wealth than their parents did at the same age."[34]

A different question addressed by the Pew studies is how "a person's rank on the income, earnings, or wealth ladder compared to his or her parents' rank at the same age."[35] In other words, do the children end up in a higher or lower relative position in income among their contemporaries, compared to their parents' rankings among the contemporaries of their day? To this question, the answer from this study is: "Sixty-six percent of those raised in the bottom of the wealth ladder remain on the bottom two rungs themselves, and 66 percent of those raised in the top of the wealth ladder remain on the top two rungs."[36]

This is the crucial finding on which many commentators have based their assertion that social mobility in America is now a "myth." However, these Pew studies themselves caution that the data do not include immigrants,[37] because of a lack of historical data, such as were used for studying families that were in America for both parents' and children's generations. This is a crucial caveat because the original 2008 Pew study itself said that its findings do *not* apply to immigrant families, for whom "the American Dream is alive and well."[38]

If low-income immigrants are able to move up, even when native-born Americans tend to stay in their same relative economic positions from one generation to the next, that strongly suggests that American society continues to offer opportunities to move up economically, but that not all groups make the same use of these opportunities.

MENTAL CAPABILITIES

There is a vast, complex and inconclusive literature on the mental potential of different racial groups. But the practical question for anyone investigating current economic disparities between individuals or groups is not what their mental potential was at birth, but what human capital they developed as they grew up and can bring with them as adults to a job or a college, or to the creation of a business or a scientific endeavor.

Such developed capabilities have obviously varied enormously, not only among racial or ethnic groups, but also among people living in major urban centers, as compared to people living in isolated mountain villages or other isolated or otherwise unpromising locations. Nor is this a new phenomenon of modern times. As previously noted, the Greeks were far more advanced than the British thousands of years ago. In the days of the Roman Empire, Cicero warned his fellow Romans against buying British slaves, since they were so hard to teach.[39] Given the vast cultural gulf between the illiterate tribal Britons of that era and the complex and sophisticated society of ancient Rome, it is hard to imagine how things could have been otherwise. With the advantage of centuries of historical hindsight, we can recognize today that this disparity in human capital was not permanent— which is not to deny that it was present, and consequential, at the time.

Today, with the specter of genetic determinism hovering in the background, many are loath to admit that there are major differences in developed mental capabilities among racial or ethnic groups. Tests that show such differences are dismissed as "culturally biased" tests and historical evidence of such differences is dismissed as "stereotypes." Racial differences in patterns of employment and promotion are treated as evidence of discrimination. People who present empirical evidence of differences in current mental capabilities are often denounced as racists. Such reactions are not confined to racial or ethnic "leaders" or "spokesmen," or to politicians responsive to racial or ethnic voting blocs. Many academic scholars have had similar reactions and so have some Supreme Court justices.

Yet such attempts to evade or discredit empirical evidence are as unnecessary as they are futile, for there is other empirical evidence against genetic determinism. For example, there have been, not merely individual whites, or white families, but whole communities of whites from isolated mountain regions in America whose average IQs have been similar to, or lower than, the average IQs of black Americans.[40] Mental tests given to American soldiers during the First World War likewise showed that whites from some Southern states scored lower than blacks from some Northern states.[41] But while such evidence undermines genetic determinism, that does not make mental test differences irrelevant, any more than the great achievements of the British, many centuries after the decline and fall of the Roman Empire, deny that Britons in Roman times were not functioning at the same intellectual level as Romans.

Predictive Validity

Mental tests to measure intellectual capabilities have been caught in a crossfire of controversies. However, a distinction must be made between the *predictive validity* of a mental test and whether it measures "real" intelligence, however the latter might be defined. Clearly no current mental test can retroactively measure "native intelligence"— that is, mental potential years earlier, at birth, which is what the controversies over innate intelligence are ultimately all about. The predictive validity of a test, however, is a very different and straightforward statistical question about the extent to which a particular test's results correlate with later performances in schools, on a job or in some other endeavor.

Obvious as this might seem, the Supreme Court of the United States ruled in the landmark case of *Griggs v. Duke Power Co.* that employers must "validate" tests which have a disparate impact on minority groups, when those tests are "unrelated to measuring job capability."[42]

In other words, the *plausibility* of the test's relevance to the job, as judged by third parties with neither expertise nor experience in the jobs themselves, must be the criterion, according to the Supreme Court— *not* the objectively demonstrated statistical correlation between the scores received on a test and the scorers' subsequent performances on the job. But if scores on an IQ test correlate with the quality of pilots' subsequent performances in the air, this means that the test is predictively valid, even if there is not a single question on the IQ test that has anything to do with flying a plane. Even if an IQ test does not measure "real" intelligence— however defined— if whatever it does measure is correlated with pilots' subsequent performance, then it is predictively valid for that specific purpose, whether or not it measures innate mental potential.

Educational Tests

Employment tests are not the only tests under attack when they result in different racial or ethnic groups scoring at very different levels on these tests. The use of such tests to determine who will and will not be admitted to selective public high schools, such as Lowell

High School in San Francisco or New York City's three highly selective high schools— Stuyvesant, Bronx Science and Brooklyn Tech— has also been under attack, especially by spokesmen for racial or ethnic groups who do not gain admissions as often as others. Even larger numbers of attacks have been directed at college admissions tests across the country.

With academic admissions tests, as with tests for employment and promotions, intergroup disparities have often been extreme. At one time, Jewish students were so overrepresented among those who successfully passed admissions tests to Stuyvesant High School that Stuyvesant was referred to by critics as a "free prep school for Jews" and a "privileged little ivory tower."[43]

Today, it is Asian American students who predominate, not only at Stuyvesant but at Bronx Science and Brooklyn Tech as well. At all three of these highly selective schools, where admissions are based on academic tests, Asian American students are not only a majority of all students but outnumber white students by more than two to one.[44]

The issues raised by critics of academic admissions tests, whether at the high school or college level, raise questions that go to the heart of what education is about and what its role is in the larger society. The ultimate value of high performance schools and colleges is not determined by the benefits they confer on whatever individuals or groups constitute the students who pass through these institutions. The most important value of such institutions consists of the benefits conferred on society at large from the work in later life of people with high-powered intellectual skills— whether in medicine, science or other endeavors.

It is not a question of how many of these schools' graduates were admitted to Harvard or by the fact that, in some years, more graduates of Brooklyn Tech have been admitted to M.I.T. than the graduates of any other high school in the country.[45] The real value of highly selective and intellectually elite high schools is in what their alumni go on to achieve that benefits vastly more other people than themselves.

The many prizes and awards accumulated over the years by students from Stuyvesant, Bronx Science and Brooklyn Tech are just symptoms of their contributions to society at large. These include many Westinghouse Science awards, Intel Science awards, Pulitzer Prizes and multiple Nobel Prizes. Seven graduates from Bronx Science alone have gone on to receive Nobel Prizes in physics alone, and graduates from Stuyvesant and Brooklyn Tech have also gone on to receive Nobel Prizes.

That a particular student goes on to become a brain surgeon is of course significant in that individual's life, but it is of far greater significance to vastly more people whose lives are saved in the course of the surgeon's career. Just one graduate of New York's selective Townsend Harris High School, Jonas Salk, made an incalculable contribution to society— and to the world— by developing a vaccine that put an end to the tragic scourge of polio.

The envy and resentment of achievements that have been painful facts of life in other times and places around the world are perhaps not surprising in an educational context. But such envy and resentment are certainly nothing to be encouraged, to the ultimate detriment of society at large, whose progress is advanced disproportionately by the achievements of people with highly developed levels of human capital.

To refer to Stuyvesant High School as a "privileged little ivory tower" may be clever, but cleverness is not wisdom. Slippery use of the word "privilege" is part of a vogue of calling achievements "privileges"— a vogue which extends far beyond educational issues, spreading a toxic confusion in many other aspects of life. A privilege exists *ex ante* and is fundamentally different from an achievement, which exists *ex post*. Students whose demonstrated academic achievements earn them admission to high-powered educational institutions are fundamentally different from students admitted on the basis of demographic "diversity" or political expediency.

Whether the elite public high schools of New York were overwhelmingly Jewish in one era or overwhelmingly Asian in a later era, their lack of demographic "diversity" seems not to have adversely affected their educational performances or their graduates' achievements in later life. And that is what such schools are there for, not to present a tableau that matches fashionable preconceptions.

Passionate advocacy of the interests of lagging minorities has seldom been followed by equally dedicated empirical investigation as to whether those minorities have actually benefitted, on net balance, from the success of those advocacies. The triumph of egalitarian principles and demographic "diversity" in the rest of New York's educational system has not resulted in an increase in the number or proportion of black or Hispanic students passing the admissions tests to get into Stuyvesant, Bronx Science and Brooklyn Tech. On the contrary, the numbers and proportions of black and Hispanic students have *declined* substantially over the years at all three institutions.[46]

Back in 1938, the proportion of blacks attending Stuyvesant High School was almost as high as the proportion of blacks in the city's population.[47] But 1938 was the last year when this was true. The sharpest declines occurred in the second half of the twentieth century, when the socioeconomic position of blacks was far higher than in 1938. As of 1979, blacks were 12.9 percent of the students at Stuyvesant but, in 1995, the *New York Times* reported that only 4.8 percent of the students at Stuyvesant were black.[48] As of 2012, the *New York Times* reported that blacks were now 1.2 percent of the students at Stuyvesant High School.[49]

In short, over a period of 33 years, the proportion of blacks gaining admission to Stuyvesant High School fell to just under *one-tenth* of what it had been before. None of the usual explanations of racial disparities— genetics, racism, poverty or a "legacy of slavery"— can explain this retrogression over time. Back in 1938, both racism and poverty were worse than in later times, and the blacks of 1938 were generations closer to slavery. Clearly, something else was happening.

Such distressing and puzzling trends present a challenge to believers in either heredity or environment, where environment is defined in the usual socioeconomic terms. There is no obvious, or even plausible, genetic reason why blacks of an earlier generation should have been more able to meet demanding mental test standards to get into an elite public high school. An environmental explanation in socioeconomic terms has even worse problems, since socioeconomic conditions have clearly improved among blacks since 1938, both absolutely and relative to the general population. One of the few possibilities left is that the culture within black communities has in some respect changed for the worse over the years.

There have long been different cultures among blacks. One has been the culture of the old South, the culture which created many handicaps for white Southerners,[50] of which the low mental test scores of white soldiers from Southern states during the first World War[51] were just one symptom.

The thousands of volunteers from the North who went into the South after the Civil War to take on the formidable task of educating the children of freed slaves were led by people who operated on the premise that a major objective of that education should be displacing the Southern culture that blacks had absorbed. This premise was publicly proclaimed,[52] in contrast to the opposite premise in our times that preserving and praising the black culture is important in education.

A disproportionate share of the Northern educators who went South after the Civil War were from New England, and sought to replace the Southern culture among blacks with the contrasting culture of New England. Given the limited economic resources available, this was possible only in a relatively few educational institutions, but those few institutions produced a very disproportionate share of black leaders and pioneers in a number of fields.[53]

One of those institutions was the first black public high school in the country, founded in 1870 in Washington, D.C. In 1899, when tests were given in the city's four academic high schools— three white and one black— this black high school scored higher than two of the three white high schools.[54]

This was not an isolated fluke. Although the IQ of blacks has consistently averaged around 85 over the years, the average IQ at this school— called by various names over the years, including Dunbar

High School after 1916— was consistently at or above 100 every year from 1938 to 1955, except for 1945, when it was 99.[55] This was in the absence of preselection by IQ tests, and with many students with IQs below 100 being admitted to Dunbar on the strength of their academic records.[56] Nor was there "diversity." This school had an all-black student body during the entire 85 years of its academic ascendancy, from 1870 to 1955.

Most of its graduates went on to college during that era, which was unusual for either black or white high school graduates in those years. Some graduates began going to elite colleges in the late nineteenth century, and the school's first graduate who went to Harvard did so in 1903. From 1892 to 1954, Amherst admitted 34 of these graduates. Of these, 74 percent graduated from Amherst and 28 percent of these graduates were Phi Beta Kappas.[57] Nor was Amherst unique. Over the years, the school's graduates went on to become Phi Beta Kappas at Harvard, Yale, Amherst, Williams, Cornell, Dartmouth, and other elite institutions.[58]

In terms of their later careers, "the first black who" pioneered in a number of fields also came from this one school. These included the first black man to graduate from Annapolis,[59] the first black enlisted man in the Army to rise to become a commissioned officer,[60] the first black woman to receive a Ph.D. from an American university,[61] the first black federal judge, the first black general, the first black Cabinet member and, among other notables, Dr. Charles Drew who achieved international recognition for his pioneering work on the use of blood plasma.[62] During World War II, when black military officers were rare, there were among Dunbar High School's graduates "many captains and lieutenants, nearly a score of majors, nine colonels and lieutenant colonels, and one brigadier general."[63]

All of this from one public high school in a black community was remarkable enough. What is relevant to the issue of culture was that this was a school which, from its beginning, had a wholly different cultural orientation from that of the ghetto culture. Seven of its first ten principals were educated in a New England environment. Four had degrees from colleges located in New England and three had degrees from Oberlin College, which was established by New Englanders in Ohio as a deliberate project to plant New England culture in the midwest. Dunbar High School issued a handbook on behavior to its students that spelled out how one should act, not only in the school but in the world at large.[64] The values and deportment these students were taught would today be called by critics "acting white."

Nor did the difference in the way Dunbar students behaved go unnoticed in the local black community. Dunbar High School became so controversial among blacks in Washington that the late Pulitzer Prize-winning *Washington Post* columnist William Raspberry said that you could turn any social gathering of the city's middle-aged blacks into warring factions by simply saying the one word "Dunbar."[65] Resentments of Dunbar High School in Washington's black community were as common as resentments of New York's elite public high schools and resentments of other high achievers in other countries around the world.

The clash between proud alumni of Dunbar and other blacks antagonistic to the school became so bitter that a controversy over what to do with the original Dunbar High School building, after a more modern building was built to replace it, became literally a federal case that went up to the U.S. Circuit Court of Appeals. When the issue was first raised in Washington's City Council, one member of that Council said, "There are people in this city who say that the school represents a symbol of an élitism among blacks that should never happen again. I say we should raze it."[66] After the Dunbar alumni lost in the courts, the original Dunbar High School building was demolished. It was one of many triumphs of the ghetto culture across the country in the second half of the twentieth century, with consequences that spread far beyond educational institutions.

The changing social climate of the 1960s and beyond included a celebration of the ghetto culture, essentially an offshoot of the dysfunctional redneck culture of the South,[67] though often regarded as something uniquely black or even African, despite much evidence to the contrary.* So pervasive did the influence of this ghetto culture become that even middle-class black youngsters felt a need to adopt attitudes, values and behavior from that ghetto culture, as a sign of racial solidarity or a need to avoid the stigma of "acting white" and the social consequences which could follow, ranging from ridicule to ostracism to threats and outright violence.

Legendary basketball star Kareem Abdul-Jabbar described what it was like for him as a youngster growing up in this culture:

> I got all A's and was hated for it; I spoke correctly and was called a punk. I had to learn a new language simply to be able to deal with the threats. I had good manners and was a good little boy and paid for it with my hide.[68]

None of this was unique to a particular individual or a particular place. It was a growing influence among blacks across the country. A study of black youngsters in the racially mixed, affluent suburb of Shaker Heights, Ohio, found these youngsters far behind their white peers academically. Nor was the reason mysterious. Black students spent far less time studying and far more time watching television or engaging in other activities.[69] Nor was this simple laziness. There was an actual aversion to behaviors regarded as "acting white." According to the researcher who studied these black students, "The 'White behavior' most often singled out for criticism was 'talking proper.'"[70] In other words, speaking standard English was seen as a racial betrayal.

"What amazed me," the researcher said, "is that these kids who come from homes of doctors and lawyers are not thinking like their parents; they don't know how their parents made it." Instead they "are looking at rappers in ghettos as their role models, they are looking at entertainers."[71] The normal incentives against short-sighted young people throwing away their education— and thus, in many cases, their

---

* So-called black English, for example, has no connection with languages in Africa but very strong connections with the way English was spoken, centuries ago, in the parts of Britain from which white Southerners came. See, for example, David Hackett Fischer, *Albion's Seed: Four British Folkways in America* (New York: Oxford University Press, 1989), pp. 256–258.

chance for a decent life— are greatly reduced when schools promote them to the next grade, whether they have learned what they were supposed to have learned or not. When asked why they were not taking their school work seriously, many black students in Shaker Heights said that they knew they were going to be promoted to the next grade anyway.[72] What lay ahead of them in life after they finished school was apparently beyond their time horizon.

School teachers and administrators were not the only adults reducing the incentives for black youngsters to take school work seriously. Many black leaders and spokesmen, like leaders and spokesmen for other lagging racial or ethnic groups in various other countries, depict their group's problems as primarily or solely due to other people, and depict opposing those other groups *and their culture* as the way to advance. Moreover, many among the intelligentsia and in educational institutions go along, in the spirit of helping blacks. One of the black leaders who rejected this approach was Martin Luther King, Jr. He said, "We can't keep on blaming the white man. There are things we must do for ourselves."[73] But that has not been the prevailing view.

It is not just in elite schools that we can see educational retrogression among black youngsters. We have grown so used to seeing ghetto schools lag far behind other schools that it may be surprising for some to learn that this was not always the case. As of 1941, for example, test scores in a sample of classes in Harlem elementary schools were very similar to test scores in a sample of classes in the same grades in white schools in working class neighborhoods on New York's Lower East Side.

In April of that year, there were some questions on which sixth grade classes in some Harlem schools did marginally better than sixth grade classes in the white schools on the Lower East Side, while on other questions these white sixth graders did marginally better than their counterparts in Harlem. The same was true of third grade classes in the two neighborhoods in May 1947. December 1941 saw all sixth grade classes in the sample of Harlem schools do marginally better than sixth grade classes in the sample of Lower East Side schools on all the questions. February 1951 saw a class in a junior high school on the Lower East Side do marginally better than the average of an all-male and an all-female junior high school in Harlem.[74]

In short, there were no serious differences in test results in these samples of Harlem schools and Lower East Side schools. These were all just ordinary working-class neighborhood schools, with no real difference in educational results between those schools that were black and those that were white.

The educational retrogression to the situation today seems far more explicable by cultural retrogressions in the intervening years than by alternative theories of either heredity or environment, when environment is defined as surrounding socioeconomic conditions, as distinguished from including internal changes in cultural values. Other social retrogressions over the same years include changes from an era when most black children were raised in two-parent homes to an era when the vast majority were not.

It should also be noted that, despite the prevalence of poverty in many black communities, the poverty rate among black married couples has been in single digits every year since 1994.[75] In other words, those blacks whose behavior put them outside the pattern of the spreading ghetto culture escaped poverty to a far greater extent than other blacks.

Culture matters. The ghetto culture was not new, but it had not spread so much to other parts of the black community before the second half of the twentieth century, when it became widely celebrated, especially by both the black and the white intelligentsia.

Colleges and Universities

At the college level, egalitarian and demographic "diversity" criteria have triumphed in admissions policies and practices, even at elite institutions, so the question is how this has affected the outcomes for black and Hispanic students in college and beyond. Affirmative action policies can ensure that there are more minority students on campus, but these policies cannot ensure that they will graduate, much less graduate in challenging subjects like mathematics, science and engineering.

Despite rising numbers of black students admitted to the University of California at Berkeley during the 1980s, the number of black students *graduating* actually declined.[76] Conversely, when a ban on affirmative action in admissions to the University of California system was imposed in the following decade, the number of black students declined slightly in the system as a whole but the number of black students *graduating* increased. The number of Hispanic students who graduated also rose substantially,[77] now that minority students were being admitted to those campuses of the University of California system that matched their academic qualifications, rather than being mismatched with Berkeley or UCLA for the sake of demographic representation.

In the wake of the ban on affirmative action, the number of black and Hispanic students who graduated in four years rose 55 percent; those who graduated with degrees in science, technology, engineering and mathematics rose by 51 percent; and those who graduated with grade point averages of 3.5 or higher rose by 63 percent. These results confirmed what many critics of affirmative action in academia had long said: the students mismatched with institutions whose standards they did not meet would either fail to graduate as often as others or would manage to graduate only by avoiding difficult subjects like science, technology, engineering, and mathematics.

A widely acclaimed attempt to say that affirmative action was successful— *The Shape of the River* by former college presidents William Bowen and Derek Bok— had crucial defects:

> 1. Although the study purported to show that blacks admitted under affirmative action policies with lower academic qualifications did well, the actual samples in the statistics lumped together *all* black students— those who were admitted with the same qualifications

as other students and those admitted under affirmative action with lower qualifications than the other students.[78] The absence of data on the group specifically at issue— those particular black students who were admitted with lower qualifications— makes that study the statistical equivalent of *Hamlet* without the prince of Denmark.

2. Despite Bowen's and Bok's apparently triumphant finding that black students in their sample "graduated at *higher* rates, the more selective the school that they attended,"[79] that is *not* the mismatch hypothesis being tested. The mismatch hypothesis says that the larger the *differential* in academic qualifications between black and white students at a given institution, the larger the racial differential in failure to graduate tends to be. When this hypothesis is tested at specific, individual institutions (as was done in the Thernstroms' *America in Black and White*) rather than in aggregations of institutions from different SAT levels (as in *The Shape of the River*), the mismatch hypothesis is confirmed. Both studies use combined SAT scores as the measure of academic qualification. The data in *America in Black and White* show that the difference between the combined SAT scores of black students and other students at Harvard, for example, was 95 points— 1305 versus 1400— while the difference at Rice University was 271 points. Correspondingly, the racial difference in dropout rates was 2 percentage points at Harvard and 15 percentage points at Rice.[80] In the Bowen-Bok aggregations, Rice is included in an aggregation that also includes Princeton,[81] which has a much smaller racial differential in SAT scores than at Rice and a correspondingly smaller racial differential in dropout

rates, namely 4 percentage points— while Harvard is omitted from this selection of schools with top SAT scores. Thus confirmations of the mismatch hypothesis within the same category of institutions vanish from view when the focus is on comparisons of different aggregations. Statistical wonders can be performed with aggregations, but these wonders do not necessarily stand up when individual institutions are examined. Data from other studies of individual institutions show results very similar to those in *America in Black and White* and very different from those in *The Shape of the River*.[82]

3. Other researchers were denied access to the raw data from which Bowen and Bok derived their conclusions.[83]

The acclaim for the Bowen and Bok book may have had more to do with how welcome its conclusions were in many quarters, rather than the quality of its evidence or logic. What they said fit the prevailing vision, which was apparently enough to exempt their conclusions from the further requirement of fitting the facts.

Innate Potential

Developed mental capabilities are not only more readily measured but are more demonstrably important than innate mental potential. Indeed, the significance of innate potential derives largely from whatever role it might have as a source of, or limitation on, developed mental capabilities. Whether we are choosing a plumber or a surgeon, what we most want to know is that individual's skill at plumbing or surgery, not whether that skill was due to heredity or environment.

In the heyday of genetic determinism in the early twentieth century, it was widely assumed by genetic determinists that genetic potential put a ceiling on the mental capabilities that could be developed in some racial or ethnic groups. Because members of some groups were deemed to be intellectually capable of being no more than the proverbial "hewers of wood and drawers of water," genetic determinists supported eugenics— a term coined by Francis Galton, who advocated "the gradual extinction of an inferior race."[84]

The eugenics movement spanned the Atlantic. Perhaps even more remarkably, it spanned the ideological spectrum, from conservatives like Winston Churchill and Neville Chamberlain to people on the left like John Maynard Keynes and leading Fabian socialists in England, while a similar sweep in the United States ranged from socialist Jack London to conservative icon Henry L. Mencken.

Many American writings by genetic determinists of that era sought to show that Eastern Europeans and Southern Europeans were innately inferior intellectually to Northern Europeans.[85] This was an era when mass immigration from Europe to America had shifted from the Northern regions of Europe to its Eastern and Southern regions, provoking fears that intellectually inferior and culturally unassimilable immigrants were flooding into the United States. Belief in the innate inferiority of blacks was already so widespread and so deeply believed that literature on this subject was not comparably large.

Later empirical evidence undermined the conclusions drawn at the peak of the ascendancy of genetic determinism. As noted earlier, Jews began to score above the national average on mental tests, for example,[86] leading to mental test pioneer Carl Brigham's recantation of his earlier views.[87] Others brought out the fact that white soldiers from several Southern states scored lower on the Army's mental tests than black soldiers from several Northern states,[88] undermining the most widely accepted racial version of genetic determinism.

Not only did such results undermine the theory of a genetic basis for black-white differences in performances on mental tests, these results were also inconsistent with the presumed innate mental superiority of Northern Europeans to Southern Europeans, since the American South was settled primarily by the supposedly superior

Northern European population from Britain while the massive immigration from Eastern Europe and Southern Europe settled primarily outside the South.*

A closer examination of the performances of black soldiers on mental tests during the First World War raises questions about their cultural level at that time, just as cultural questions were raised when Carl Brigham reexamined his conclusions about white immigrants who had been raised in homes where English was not the language spoken.

For blacks who took the Army tests, their very low level of literacy at that time was likewise a factor to be considered, though few commentators took that into account. One sign of the effect of the low level of literacy among black soldiers taking the Army mental tests, and how that could affect the results, was that a larger proportion of black soldiers were able to answer some of the more difficult test questions that did not require understanding the meaning of written words than were able to answer much simpler questions that did.

In many parts of the Army Alpha test used during the First World War, the modal score of black soldiers was *zero*— derived by subtracting incorrect answers from correct answers, in order to neutralize the effect of guessing. These results were despite the fact that the actual intellectual substance of some of these questions involved only knowing that "yes" and "no" were opposites, as were "night" and "day," "bitter" and "sweet" and other similarly extremely easy questions— questions too simple to be missed by anyone who knew what the word "opposite" meant.

In the Army Beta test, given to soldiers who could not read, some of the questions involved looking at pictures of a pile of blocks and

---

* The lower mental test scores of Southern whites are consistent with the fact that many, if not most, white Southerners emigrated from culturally isolated regions of Britain *before* those regions were incorporated into the mainstream culture of the country and before the spectacular rise of Scotland to the forefront of achievements after having been what historian Henry Buckle called "poor and ignorant" people. See Grady McWhiney, *Cracker Culture: Celtic Ways in the Old South* (Tuscaloosa: University of Alabama Press, 1988), p. 56.

determining how many blocks there were, including blocks that were not visible, but whose presence had to be inferred (and counted) from the shape of the piles. Yet fewer than half of the illiterate black soldiers who took the Army's Beta test received a score of zero on such questions, which were more intellectually demanding, but did not require the ability to understand written words like "opposite" or written directions that may have been challenging to literate black soldiers whose literacy might have been very thin during that era, when many blacks had very little education— either quantitatively or qualitatively— in inferior Southern schools.

Given the very small quantity and low quality of education received by that generation of blacks, even those who were technically literate were unlikely to have a substantial vocabulary of written words. So it is hardly surprising that the completely illiterate black soldiers did better on substantively more challenging questions than blacks with some ability to read did on simpler questions.[89]

Decades later, the research of Professor James R. Flynn, an American expatriate in New Zealand, brought out the fact that the raw scores on IQ tests had risen in a generation or two by a standard deviation or more, in more than a dozen countries,[90] calling into question the belief that scores on these tests measured some fixed genetic endowment.

The repeated re-norming of IQ tests, in order to maintain the definitional average IQ at 100 while the number of questions answered correctly changed, had previously concealed this huge rise in the raw scores on IQ tests. These rises in raw scores included the raw scores of black Americans, whose IQs had remained at about 85 over the years as the tests were renormed. But the average number of questions answered correctly on IQ tests by blacks in 2002 would have given them an average IQ of 104 by the norms used in 1947–1948, which is to say, slightly higher than the average performance of Americans in general during the earlier period.[91]

Whether, or to what extent, existing gaps in IQ are due to heredity is by no means a settled issue. But even with something that is generally agreed to be determined primarily by heredity, such as height, that does not mean that all existing differences in height are due to heredity, much less that heights cannot vary for other reasons besides heredity in particular cases or change over time.

The average height of Britons, for example, was once greater than the average height of the French, as far back as the early eighteenth century, and continuing on into the twentieth century. However, after 1967, the average height of the French equaled the average height of Britons.[92] While the gap in height between the British and the French closed, a gap between the heights of North Koreans and South Koreans opened up after the country was partitioned following the Second World War,[93] with people in North Korea living under a draconian dictatorship that kept them poverty-stricken and ill-fed. In Holland, the average height of young males increased from 5 feet, 4 inches to 6 feet between the middle of the nineteenth century and the early twenty-first century.[94]

Even in the absence of these various empirical findings, the theories of genetic determinism that prevailed in the early twentieth century suffered from the relatively narrow slice of the millennia of human history from which they generalized. The recurring theme in discussions of American immigration laws during that era was that immigrants from Southern Europe were mentally inferior to those from Northern Europe— inferior not just in education or various other contemporary accomplishments, but innately, genetically and permanently inferior.[95]

In the past few centuries, Northern Europe has in fact outperformed Southern Europe in many ways— in its economies, in science and in technology, for example. But, in ancient times, Southern Europe outperformed Northern Europe by a far wider margin— and there is no indication that the genes of people in either part of Europe changed. Meanwhile, China over the centuries lost its once commanding lead over all the Europeans— and over Japan, which much later overtook China, again without any indication that genes had changed in any of these races.

Looked at another way, strongly similar economic and social patterns have been found among people in certain geographic settings, such as mountain communities in various parts of the world— which is to say, among people of different races, with no genetic connection to one another. Believers in genetic determinism will have to explain not only the coincidence of such non-genetically based similarities among these groups, but also why persistently lagging groups, from Canary Islanders in the past to various sub-Saharan Africans to Australian aborigines, have shared an unusually severe degree of isolation.

There have been not only individual whites, but whole communities of whites, who scored at the same average IQ level as American blacks, or lower. The national average is itself an amalgam of very different IQs among groups as well as individuals, so that comparison of any given group with the national average can suggest a uniqueness that is simply not there. During the era of mass immigration to America from Europe, immigrants from Spain, Italy, Greece, Portugal and Poland scored at or below the IQs of American blacks.[96] Other groups of whites with average IQs no higher than those of blacks have included white mountaineer communities in the United States, canal boat people in Britain, and the Gaelic-speaking inhabitants of the Hebrides Islands off Scotland.[97]

In short, genes are neither necessary nor sufficient to explain most of the social patterns of disparate achievements that genetic determinists tried to explain. However important genetics may be in a medical or other scientific context, the relative influence of heredity and environment on the intelligence of different races remains an unresolved issue.

Even if we were to accept IQ tests as a universally valid measure of intelligence, for the sake of argument, the existing *range* of IQ scores among blacks goes far above the average IQ of whites, even though whites as a group have higher average IQs than blacks as a group. The eugenics agenda of the genetic determinists in the early twentieth century seemed to be based on an implicit assumption that there was a *ceiling* on the intelligence of particular racial or ethnic groups, not simply that the *average* of their intelligence was lower at a particular time or place.

Groups with identical ranges of innate intellectual potential can still end up with different averages if environmental circumstances cause different rates of reproduction or survival in various segments of their respective populations. In other words, environments can change the statistical average of IQs, even if the range of IQs remains unchanged. It has been suggested, for example, that the failure to reconsider "current welfare policies"— which may be promoting a higher rate of reproduction of lower classes within the black community— may be "our society's greatest injustice" to the black population. It was pointed out that three-fourths of the blacks who failed mental tests given by the armed forces "come from families of four or more children."[98]

Few American professional families of any race have four or more children, which may be more common among unwed teenage mothers who are high school dropouts, for whom the children are their meal ticket in a world with very few better options for them, by the time they have frittered away their educational opportunities. To have the proportion of the black population that is born to unwed teenage dropouts artificially increased by government policies is hardly a benefit to either the black population or to the society at large.

The backlash against genetic determinism in later years has produced social philosophies lacking even as much evidence as the genetic determinists had. Multiculturalists today decry any recognition that some peoples have superior achievements or inferior achievements at a given time and place, though it is blatantly clear that Greeks were far more advanced than Britons in ancient times and Britons were more advanced than Greeks in the nineteenth century. Today, tests that show some groups far better at some things than other groups are often dismissed as biased tests. Apparently, according to that view, some groups cannot possibly be better or worse than other groups at a given time or place, or at least we cannot publicly admit it.

Such reactions, or over-reactions, to genetic determinism can be especially harmful to groups that are lagging, since it turns their attention and energies away from the many available ways in which they can improve themselves and their prospects, as other lagging groups have done before them— sometimes rising dramatically— and instead leads them into the blind alley of resentments and lashing out at others.

Chapter 5

POLITICAL FACTORS

> *The worst political blunder in the history of civilization was probably the decision of the emperor of China in the year 1433 to stop exploring the oceans and to destroy the ships capable of exploration and the written records of their voyages. . . The decision was the result of powerful people pursuing partisan squabbles and neglecting the long-range interests of the empire. This is a disease to which governments of all kinds, including democracies, are fatally susceptible.*
>
> *Freeman Dyson*[1]

In addition to the influence of such long-run or general factors as geography and culture, particular economic and other social outcomes can be influenced— or even determined— by particular individual happenstances at particular junctures in history. The decision of the fifteenth century emperor of China to isolate his country from the outside world was just one of those fateful political decisions with unforeseen repercussions that changed the course of history for a whole civilization. Such happenstances cut across such general influences as geography or culture, preventing either geographic determinism or cultural determinism.

The decision of the Spanish government to finance Columbus' voyage across the Atlantic, in search of an alternate route to India, obviously changed the course of history for the entire Western Hemisphere and, to a considerable extent, for Europe as well. Had the Japanese government not made the fateful decision to bomb Pearl Harbor, Japan today might be a very different country, without the fundamental and enduring social and institutional changes that took place during the years of American occupation after Japan's defeat in the Second World War.

Sometimes the happenstance that changes the course of history is not a conscious decision but the unpredictable outcome of a crucial military battle between closely matched armies on a chaotic battlefield, where victory could easily have gone to either side. Such was the battle of Waterloo in 1815, which the victor— the Duke of Wellington— afterwards called "a near run thing." But his victory over Napoleon determined the fate of generations yet unborn, in countries across the continent of Europe.

Had Hitler not been a fanatical anti-Semite, at a time when many of the world's leading nuclear physicists were Jewish, the United States might not have become the first nation with a nuclear bomb, as a result of the Manhattan Project, which was created in response to the initiative of Jewish physicists who had fled to America to escape mortal dangers in Europe.

Whatever the geographic, cultural or other influences in a given society, they are all ultimately constrained by power, whether governmental power or military power. The Roman Empire was destroyed by barbarians, setting back the economic, cultural and technological level of Western Europe for centuries. It has been estimated that a thousand years passed before Western Europe regained the standard of living it once had, back in the days of the Roman Empire.[2]

Political factors affecting the economic level of nations include both the presence and the effectiveness of government as an institution, as well as the particular policies of particular governments.

We take national governments so much for granted today that it is easy to forget how long it took for ancient village, clan or tribal societies to coalesce into successively larger groupings over the millennia, until eventually such entities as Greece, China or France could emerge on the world stage.

Although China emerged in what are, from our perspective today, ancient times, this emergence of nations in general began, like most of what we recognize as civilization, in a late and small fraction of the existence of the human species. Moreover, the emergence of nations was not the same everywhere, either in timing or completeness. We need to consider the process by which nations have emerged— and the economic and social consequences of differences in the pace and completeness of that political process among different peoples in different places and times.

THE EMERGENCE OF NATIONS

There was a China many centuries before there was a Britain or France, and these European nations in turn predated the United States by centuries. Moreover, the process of forming nations has by no means been irreversible. Not only was Carthage obliterated by the Romans, Poland was just one of the many nations swallowed up by larger empires, and one of the few that was later reconstituted, after the breakup of dynastic empires in Europe and the Middle East, in the wake of the First World War.

The incentives for moving beyond the ancient bands of hunter-gatherers, and forming successively larger political units over the millennia, were both political and economic. Larger governing units usually mean more powerful units protecting the society or advancing its interests. Larger political units also offer economic benefits. Tribes or villages can seldom, if ever, produce and sell in a large enough volume to reap the full benefits of lower costs per unit, which result from specialization and economies of scale that mass production firms and industries reap— if they have a large enough market for a vast outpouring of their products.

Cities may be able to reap some of the benefits of specialization, when there has been a large enough local market for the resulting product, so that specialized workers are able to devote themselves, full-time, to producing one particular product or engaging in one particular process, such as printing or weaving. But cities have usually been way stations on the road to the creation of nations, though there are still a few city-states, even today, such as Singapore or Monaco.

The economic and social benefits of larger societies do not ensure that such societies will emerge everywhere. In some places and times, the spontaneous coalescing of smaller groupings into successively larger groupings has lagged so far behind the pace of the same process in other contemporary societies that people living in small and vulnerable societies have been simply conquered or enslaved by larger and more powerful societies.

Among the reasons why some societies coalesce into larger political units at different paces is that some societies are more in communication and interaction with other societies, with greater frequency or over wider areas, so that their peoples and rulers can come to know and work with other peoples and rulers over long periods of time, slowly resolving their differences through trial and error, and gradually building up ties that create mutual benefits which all have incentives to preserve and expand.

This process, however, may be much slower, or even non-existent, in regions fragmented geographically, as in the Balkan mountains, or on small islands scattered across a vast sea, or in much of sub-Saharan Africa, with its many limitations on communication and transportation. Peoples in such isolated places have usually been slow to create nations on a scale like that of ancient China or the Roman Empire, or even on a scale like that of modest-sized nations like Italy or Thailand.

The radius of trust can be a major factor in the pace and extent to which small social groupings coalesce into successively larger political units, just as it has been a factor in creating larger economic units.

Small mountain communities, for example, have been especially slow to coalesce into larger governmental units. As one geographic study put it, "Political solidarity has a hard, slow birth in the mountains" because of various "forces working against political consolidation."[3]

These forces working against consolidation into larger political units include a multiplicity of languages and dialects among fragmented mountain populations,[4] impeding even simple communication. Clan, tribal and religious differences have likewise fragmented mountain populations, along with the geographic isolation of mountain communities from one another, whether with or without cultural contrasts among the different settlements. The limited economic benefits of cooperation between very poor mountain communities can also mean reduced incentives to consolidate. There is not the same reward for cooperation or consolidation as in richer places, especially those with contrasting skills and very different natural resources, such as make trade beneficial to all the parties involved.

Family and tribal feuds have long been common among mountain peoples around the world,[5] whether in the mountains of Taiwan or Afghanistan or in America's Appalachian Mountains. The geographic fragmentation of mountain peoples has been an obstacle to developing a wider radius of trust, or even a wider radius of toleration. Among the consequences of such social fragmentation of populations have been "minute mountain states" and "dwarf republics" in the words of a noted geographer.[6]

Even where there are, formally speaking, large mountain nations such as Afghanistan, these are not necessarily nations whose national governments actually have effective control over all the territory they nominally govern. More than a hundred years ago, mountainous Afghanistan was described as a region with "no sense of unity" among its numerous tribes— a situation which "offers little hope of Afghanistan ever developing national cohesion."[7] Little that has happened in more than a century since then would contradict that assessment.

Political consolidation has sometimes been forced upon fragmented mountain peoples by foreign conquest or by the threat of such conquest, which sometimes led to defensive alliances against that outside threat. But these temporary alliances seldom led to permanent consolidations into nationhood.

Switzerland has been a rare exception, perhaps due to the many mountain passes into the Swiss Alps[8] that kept the people in these mountains from being as isolated as peoples in many other mountains around the world, while the large valleys in the Swiss Alps presented better opportunities for large settlements, more in touch with each other and with the outside world.[9] The dearth of navigable waterways in other mountain regions is not the case in Switzerland, which has such waterways as Lake Geneva and Lake Lucerne— lakes, as enclosed waterways, being inherently navigable, unlike rivers and streams that pour down steep mountain terrain.

The empire of the Incas in the Andes Mountains of South America was another, and even more striking, exception to the small size of nations in mountainous terrain. The Inca Empire covered 906,000 square kilometers— more than 20 times the size of Switzerland and roughly the size of France and Germany put together.[10] There were long and large valleys between the mountain ranges, those valleys in the lower elevations being suitable for agriculture.[11] This created a very different geographic setting from those in other mountains where people are more fragmented geographically in small communities, kept small by the very limited amount of arable land in many mountain valleys and by formidable geographic obstacles to communication and transportation.

Unlike other mountains lacking major navigable waterways, the Andes include Lake Titicaca, more than 100 miles long, more than 900 feet deep and with a surface area of more than 3,000 square miles.[12] The peoples living around the enormous perimeter of this lake had ready communication with each other across a navigable waterway. Lake Titicaca has been called "the cradle of the Inca Empire"[13] and its capital, Cuzco, was situated between two rivers.

The presence of vast numbers of llamas in some of the mountain valleys of the Andes gave the Incas small but numerous pack animals that were lacking elsewhere in the Western Hemisphere before Europeans arrived with their animals. In these settings, the Inca Empire began and later spread to other geographic settings in western South America, for a distance of 4,000 kilometers from north to south.[14]

The imperative to produce specific crops at specific times of the year, and to preserve the resulting food, which peoples in temperate zone climates felt for millennia, were in the Inca Empire challenges supplied by the peculiar climate of the region where that empire originated. The unique situation of a vast and high mountain range, located in the tropics, gave the Incas a unique climate that was quite different from that common in either temperate or tropical zones. This climate had a seasonality based on great differences in the amount of rainfall at different times of the year, even though average daytime high temperatures ranged only from 68 degrees to 73 degrees in the Inca capital of Cuzco.

This rainfall seasonality, plus the vulnerability of crops to drought and hard frosts, due to overnight temperatures that could fall to freezing levels during the winter, as well as changing weather conditions from one year to the next, created the same life-threatening challenge faced for millennia by peoples located in the temperate zones. The Incas met this challenge by creating large networks of food storage facilities, scattered throughout their far flung empire, and by developing ways of making some perishable foods storable.[15] Thus the geographic environment of the Incas produced the same necessity for developing self-discipline, and human capital in general, that peoples in the temperate zones had to create in order to survive. The Inca Empire was not tropical in any meaningful climatic sense.

Special local geographic conditions made Switzerland and the Inca Empire exceptions to the handicaps that kept the peoples in many other mountains poor, backward and unable to create large, well-functioning political units. However, mountains are not the only geographic feature that can fragment a population and isolate the fragments from one another, impeding the formation of nation-states. Other geographically isolated and fragmented regions, such as the Canary Islands and much of sub-Saharan Africa, have likewise been culturally divided, with far more different languages than among similar numbers of people living on a broad mainland in ready communication with each other.

The Canary Islanders, for example, were not only poor and backward, ignorant of iron and other metals when the Spaniards discovered them, but were also speaking languages in some of these islands that were unintelligible to people on some other islands in the same group.[16] The peoples of sub-Saharan Africa produced iron more than a thousand years earlier, but were likewise handicapped by a multiplicity of languages. In those parts of sub-Saharan Africa with less severe geographical handicaps, larger communities arose than in other parts of tropical Africa. As in other regions of the world, these larger and more advanced peoples in sub-Saharan Africa often conquered or enslaved their smaller or less advanced neighbors.

In China, one of the advantages of the written Chinese language is that it is a non-phonetic language, so that peoples who cannot understand each other's spoken languages or dialects can nevertheless communicate with each other in written Chinese. From a political standpoint, this can facilitate the consolidation of linguistically different peoples into a larger nation.

Since power is inherently relative, the ability of small political units to survive independently depends on the size and power of other political units within striking distance of them. As already noted, impediments to political consolidation have made small societies vulnerable to both conquest and enslavement. Despite widespread misconceptions in the United States today that the institution of slavery was based on race, for most of the thousands of years in which slavery existed around the world, it was based on whoever was vulnerable to enslavement and within striking distance.

Thus Europeans enslaved other Europeans, just as Asians enslaved other Asians and Africans enslaved other Africans, while Polynesians enslaved other Polynesians and the indigenous peoples of the Western Hemisphere enslaved other indigenous peoples of the Western Hemisphere. The very word "slave" derived from the word for Slavs, who were enslaved by fellow Europeans for centuries before Africans began to be brought in chains to the Western Hemisphere.[17]

Africans were not singled out by race for ownership by Europeans, they were resorted to after the rise of nation-states with armies and navies in other parts of the world reduced the number of places that could be raided for slaves without great costs and risks. Slave-raiding continued in Africa, primarily by Africans enslaving other Africans and then, in West Africa, selling some of their slaves to whites to take to the Western Hemisphere. Meanwhile, the growing range of ships and the growing wealth of nations eventually made economically feasible the transportation of vast numbers of slaves from one continent to another, creating racial differences between the enslaved and their owners as a dominant pattern in the Western Hemisphere.

Such a pattern was by no means limited to Europeans owning non-Europeans, however. There were many examples of the reverse, quite aside from vast regions of the earth where neither the slaves nor their owners were either black or white.

Unprotected coastal settlements in Europe, and European sailors at sea, were long vulnerable to slave raids by pirates from the Barbary Coast of North Africa. These pirates enslaved at least a million Europeans between 1500 and 1800.[18] That is more than the number of African slaves transported to the United States and to the American colonies from which it was formed.[19] The Ottoman Empire set a levy of a certain percentage of young boys from the conquered peoples in Southeastern Europe, these boys being taken away as slaves, converted to Islam, trained and assigned civil and military duties in the empire.[20] Nor were these the only white slaves in the Ottoman Empire. Among others, Circassian women from the Caucasus region were highly prized as concubines by wealthy men in the Ottoman Empire, and such positions were sufficiently prized by Circassians that mothers groomed their daughters for such roles.[21]

The slow pace of political consolidation in much of sub-Saharan Africa left many small and vulnerable societies there, whose people were raided and enslaved, largely by other Africans from more geographically favored settings— coastal peoples enslaving less advanced and less consolidated inland peoples, for example.[22] It was from the coastal peoples of West Africa that whites purchased slaves for shipment to the Western Hemisphere.[23] In East Africa, both Africans and Arabs raided the more vulnerable tribes and enslaved them.[24]

Conquest was another fate of smaller or less powerful peoples in countries around the world. One of the consequences of imperialism, whether ancient or modern, has been that an empire can combine peoples into larger governmental units than the conquered peoples ever combined into themselves. Thus the Roman Empire, for example, combined independent tribes in ancient Britain into Roman Britain, within a government that covered a great part of the island. Then, when the Romans withdrew, four centuries later, to go defend the empire that was under attack on the continent of Europe, Britain fragmented into tribal areas again and retrogressed economically.

This pattern would be repeated, more than a thousand years later, when European imperialism in Asia and Africa collapsed after the Second World War. In Nigeria, for example, the Hausa-Fulani tribes of the north had never been combined in the same country with the Ibos, Yorubas and various other tribes in other parts of the country before the British began taking over that region of Africa in the late nineteenth century and named it Nigeria.

After the British pulled out in 1960, independent Nigeria was repeatedly racked by inter-tribal mob violence, a ghastly civil war and a series of military coups and counter-coups, all of these reflecting tribal hostilities in a country the indigenous peoples never created, but where they were thrown together under outside imperial rule. This pattern of post-independence polarization and violence was not unique to Nigeria. As the international treatise *Ethnic Groups in Conflict* by Donald L. Horowitz put it: "In a large number of ex-colonial states, the independence rally gave way to the ethnic riot."[25]

Geographically, Nigeria has been one of the more fortunate regions of sub-Saharan Africa. Watered by the great Niger River and its principal tributary, the Benue, and blessed with natural resources, including iron ore and large petroleum deposits, the peoples of that region had produced iron centuries before the Christian era, and had developed their own cities and countries before the British arrived— but nothing on the scale of the Nigeria that the British created, with its tribal antagonisms that had never been resolved, but only suppressed, under British rule. According to Professor Horowitz's treatise:

> What the colonialists did that was truly profound, and far more important for ethnicity, was to change the scale of the polity by several fold. The colonies were artificial, not because their borders were indifferent to their ethnic composition, but because they were, on the average, many times larger than the political systems they displaced or encapsulated.[26]

Like Roman Britain more than a thousand years earlier, Nigeria was an artificial creation of the conquerors, and its prosperity and viability were in jeopardy, once the conquerors pulled out. Nigeria has managed to remain one country but one of the poorest and most turbulent countries in the world. That this is more a product of political factors than of either geographic handicaps or inherent deficiencies of its people is suggested by the fact that Nigerians living in the United States have had an impressive record of success:

> In 2010, there were some 260,000 Nigerians in the U.S., a mere 0.7 percent of the black American population. Yet in 2013, 20 to 25 percent of the 120 black students at Harvard Business School were Nigerian. As early as 1999, Nigerians were overrepresented among black students at elite American colleges and universities by a factor of about ten.[27]

Nearly one-fourth of Nigerian households in the United States have incomes of more than $100,000.[28] With all due allowance for the fact that immigrants may be different from the people left behind, the contrast between the way Nigerians progress under American institutions and the way they fail to make comparable progress under the institutions in their homeland is much like the way the overseas

Chinese and the overseas Indians long progressed far better outside their respective homelands. This suggests that there may well be similar reasons, that the political structures and practices in Nigeria may be a major handicap that nullifies the potential of both its people and its geographic setting.

In Asia, British India was a similar story on a larger scale. The extremely heterogeneous peoples living on the Indian subcontinent were lumped together by their conquerors, for their conquerors' convenience— but without the indigenous peoples' having resolved their differences and coalesced voluntarily over time into this political entity. After the British pulled out in 1947, the carnage was even greater than in Nigeria. The number of people killed in the 1947 mob violence between Hindus and Muslims has been estimated in the vicinity of a million, as British India split into a predominantly Hindu India and a predominantly Muslim Pakistan.

Nevertheless, despite this split, aimed at reducing Hindu-Muslim conflict, both India and Pakistan have subsequently been racked sporadically by internal conflicts between various groups, with East Pakistan eventually breaking off to form the new nation of Bangladesh. Overseas Indians, like the overseas Chinese and like the Nigerians living in America, have long prospered in many other countries around the world, where they were free from the political and other constraints, deficiencies and conflicts of their native land. Despite the widespread poverty in India, Americans of Indian ancestry have the highest incomes of any group tracked by the U.S. Bureau of the Census.[29] (Religious groups like Mormons and Jews are not tracked).

Other multi-ethnic, post-colonial nations that emerged after being freed by the breakup of empires have had similar internal turmoils. Whether these nations subsequently split internally, as happened with India, Yugoslavia and Czechoslovakia, or remained intact like Nigeria, Sri Lanka and the Philippines, their internal strife has taken its toll, both economically and socially.

While such historical patterns demonstrate once more the powerful negative force of isolation on economic and social development, these patterns also show why the transportation and communications revolutions of the past two centuries cannot undo the effects of earlier centuries or millennia of isolation. Even if the transportation and communications revolutions were to become as complete in formerly isolated parts of the world as in other regions that have long had a wider cultural universe, that cannot undo the fact that peoples living in a wider cultural universe have had centuries or millennia to become acquainted with other peoples and to work out cooperative relationships with them, while those living in isolation have not.

The fact that isolated peoples have usually been poorer and more backward has often meant that transportation and communications advances reached them belatedly and on a smaller scale. A life-changing advance like railroads, for example, reached parts of Eastern Europe and the Balkans only after trains had spread rapidly across Western Europe in the first half of the nineteenth century.

As late as 1860, there was not a single mile of railroad track south of the Danube and the Sava rivers.[30] We have already noted that a train was a complete mystery to people in Japan in 1853, when that country was a poor and backward nation. It was a quarter of a century later before the first railroad reached Serbia.[31] Meanwhile, in the United States, even the less industrialized South had a railroad hub in Atlanta, which made it a target for General William T. Sherman's army in its devastating march through Georgia during the Civil War.

The often tragic histories of the emergence of multi-ethnic nations created by imperial conquerors should call into question the extent to which "nation-building" by outsiders is a promising prospect. It should also cause some second thoughts— or perhaps first thoughts— about the endlessly repeated mantra of ethnic "diversity" as such a source of societal strength that it is a "compelling interest" for government, in the words of the Supreme Court of the United States.[32] Few words have been repeated so often or so insistently as "diversity," without a speck of evidence being offered or asked for to substantiate its claims of economic or social benefits. And the evidence to the contrary is huge.

Seldom, if ever, do advocates of demographic diversity compare the actual empirical record of the costs and benefits of such diversity in countries around the world. India, with its vast array of ethnic, linguistic, caste and other subdivisions of its population should have great advantages over an extremely homogeneous society like Japan, if diversity is such a benefit, but there is little empirical evidence that this is so, and much empirical evidence to the contrary. In India, as in a number of sub-Saharan nations, there is no given language spoken by even half the population, and mass intergroup violence has by no means been unusual.

It is an important and commendable achievement for a nation to overcome problems common to multi-ethnic societies, but that is very different from claiming that multiple ethnicities in a nation are automatically a net benefit. A closer look at politically polarized multi-ethnic societies raises many painful questions. This is nowhere more clearly or more distressingly apparent than in countries where one racial or ethnic group is strikingly more prosperous than others, and where that fact is politicized.

THE POLITICS OF POLARIZATION

Disparities in income and wealth, whether within nations or between nations, can arise from many causes. However, the presumed causes that are politically popular have tended to be those which involve the less fortunate being victims of the more fortunate. General causes, such as geography, demography and culture have no such political attraction as explanations, despite whatever causal weight they may have in fact.

It might seem as if every society, whether rich or poor, can always use greater productivity, wherever it is available. But it only *seems* that way. Politically, there is a major problem, especially in a poor country, when some racially or socially distinct group has markedly higher levels of skills or economic experience than that in the rest of the population.

From an economic perspective, this situation presents a valuable opportunity for the more productive portion of the population to supply much needed human capital to enable the economy as a whole to become more productive, creating benefits for the population at large. Moreover, the presence of people with such human capital also presents an opportunity for individuals in the rest of a society to acquire some of this human capital themselves, whether by example, by working with or observing the more productive group, or by studying to acquire such skills in educational institutions. Knowledge is one of the few things that can be transferred to others without those from whom it is transferred having any less remaining for themselves.

From a *political* perspective, however, the situation is entirely different. As noted in Chapter 3, when more productive groups freely compete in a market economy, this leads to visible disparities in economic outcomes that are resented by the less successful groups. Political leaders in many lagging countries have been keenly aware of this prospect.

A political leader of the Malays in Malaysia, for example, said candidly, "Whatever the Malays could do, the Chinese could do better and more cheaply."[33] This provided a political rationale for imposing preferential policies for the benefit of the Malays, which is to say, discrimination against the Chinese in Malaysia. This same political leader observed:

> These few Malays, for they are still only very few, have waxed rich not because of themselves but because of the policy of a Government supported by a huge majority of poor Malays. It would seem that the efforts of the poor Malays have gone to enrich a select few of their own people. The poor Malays themselves have not gained one iota. But if these few Malays are not enriched the poor Malays will not gain either. It is the Chinese who will continue to live in huge houses and regard the Malays as only fit to drive their cars. With the existence of the few rich Malays at least the poor Malays can say that their fate is not entirely to serve rich non-Malays. From the point of view of racial ego, and this ego is still strong, the unseemly existence of Malay tycoons is essential.[34]

What is involved in such reactions is not simply poverty or envy, but *resentment*. If the issue was envy, then it would be hard to explain the pride that Malays have had in their own wealthy Malay sultans.[35] Sultans are in a much more enviable position than most Chinese in Malaysia. The sultans are likely to be wealthier, and their wealth has come by inheritance, rather than by personal achievement. But personal achievement is much more of a threat to the egos of others than inheritance is, not only in Malaysia but elsewhere.

In the United States, for example, three heirs to the Rockefeller fortune have been elected governors of three different states, and two Roosevelts with inherited wealth have been elected President of the United States. It is the Asian immigrants of a later time, many of whom have been refugees, who in many cases arrived on American shores with little money and a few words of broken English, but who have worked their way up from the bottom to a modest prosperity, and whose children excel in school and then head off to prestigious universities, who are threats to the egos of lagging groups in America who have made nothing like the same use of their own opportunities.

Korean immigrants to the United States, for example, worked an average of 63 hours per week as storekeepers in Atlanta, with one-fifth of them working 80 hours or more.[36] In New York, Korean greengrocers have gone out to pick up their fruits and vegetables from wholesalers at 4:00 AM, enabling them to select the best of these fruits and vegetables and to save on delivery charges that other greengrocers had to pay.[37]

The children of such Asian families have shown a similar work ethic in school— and have provoked the same resentments by their superior academic achievements as adult high achievers have provoked in members of lagging groups in countries around the world. Children of Asian families have for years been beaten up by black classmates in the public schools of New York and Philadelphia[38]— with little or nothing being done by the authorities to stop it, and no editorial indignation about it from people in the media who are quick to cry "racism" at any passing remark that can be construed as critical of any of the groups currently in favor among the intelligentsia.

Like the Asian immigrants to America today, Jewish, Lebanese and Japanese immigrants have at various times in the past arrived in various countries around the world with little money, but much human capital, and prospered as a result— provoking resentments among those who were there before them, and who made no similar use of their own opportunities. There have also been examples of the same social phenomena among groups who migrated within their own country and rose to prosperity, and who were likewise resented. The Marwaris and Bengalis in various parts of India, Armenians in the Ottoman Empire, as well as Ibos in Nigeria and Tamils in Sri Lanka are among other examples of the same social phenomenon.[39]

In many countries, the political priority of protecting majority group egos has trumped the economic or other benefits of making use of the best skills and talents available in the economy. After Nigeria became independent in 1960, a high political priority among the Hausa-Fulani peoples in northern Nigeria was to get rid of the Ibos from southern Nigeria, who had dominated professions and skilled occupations in northern Nigeria under British rule. Ibos were driven out of northern Nigeria, often to the accompaniment of lethal mob violence, even when there were not enough qualified northern Nigerians to replace the Ibos, and European expatriates had to be hired to take their place instead.[40]

In the same vein, when Romania acquired territory from the defeated Central Powers after the First World War, this territory included universities that were culturally German or culturally Hungarian. The Romanian government made it a political priority to force Germans and Hungarians out of these universities, even though most Romanians were still illiterate at that point, and so could not replace the Germans or Hungarians.[41] The expulsion of Asians from Uganda in the 1970s led to the collapse of the Ugandan economy, because there were not nearly enough qualified Ugandans to replace them in the business sector that people from the Indian subcontinent had dominated for generations.[42]

These were not isolated examples. Distinguished development economist Peter Bauer of the London School of Economics, who studied Third World countries for years, reported a general pattern in those countries of "persecution of the most productive groups, especially minorities, and sometimes their expulsion."[43]

However much productive minority groups might benefit a national economy in a poor country, their marked success threatens the egos of the lagging majority, provoking often bitter resentments. In Bolivia, a terrorist of indigenous descent, when asked why he was engaging in terrorist activity, replied: "So that my daughter will not have to be your maid."[44] When the new nation of Czechoslovakia was created out of the dissolution of the Habsburg Empire after the First World War, one of the new Czech leaders' first political priorities was preferential treatment of Czechs— which meant discrimination against Germans, setting in motion a series of major tragedies for both Czechs and Germans over the next three decades.[45]

If poverty or envy were the fundamental problem, then a more productive economy and a spreading of productive skills to those without them might seem to be the answer. But neither of these things can cure resentments at being in a galling inferior position.

For those seething with such resentments, it is not sufficient to have a rising standard of living. From the standpoint of resenters, the priority is that those in a superior position must be brought down. Even the killing of the more fortunate is often not considered sufficient. They must be made to suffer both physical agonies and personal humiliations to bring them down to the level of those who attack them— and below. That has been a common pattern, whether the targets of violent actions have been the Chinese in the Philippines, Armenians in the Ottoman Empire, Jews in Nazi Germany or Tutsis in Rwanda, among others.

The Chinese in the Philippines are among the many productive groups whose economic success has led to violent backlashes. As an international study noted:

> In the Philippines, millions of Filipinos work for Chinese; almost no Chinese work for Filipinos. The Chinese dominate industry and commerce at every level of society. Global markets intensify this dominance: When foreign investors do business in the Philippines, they deal almost exclusively with Chinese. Apart from a handful of corrupt politicians and a few aristocratic Spanish mestizo families, all of the Philippines' billionaires are of Chinese descent. By contrast, all menial jobs in the Philippines are filled by Filipinos. All peasants are Filipinos. All domestic servants and squatters are Filipinos.[46]

The same study also noted: "Hundreds of Chinese in the Philippines are kidnapped every year, almost invariably by ethnic Filipinos. Many victims, often children, are brutally murdered, even after ransom is paid."[47]

A study of the Ottoman Empire described the mass slaughters of Armenians by Turkish mobs in 1894, including "bayoneting the men to death, raping the women, dashing their children against the rocks."[48] In 1915 there was a death march imposed on Armenians, in which thousands perished, many of the women were stripped naked and forced to walk into the city that way.[49]

It was much the same pattern in Rwanda in the late twentieth century, when the Hutus slaughtered hundreds of thousands of Tutsis. Young children were often killed in front of their parents, by cutting off one arm, then the other. A United Nations official reported: "They would then gash the neck with a machete to bleed the child slowly to death but, while they were still alive, they would cut off the private parts and throw them at the faces of the terrified parents, who would then be murdered with slightly greater dispatch."[50]

Such atrocities reflect vengeful resentments that cannot be assuaged by a higher Gross Domestic Product per capita. The feelings behind ghastly acts of revenge are not simply envy, but resentments— lashing out at those whose success has inflicted a galling position of inferiority, and wounded feelings of inferiority, on those who resent.

Yet it is also a puzzling and disturbing fact that some groups who inflicted horrific atrocities on others had previously co-existed peacefully for years, or even generations, with those who eventually became targets of their rage. *The Times of India*, for example, referred to "neighbours leading long-time friends to gory deaths" during intergroup outbreaks of violence in Mumbai (Bombay) in 1992–1993.[51]

Such disturbing patterns not only raise sobering questions about how secure any apparent *detente* between racial or ethnic groups is in fact. These patterns also suggest that some catalyst may be needed to arouse the feelings behind the horrors— and of course no one can know in advance when any such catalyst may arise, even in the most tranquil settings, whether that catalyst appears in the form of a particular episode or a particular skilled and talented demagogue.

When Sri Lanka achieved independence in 1948, its main ethnic groups were seen by observers, both inside and outside the country, as having good— even "cordial" relations with one another.[52] There had been no riot between the Sinhalese majority and the Tamil minority during the previous half-century. The educated and Westernized elites of both groups lived peacefully in the same Westernized residential enclaves.

Nevertheless, within a decade after Sri Lanka emerged from British rule as an independent nation in 1948, an ambitious politician named Solomon Bandaranaike, seeking the prime ministership by turning the Sinhalese majority against the more prosperous Tamil minority, set in motion group polarizations that escalated into mob violence, and then a civil war that lasted a quarter of a century, with unspeakable atrocities on both sides. Bandaranaike was the catalyst. Like many others who played that deadly role in other countries, Bandaranaike was by no means one of the embittered poor himself. He was from an elite background and was skilled in whipping up other people's emotions for his own political purposes.*

Much discussion of policies toward Third World countries proceeds as if the fundamental problem in such countries is poverty

---

* Once his purposes were served— that is, he became prime minister— Bandaranaike was willing to back off the extremism he had aroused. But the emotions he had whipped up could not be turned off, and acquired a life of their own. When Bandaranaike moderated his stance toward the Tamils after getting elected, he was assassinated by a Buddhist extremist and the polarization process continued to escalate into a devastating civil war.

and a lack of the skills and knowledge required to raise their standard of living. Supplying money, physical equipment and technocrats with skills might seem to be the answer, as policies to help Third World countries advance. But many, if not most, poor countries already have within their own borders people with the human capital to advance the nation's economy. Yet there are formidable political obstacles to using that human capital, and many political incentives to avoid letting minorities with skills lacking in the majority population have free rein to put their skills to work, with resulting disparities in performances and rewards.

In the most varied conditions in countries around the world— whether in Third World countries or in economically more advanced countries, and whether in countries where the majority or the minority has the higher skills— those seeking either the leadership or the votes of lagging groups tend to offer them four things:

1. Assurance that their lags are not their fault.
2. Assurance that their lags are the fault of some advanced group that they already envy and resent.
3. Assurance that the lagging group and their culture are just as good as anybody else's, if not better.
4. Assurance that what the lagging group needs and deserves is a demographically defined "fair share" of the economic and other benefits of society, sometimes supplemented with some kind of reparations for past injustices or some special reward for being indigenous "sons of the soil."

Economic competition in the marketplace can financially punish people whose beliefs differ from reality, but competition for votes at election time can politically punish people who assert a reality that differs from popular beliefs. In addition, racial or ethnic leaders have every incentive to promote the isolation of the groups they lead—

despite the fact that isolation has been a major factor in the poverty and backwardness of many different peoples around the world.

Where a lagging group is concentrated in a particular region of a country, leaders of such groups have incentives to promote secession from the more advanced part of the country, as Slovaks seceded from Czechoslovakia and as East Pakistanis seceded from Pakistan to create the new nation of Bangladesh. Despite the economic losses that poorer groups may sustain when they are no longer part of a more advanced economy, their political leaders gain from acquiring more power as leaders of a nation, and have every incentive to promote national pride in independent nationhood, whether or not that has made the people they lead better off or worse off economically. The people themselves may also benefit psychically by being spared the public embarrassment and private shame of being visibly outperformed repeatedly by others in the same economy and society.

Where the political situation makes secession unlikely to happen, leaders of lagging groups have every incentive to promote cultural isolation, such as laws or policies in parts of the United States requiring the teaching of Hispanic children in the Spanish language, even when their parents want them taught in English, so as to facilitate their rise in the American economy and society.[53]

Perhaps the most culturally isolated of all American ethnic groups are those descendants of the indigenous American Indian population who still live on reservations with great legal autonomy, but with lower per capita incomes than blacks, Hispanics or other American Indians who are not living on reservations. Since the 1980s, American Indians living off reservations— who are a substantial majority of all American Indians— have had per capita incomes slightly higher than those of Hispanic Americans, while American Indians living on reservations have had substantially lower per capita incomes than black or Hispanic Americans and less than half that of the American population as a whole.[54] Yet leaders of American Indian reservations jealously guard their prerogatives and promote the perpetuation of separate cultures among the populations of these reservations.

Racial or ethnic leaders also have incentives to blame advanced groups for the lags of lagging groups. The behavior of advanced groups toward lagging groups has by no means always been exemplary, nor necessarily even decent, so the leaders of lagging groups may have many things to complain about— without those things necessarily being the reasons for the economic, educational or other gaps between the advanced groups and the lagging groups.

In particular circumstances, some advanced group may in fact be the cause of holding back some lagging group. But that cannot be assumed *a priori* from the fact that one group is demonstrably more successful economically or in other ways. Even where the advanced group has behaved badly toward the lagging group, as has often happened in many countries around the world, that is still not proof that the lagging group would have been better off economically in the absence of the advanced group.

The ancient Romans certainly behaved abominably toward the ancient Britons whom they conquered. But that is not to say that the Romans were the reason that the Britons lagged. It was only the fact that the Britons lagged *before* the Romans arrived and conquered them that permitted a numerically smaller Roman military force to overwhelm a numerically larger British force, both during the conquest and later, when there was a mass uprising of the British, provoked by the Romans' oppression. In putting down that uprising, the Romans slaughtered Britons by the thousands, and the queen who had led the uprising committed suicide to avoid the retribution she knew she could expect from the Romans. Yet, in modern times, even such a British patriot as Winston Churchill could say, "We owe London to Rome"[55] because the ancient Britons were not yet capable of creating such a city themselves.

No one believes that slaves were always treated well, in the many times and places around the world where there were slaves. There is too much documented evidence that they were not. But the fact that black Americans today have a far higher standard of living than the peoples of sub-Saharan Africa from which they are descended is not a happenstance. Nor can this outcome retroactively justify slavery, any more than the valuable advantages that Western Europeans' descendants received as a cultural legacy from Roman conquests can retroactively justify the Romans' brutal oppression of their ancestors.

Neither can individuals or groups lagging today automatically blame their lags on the injustices inflicted on their ancestors, when the cultural benefits available to them in later times were an unintended by-product of those injustices. *Moral* condemnation is not *causal* explanation, despite how often the two have been combined in a politically attractive package. Despite the tendency of political, and especially ideological, explanations of economic disparities to combine moral and causal factors, the reason so many mountain peoples around the world have been poor has not been that others went up into those mountains and took away their wealth, but that the mountain peoples seldom produced much wealth in the first place. The Spaniards seizing the wealth of the Incas was an exception on a horrific scale, but empirically it was not the rule.

The one thing that can be said unequivocally about the past is that it is irrevocable. When both history and the contemporary world scene show what a challenge it can be to create or maintain decent relations among contemporaries, it is staggering that some people imagine that they can take on the far larger task of righting the wrongs of the past, committed by people long dead, without igniting dangerous new hostilities among the living.

THE WELFARE STATE

The welfare state is often seen in terms of its effects on the material well-being of individuals or groups. However, it can also have an effect on the productivity of a nation as a whole, and therefore on the standard of living of its people in general. Moreover, the welfare state's effects extend beyond economics to social behavior with major impacts on both the recipients of welfare benefits and those who interact with them. These effects are not due solely to the welfare state, as such, but often to the social vision that accompanies the welfare state and changes the way many people see the world.

The Welfare State Vision

In a democratic country, a welfare state can be created only after a welfare state vision is created and prevails politically. Therefore, in assessing the effect of a welfare state, we must include the effects of that vision, as well as the effects of the particular institutions and policies created. Among the assumptions behind the welfare state vision, two seem crucial: (1) many people are mired in a degree of poverty that a prosperous society can and should relieve, and (2) many, if not most, of the people in poverty never had the same chance of a better life as others who ended up more prosperous.

Even in a society with rules that are fair, in the sense of judging everyone by the same standards and rewarding or punishing them according to the same criteria, it would still be true that someone born in the South Bronx would have nothing like the same probability of achieving economic success— however defined— as someone born in an elegant Park Avenue neighborhood. To be fair in the sense of providing equal probabilities of success for people born in unequal social circumstances would be very different. In that sense, life has been unfair in virtually every society of the past or the present.

The case for the welfare state vision has seldom been made more clearly than by Nicholas Kristof of the *New York Times*:

> One delusion common among America's successful people is that they triumphed just because of hard work and intelligence.
> In fact, their big break came when they were conceived in middle-class American families who loved them, read them stories, and nurtured them with Little League sports, library cards and music lessons. They were programmed for success by the time they were zygotes.[56]

The social conditions into which individuals are born and raised are of course not equal, just as the geographic, demographic and cultural conditions in which individuals, groups and nations find themselves are not equal in their economic prospects. This has been true throughout recorded history. No doubt many of us wish that things were different, and some want to "do something" about it. But everything depends on just what specifically is the "something" that is done. The welfare state is just one option among many.

Mr. Kristof's response to the unfairness of life is to criticize those "who are oblivious of their own advantages, and of other people's disadvantages." He accuses them of "a mean-spiritedness in the political world or, at best, a lack of empathy toward those struggling— partly explaining the hostility to state expansion of Medicaid, to long-term unemployment benefits, or to raising the minimum wage to keep up with inflation."[57] In short, Kristof's response to the unfairness of life is a government transfer of resources from those who are more prosperous to those who are less prosperous— with no caveats about the further consequences of such welfare state policies or its accompanying vision, and no apparent apprehension about whether those consequences will make either the less prosperous, or society at large, better off or worse off on net balance.

To blithely assume that the only reason to be against minimum wage laws is a lack of empathy with the poor is to ignore a vast literature on the negative repercussions of minimum wage laws. These repercussions include increased numbers of unemployed young males idle on the streets, which is seldom a benefit to any community.

Ten years after passage of the federal minimum wage law in the United States— the Fair Labor Standards Act of 1938— the wartime inflation in the intervening years had so raised prices and wages that the minimum wage specified in that law was below what inexperienced and unskilled workers were already being paid, so that by 1948 the economic situation in most places was the same as if there were no minimum wage law. The unemployment rate among black 16- and 17-year-olds that year was just under 10 percent. But, in later years, as the minimum wage was repeatedly raised to keep up with inflation, unemployment among blacks this age never again fell below

20 percent. It was 27 percent a decade later in 1958 and 45 percent in 1975.[58] It is one of the most elementary principles of economics that prices artificially raised above the level set by supply and demand creates unsaleable surpluses, whether what is being sold is agricultural produce or labor— regardless of the presence or absence of empathy.

Despite a common claim, advanced by Kristof among many others, that "Slavery and post-slavery oppression left a legacy of broken families" among blacks,[59] the plain fact is that the proportion of black children living with only one parent was never as large during the first hundred years after slavery as it became in the first thirty years after the great expansion of the welfare state, beginning in the 1960s. Yet the "legacy of slavery" argument continues to be blithely repeated and the legacy of the welfare state ignored.

The proportion of black children being raised by a single mother in 1960 was 22 percent. Thirty-five years later, that proportion had risen to 52 percent being raised by a mother alone, 4 percent being raised by a father alone and another 11 percent being raised with neither parent present— altogether, 67 percent of all black children.[60] By 1995, the proportion of black children in poverty-level families who were being raised without a father present was 85 percent.[61]

The central rationale for the welfare state is poverty. But, if the word is to have any specific meaning, someone must define it in specific terms. Once that is done, "poverty" means *no more and no less* than those specifications, however much the word may conjure up images from a past era when poverty meant hunger, ragged clothing, cramped housing and the like. Today, poverty in America means whatever government statisticians in Washington say it means— and they are unlikely to define it in ways that would jeopardize the welfare state of which they are part.

Most people living below the official poverty line in the United States in 2001 had central air conditioning and a microwave oven, for example. In fact, these items were more common among the officially poor in 2001 than they were among the American population as a whole in 1980. Most poverty-level households in 2001 had cable television and two or more television sets. As of 2003, nearly three-fourths of officially poverty-level households owned at least one motor vehicle and 14 percent owned two or more.[62] In contrast to times past when low-income people lived in overcrowded dwellings, Americans living below the official poverty level today have more housing space per person than the average European— not poor Europeans, but the average European.[63] As a scholar who spent years studying Latin America put it, "the poverty line in the United States is the upper-middle class in Mexico."[64]

This is not to say that Americans living in official poverty have no problems. They have serious and often catastrophic social problems, but these are seldom the result of material deprivation— and are far more often a result of social degeneration, much of it representing social retrogressions during the era of the rising welfare state and of the pervasive, non-judgmental welfare state ideology.

Progress and Retrogressions

Black Americans, a group often identified as beneficiaries of the welfare state in America, made considerable economic progress in the twentieth century but much, if not most, of it was *prior* to the massive expansion of the American welfare state, beginning with the "war on poverty" programs of the 1960s.

Progress, for most blacks, can be measured from the time of the Emancipation Proclamation of 1863. That progress was slow but steady. By 1900, a majority of black Americans were literate— something that would not be true of the population of Romania until decades later, and of the population of India until more than half a century after that. As of 1910, about one-fourth of black farmers were owners or buyers of their land, rather than renters or sharecroppers.[65] Herbert Gutman's monumental treatise, *The Black Family in Slavery and Freedom, 1750–1925* showed that, during the era from 1880 to 1925, "the typical Afro-American family was lower-class in status and headed by two parents." In 1925, just 3 percent of black families in

New York were headed by a woman under thirty.[66] The unwed teenage mother became common in a later generation, during the era of the expanded welfare state.

The reasons for black poverty— often very real poverty, in earlier years especially— are not hard to find. It was 1930 before the average black adult had six years of education,[67] mostly in inferior Southern schools. At that time, only 19 percent of black children of high school age in the South actually went to high school.[68] It was 1924 before the first permanent public high school for black children was built in Atlanta,[69] after years of campaigns by the local black community.

As of 1940, 87 percent of black families in the United States lived below the poverty line. But this declined to 47 percent by 1960, as black education and urban job experience increased in the wake of the mass migrations of blacks out of the South. This 40 percentage point drop in the black poverty rate occurred *prior* to both the civil rights laws and the "war on poverty" social welfare programs of the 1960s. Over the next 20 years, from 1960 to 1980, the black poverty rate dropped an additional 18 points[70]— significant, but the continuation of a pre-existing trend at a slower pace, rather than being a new result from new civil rights laws and welfare state policies, as so often claimed.

There were dramatic increases in the number of black elected officials in the South after passage of the Voting Rights Act of 1965. But nothing similarly dramatic occurred in black economic advancement as a result of the civil rights laws of the 1960s. In some important social ways, actual retrogressions set in.

Arguably the most consequential of these social retrogressions was the decline in two-parent families. We have also seen in Chapter 4 some declines in black educational achievements during this later era, such as a decline in the proportion of black students in New York's Stuyvesant High School to *one-tenth* of what they had been in earlier years. In addition, there was an increase in crime and violence, including ghetto riots. The first in a series of such riots across the country erupted in Los Angeles, just days after the Voting Rights Act of 1965 was passed.

This eruption of violence was contrary to the prevailing political and social vision of the times, in which problems among blacks were automatically assumed to be due to deficiencies in the way white people treated them. But such riots were less common in the South,[71] where racial discrimination in laws and practices remained more common. By contrast, the worst of these riots— with 43 people killed, 33 of whom were black— occurred in Detroit, where the black unemployment rate was 3.4 percent and black home ownership was higher than in any other major city.[72] Yet no such facts made a dent in the prevailing social vision.

The proliferation of black politicians and of community activists provided a great increase of "leaders" promoting the same kind of vision that ethnic leaders have promoted to many other lagging groups in many other countries around the world. That vision is one in which the lagging group's problems are due primarily, if not solely, to the malign actions of other groups. The answers offered to blacks in America have been in principle— despite local variations— very much like the answers offered to Czechs in nineteenth century Bohemia, Sinhalese in twentieth century Sri Lanka, Maoris in New Zealand and many others elsewhere: group solidarity in pursuit of collective political solutions and, in the meantime, resistance to the cultures of those who are more fortunate.

The actual track record of that approach, as compared to other approaches used by other groups, has received virtually no attention from either black leaders or the black or white intelligentsia in either the media or academia. A list of groups that have risen from poverty to prosperity, in countries around the world— the Chinese, Lebanese, Jews, and Japanese, for example— would usually also be a list of groups that played very little role in politics during their rise, though a few of their members in later times could afford the luxury of political careers. But, even then, those political careers were seldom based on being spokesmen for their respective groups in the political arena.

Germans in Australia, Brazil and the United States were long noted for their unusually *low* interest in politics, while their interest in education and in otherwise advancing themselves economically was the focus of their attention. Even when some Americans of German ancestry became prominent in politics— the Muhlenbergs in the eighteenth century, Carl Schurz and John Peter Altgeld in the nineteenth century, and Herbert Hoover and Dwight D. Eisenhower in the twentieth century— they did *not* do so as spokesmen for the German American community, but as people addressing issues facing the American population as a whole. In the period up through the First World War, Germans in Brazil seldom bothered to vote.[73] Even when Germans were politically attacked as a group in nineteenth century Bohemia, their first response was to defend a cosmopolitan outlook, and only belatedly did they defend themselves specifically as Germans.[74]

It was very much the same story with the overseas Chinese in Southeast Asia and the Western Hemisphere— political apathy and fierce concentration on work, education and saving. The same unromantic but very effective concentration on work, education and saving lifted Jewish, Japanese and Lebanese immigrants from poverty to prosperity in various countries around the world. It also lifted indigenous minorities like the Ibos in Nigeria, Tamils in Sri Lanka and Armenians in the Ottoman Empire, among others.

Conversely, one of the most politically successful groups in America— the Irish— did not rise from poverty as fast as other groups that were neither as involved politically, nor as successful in politics as the Irish were. Irish politicians reached influential positions in mid-nineteenth century American cities and, within a few decades, the Irish were dominant in big city political machines in Boston, New York and other cities across the country, and remained so well into the twentieth century. This brought prosperity, prominence and power to a few, but the great majority of the Irish continued to lag behind other Americans economically, and even behind some other immigrant groups.

At the beginning of the twentieth century, 39 percent of the Irish in New York City were unskilled laborers— the highest percentage for any ethnic group in New York at that time. An additional 25 percent were classified as semi-skilled.[75] At the same time, 71 percent of first-generation Irish women in New York worked as domestic or personal servants, as did 25 percent of second-generation Irish women.[76] As of 1930, the proportion of the Irish who paid more than a hundred dollars a month in rent was barely more than half the proportion among Russians— most of whom were Jews during this era— and less than half the proportion among Germans.[77] This was despite the fact that the peak of Irish immigration to America came decades before the peak of Jewish immigration, so that the Irish had had a longer time to rise in American society.

However plausible, or even inspiring, it might seem that a lagging minority needs to unite in solidarity behind political leaders representing their interests to the larger society, in order to get ahead, the historical record shows no such pattern of success for politics, as compared to education, job skills and intact families.

Despite the ease with which some use the "legacy of slavery" argument to explain negative features of black communities today, there is seldom any attempt to examine the facts as to whether whatever is complained of— whether fatherless families, crime rates or other social pathology— was in fact worse in the first hundred years after slavery or in the first generation after the triumph of the welfare state vision in the 1960s. The homicide fatality rate among non-whites— the vast majority of whom in this era were blacks killed by other blacks— rose sharply during the 1960s, *after having declined substantially during the 1950s*. In 1950, the homicides per 100,000 people were 45.5 among non-white males, and this fell to 34.5 in 1960, followed by a rise to 60.8 in 1970.[78]

Other retrogressions followed in the wake of the disintegration of two-parent families. These retrogressions included rising rates of welfare dependency,[79] unemployment,[80] crimes[81] and organized mob violence against whites and Asians in dozens of cities and towns across the country.[82] While black civil rights organizations and the black public had long been opposed to racism, nevertheless group identity politics eventually led to a situation in which a public opinion poll in 2013 found that more blacks saw their fellow blacks as racist than saw whites as racist.[83]

During the first half of the twentieth century, black migrants from the South were ridiculed by Northern blacks when they did not speak standard English, or when their behavior in other respects betrayed a lower level of education or sophistication. Black newspapers and black civic organizations like the Urban League tried to acculturate less educated, lower-class blacks to the norms of the larger society,[84] much as Irish and Jewish civic organizations during the immigrant era tried to acculturate their respective compatriots to the norms of the larger society.[85]

In the second half of the twentieth century, however, with the spread of the non-judgmental multicultural doctrine that all cultures are equally valid, and equally deserved to be celebrated, to repudiate the ghetto culture was now seen as a racial betrayal by blacks who were "acting white." Now even more educated and more acculturated blacks, especially among the young, felt a need to adopt, or affect, some patterns or norms from the ghetto culture, as a sign of racial solidarity, or at least to avoid social friction. In short, the acculturation process now reversed, in favor of the lowest common denominator, as the influence of the ghetto culture spread up the social scale, leading to social retrogressions visible in many ways.

Television documentaries about black communities in the first half of the twentieth century may show noticeably poorer neighborhoods than today, with fewer cars parked on the streets, but usually neighborhoods without graffiti or bars on windows. Neither the residents of Harlem nor whites who visited Harlem faced the level of dangers in the first half of the twentieth century that became common and pervasive in Harlem and other black communities in later years.

During the 1920s, for example, many white celebrities frequented Harlem's entertainment centers and private parties into the wee hours of the morning, before returning to their homes downtown, often just before dawn. Many had their own cars but music critic Carl Van Vechten— a frequent visitor to Harlem— simply went out on the streets, often intoxicated, to hail a cab to take him back to his west 55th Street apartment.[86] In the early 1930s, when Milton Friedman was a graduate student at Columbia University, he and his future wife went dancing at the Savoy Ballroom in Harlem, "with no fear of being mugged or accosted," as he said in later years.[87] A black actress who lived in Harlem and performed in Manhattan's midtown theater district during the 1940s said: "At one in the morning I would be taking the Eighth Avenue subway up, getting off at the top of the Hill. I had no fears whatsoever."[88] It is hard even to imagine such things in Harlem or other ghettos across the country today.

Public housing projects were a particularly striking setting in which social retrogressions among blacks took place. The filthy, crime-ridden, violence-prone housing projects, full of single-parent families on welfare, that became common across the country in the second half of the twentieth century, were by no means the norm during the first half of the twentieth century. There were *de facto* racially segregated projects in both eras. Yet the earlier projects were a striking contrast with the later projects, during an era of non-judgmental admissions policies toward applicants for apartments in the projects. As the *New York Times* reported, looking back on New York's earlier projects:

> These were not the projects of idle, stinky elevators, of gang-controlled stairwells where drug deals go down. In the 1940s, '50s and '60s, when most of the city's public housing was built, a sense of pride and community permeated well-kept corridors, apartments and grounds.[89]

It was not simply the physical setting that was different. So was the way of life in those early housing projects:

> Doors were kept unlocked as kids bounced from one apartment to the next on rainy Saturdays to watch Laurel and Hardy and Hopalong Cassidy on television.[90]

This was an era when not everyone could afford a television set, but when many people in the housing projects of that era who did have a television set felt safe enough to leave their apartment doors unlocked on Saturday mornings, so that their children's friends could come visit to watch television with them.*

There was a similar atmosphere in Philadelphia housing projects of that era, as described by black economist Walter Williams, who grew up in a housing project there:

> Back in the '40s the Homes were not what they were to become— a location known for drugs, killings, and nighttime sounds of gunfire. One of the most noticeable differences back then compared to today was the makeup of the resident families. Most of the children we played with, unlike my sister and I, lived with both parents. More than likely, there were other single-parent households but I can recall none. Fathers worked, and the mothers often did as well. The buildings and yards were well kept.[91]

There was no graffiti in this project. On hot summer nights it was not uncommon for people to sleep out on the balconies or, in the case of first-floor apartments, in their yards. In the adjoining local black neighborhood, it was not uncommon to see old men sitting around a table out on the street on hot summer nights, playing checkers or cards, during an era when most people could not afford air conditioning.[92] The contrast with the housing projects and ghetto neighborhoods of later years could hardly be more stark:

> When the shooting gets bad, children are put to sleep in bathtubs and under beds so they won't be struck by random bullets. Residents must pay tribute to gun-toting teenagers in order to enter their own buildings, get mail, and ride the elevator. Many have become prisoners in their own apartments, afraid to walk hallways strewn with empty crack vials, used condoms, and excrement where the lights have been put out by muggers and drug dealers. The buildings themselves crumble in decay from neglect and vandalism. Those who can escape do, leaving behind an increasingly poor and demoralized underclass. The projects are increasingly seen as some other America— isolated and feared havens of addiction, violence and "problem" people.[93]

---

* Contrast that with today, when most people living in officially defined poverty have central air conditioning, cable television and multiple television sets per household, but who would not dare to leave their apartment doors unlooked.

The demographic makeup of the housing project's residents was also a contrast with that in earlier times:

> Women headed 90 percent of the families with children, and 81 percent of the households received aid to families with dependent children (AFDC). Unemployment was estimated to be 47 percent in 1980. Although only a little more than 0.5 percent of Chicago's more than 3 million people live in Robert Taylor Homes, "11 percent of the city's murders, 9 percent of its rapes, and 10 percent of its aggravated assaults were committed in the project."[94]

The retrogressions in educational achievement among blacks in parts of the United States, as well as the retrogressions represented by family disintegration, rising drug addiction, violence and criminal behavior, have been strikingly similar among lower-class whites in England. Moreover, these and other social retrogressions proliferated during the same time period— from the 1960s onward— on both sides of the Atlantic. A whole way of life among lower-class whites in England, remarkably similar to the way of life in black ghettos in the United States, has been detailed in a classic account, *Life at the Bottom* by Theodore Dalrymple, a British physician who worked in a hospital near a low-income housing project and in a prison.

As regards the housing projects, he observed: "The public spaces and elevators of all public housing blocks I know are so deeply impregnated with urine that the odor is ineradicable. And anything smashable has been smashed."[95] The physical degeneration of the premises has been matched by social degeneration among the people living in them. The unmarried mother with multiple children by multiple fathers— none of whom support their children financially or in any other way— has become common in low-income white neighborhoods in England. As for the behavior of such children in England, Dr. Dalrymple recounted the troubles of a 50-year-old lady who lived alone in a slum and was a patient of his:

> The children in her street mock her unceasingly when she leaves her house; they push excrement through her mailbox as a joke. She has long since given up appealing to their mothers for help, since they always side

with their children and consider any adverse comment on their behavior as an insult to them personally. Far from correcting their children, they threaten her with further violence.[96]

Putting excrement through someone's mailbox was not an isolated aberration but "a common expression of social disapproval" among such people.[97] In the schools, a common expression of social disapproval of those few students who seriously try to learn is beating them up— the same treatment meted out in America to some ghetto children who are accused of "acting white." Some of the low-income white children in England were beaten so badly by other low-income white children as to require medical treatment at the hospital where Dr. Dalrymple worked.[98]

Crime in England likewise skyrocketed in the second half of the twentieth century. In 1954 there was a total of 12 armed robberies in London— including 8 where the weapon was not real— at a time when anybody could buy a shotgun there. England had long been known as one of the world's most law-abiding nations. But the number of armed robberies rose to 1,400 in 1981 and 1,600 in 1991,[99] in an era of severe restrictions on the purchase of all firearms. A scholarly study found, "In the decade after 1957 the use of guns in serious crime increased a hundredfold."[100]

In England, as in the United States, crime rates had been going down for years, before they suddenly reversed and rose during the second half of the twentieth century,[101] as the social vision of the intelligentsia triumphed in both countries, not only as regards the welfare state but also as regards a more lenient, non-judgmental attitude toward criminals. This was all part of a pattern of serious social retrogressions in both countries. A non-judgmental society is a society where common decency is optional— and therefore not likely to remain as common.

Another parallel with the situation in the United States is that low-income children of immigrants in England outperformed low-income, native-born children educationally. A study in Britain in 2013 compared test results among children of various ethnic and national backgrounds, all of whom were from families with incomes low enough to qualify for free lunches in school.

Children of African immigrants in this economic bracket met the test standards nearly 60 percent of the time, as did children of immigrants from Bangladesh living at the same economic level. Children of black immigrants from the Caribbean at the same economic level met the standards under 50 percent of the time. *White, native-born children from families at the same economic level met the standards 30 percent of the time.* In the borough of Knowsley, such white children scored lower than black children in any London borough.[102]

While these educational results in England may seem very different from those in the United States, in terms of the race of those doing better and those doing worse, they are remarkably similar in terms of children from a different foreign culture doing better in school than native-born children from a lower-class culture, whether in England or America. The usual explanations of substandard educational performances in black ghetto schools— whether genetics, racial discrimination or "a legacy of slavery"— obviously do not apply to lower-class whites in England. But the outcomes are strikingly similar.

What lower-class whites in England and ghetto blacks in the United States have in common is a legacy of a generations-long indoctrination in a welfare state ideology of victimhood, grievances and a vision of barriers stacked against them that make their prospects hopeless. This welfare state ideology is backed up by welfare state programs that subsidize an economically counterproductive and socially destructive lifestyle.

Meanwhile, the children of low-income immigrants, not burdened by the ideology that generations of the low-income, native-born population have been steeped in, do far better in both countries. In *Life at the Bottom*, Dr. Dalrymple said, "I cannot recall meeting a sixteen-year-old white from the public housing estates that are near my hospital who could multiply nine by seven (I do not exaggerate). Even three by seven often defeats them."[103] Genetic determinism can hardly explain abysmal educational results in children from a race that produced such mental giants as Shakespeare and Newton, but which now turns out many youngsters unable to cope with simple arithmetic. Nor is there a "legacy of slavery" or racial discrimination excuse that would apply.

While the white students who do so badly in England are from that country's lower-income class, poverty is not a sufficient explanation, because such children represent a retrogression from previous generations of children from low-income families,[104] just as in the United States. Dr. Dalrymple's father was born in a slum. But that was in an earlier time, when even a school in the slums maintained educational standards* and did not pander to the poor by nurturing a sense of grievance and of unfair barriers blocking their rise, as schools have in later times.[105] Instead, schools of the earlier era sought to equip youngsters with the human capital needed to rise out of poverty.[106]

Among the consequences of the welfare state in both England and America is making it unnecessary for many people to develop their own productive capacities— their human capital— when they can live on what was produced by others. The economic loss to society at large is not simply the cost of welfare state benefits that are transferred to non-producing members of society, but includes the perhaps larger value of output that the recipients could produce if they had to support themselves.

In addition, the counterproductive lifestyles developed in subsidized idleness in a non-judgmental world impose serious psychic costs on other members of society, especially those financially unable to escape neighborhoods where the offensive and dangerous behavior of those whom the welfare state and its accompanying social vision have relieved from the norms of civilized behavior on both sides of the Atlantic. This is in addition to the increased financial costs of prisons,

---

* "When he died, I found his school textbooks still among his possessions, and they were of a rigor and difficulty that would terrify a modern teacher, let alone a child." Theodore Dalrymple, *Life at the Bottom*, p. 155. See also Peter Hitchens, *The Abolition of Britain*, Chapter 3.

drug rehabilitation facilities, foster care for neglected or abused children, and the like.

More than simple mistakes are involved in promoting a culture of dependency among those whom government statisticians have chosen to define as living in poverty. A dependent voting constituency is very valuable to politicians, and a paranoid constituency— resentful of social enemies supposedly dedicated to keeping them down— is even more valuable to politicians who play the role of defenders of the downtrodden, in exchange for their votes.

The many welfare state programs to support low productivity people in their officially defined poverty serve the interests of welfare state institutions, as well as politicians. American welfare state bureaucracies whose jobs, budgets and power are advanced by the existence of a large dependent population have not only created advertising campaigns to promote greater use of their programs, they have also dispatched their employees to supermarkets in low-income neighborhoods, to point out to people buying food that there are government programs that will pay for their food.

Although promoted as a means of helping people trapped by misfortunes beyond their control, welfare state institutions have themselves become traps, even for people who have in fact been victims of unforeseen but transient misfortunes, such as having a costly illness or losing a job. The multiplicity of uncoordinated welfare state benefits available have, in many American states, added up to a total value far exceeding the official poverty level of income, and exceeding what low-productivity people could earn in the labor market.[107] After recovery from an illness or other transient misfortunes— after jobs become available again, for example— for many who have been absorbed into welfare state dependency, a return to the labor market could involve a significant reduction in their standard of living.

If increasing one's earned income by $10,000 would involve a loss of eligibility for $15,000 worth of government-provided benefits, that would be in effect an implicit "tax" rate of more than 100 percent on earned income. Even in less extreme cases, welfare state beneficiaries can face an implicit "tax" rate on earned income that is higher than that facing millionaires, if the welfare state beneficiaries were to return to gainful employment at the cost of losing their eligibility for government benefits. Such disincentives have long been known and understood, but neither politicians who benefit from welfare state dependency nor the people whose jobs are in the welfare state bureaucracies have any incentive to correct what is a problem only for others— these others including both the welfare state beneficiaries and the taxpayers.

We have seen how ethnic leaders in many countries have promoted notions beneficial to themselves but counterproductive for the groups they lead. Perhaps it is significant that groups which have risen from poverty to prosperity, in various countries around the world, have seldom had as many, or as prominent, ethnic leaders as groups that remain at the bottom. Any reasonably well-informed American can name at least three or four black leaders of the past or present, but would find it hard to name even a single comparable Asian or Jewish ethnic leader to whom these groups' dramatic rises from poverty could be attributed.

The welfare state is also an often overlooked factor in the income disparities lamented by people who promote income redistribution in general and the welfare state in particular. In the United States, most households in the lowest 20 percent of income recipients have *no one* working.[108] Most of the economic resources transferred to them are transferred in kind— subsidized housing, medical care and other such benefits— rather than in money. Therefore disparities expressed in money income statistics greatly exaggerate disparities in standards of living, especially for people living in what the welfare state chooses to define as poverty.

To the extent that the expanding welfare state allows more people to live without working— and therefore without earning income or developing their own human capital— supporters of the welfare state are contributing to the very income disparities they so much decry. The welfare state ideology, so essential to creating and maintaining a welfare state, can also have negative effects of its own on attitudes and behavior, as apparently that ideology has had in both England and the

United States. However, this is not to say that all welfare states must have the same effects in all countries or that the welfare state ideology must be identical in all countries. After all, *interactions* matter here as in other contexts.

The pre-existing cultural values of different societies, or of different groups within the same society, can interact differently with the same opportunities presented by the welfare state. After all, Asian Americans live in the same welfare state as black Americans and Hispanic Americans, but have not succumbed to its temptations. It may be no coincidence that the group that has longest been wards of the federal government— American Indians living on reservations— have, by a substantial amount, the lowest per capita incomes.

The cultural context of the welfare state can differ among nations, as well as among groups within a given nation. The fact that sons born to families in the bottom 20 percent of income earners in Sweden, Norway, Finland and Denmark do not end up in the bottom 20 percent as adults as often as happens in the United States[109] may reflect a different cultural context for the welfare state in these Scandinavian countries. That is ultimately an empirical question. But the situation at least serves as an illustration of the larger point that a welfare state— like geographic, cultural, demographic and other factors— does not operate in a vacuum but interacts with other factors. We need not try to universalize the welfare state as it exists in the United States, just as we need not presume it to be unique.

A more deadly consequence of a pervasive sense of victimhood, grievance and entitlement has been a lashing out at others. The international treatise *Ethnic Groups in Conflict* noted how common such lashing out has been, in countries around the world, and that "backward groups are overwhelmingly initiators and advanced groups are targets of ethnic riot behavior."[110]

Ghetto riots that swept across the United States during the 1960s— the triumphant decade of the welfare state vision— certainly fit that pattern. In later years, there have been various repetitions of such riots. But a new pattern has also emerged in more recent years— organized black physical attacks on whites in such public places as shopping malls, parks and beaches, usually places *not* located in ghettos.

Unlike ghetto riots that erupt as more or less spontaneous reactions to particular incidents— even if later intensified by hoodlums who join in the mayhem and looting, or career racial activists who stir up mob emotions— the new organized attacks on whites are clearly pre-planned and coordinated, as large numbers of young black males suddenly converge in locally overwhelming numbers to physically attack whites at random.

Often the atmosphere among the attackers is more festive than angry,[111] even though serious and sometimes fatal injuries have been inflicted. One victim of such an attack said afterwards, "I heard laughing as they were beating everybody up. They were eating chips like it was a picnic."[112] Nevertheless, some among the intelligentsia continue to use the pat phrase "troubled youths" to describe exultant young hoodlums.

Such racial attacks have occurred in dozens of cities and smaller communities in every region of the United States, from coast to coast.[113] There has been a pattern not only to these attacks but also to media and political responses. The most common response might be summarized in one word, *denial*.

Where the attacks have been too large, too frequent, or too widely known in a given community to be ignored, the media response has almost invariably been to omit the racial aspect[114] that was central to the attackers themselves, who often referred to their victims as "crackers" or said such things as "This is for Trayvon Martin." Where such attacks across the country over the years have been reported in the media, it has usually been as if each attack was an isolated local incident involving unspecified "young people" attacking unspecified "victims" for unspecified reasons.

Where surveillance cameras reveal the racial makeup of the attackers and their victims, mayors and police officials in community after community across the country have been quick to deny that these were racial attacks.[115] It is usually unnecessary for the media to deny that these attacks are occurring nationwide because few in the media have ever connected the dots, in the first place. *Investor's Business Daily* is one of the very few media outlets to call attention to a nationwide pattern of unprovoked and organized racial attacks: "Across the U.S., mobs of black youths are organizing on Facebook to loot stores and beat whites."[116] This same information was available to others in the media, but it seldom reached the public.

One variant of these black-on-white attacks caught the media's attention briefly— the so-called "knockout game" in which an individual attacker suddenly lets loose a hard punch to the head of an unsuspecting passerby, in an attempt to knock him down and, if possible, out. A series of such knockout punch attacks by blacks against Jews in the New York area seemed to catch everyone by surprise in 2013,[117] even though a 2012 book about black-on-white violence already had a chapter titled "The Knockout Game, St. Louis Style."[118] While it may be a game to the attackers, the victims have often ended up in the hospital, or dead. Someone knocked out in a boxing ring lands on canvas; someone knocked out on a city street usually lands on concrete.

Many who deny or downplay such racial attacks may believe that such denials or downplaying will avoid a white backlash that could escalate into a truly disastrous race war. But such attacks seem unlikely to stop unless they get stopped. That is unlikely to happen without wider and more honest recognition of the dangers, followed by public pressure on elected officials to do something more substantive— and more honest— than denying that these attacks are racial.

Some people may imagine that one way of showing empathy with less fortunate people, whether blacks in the United States or low-income whites in England, is to take a non-judgmental attitude toward their transgressions, as if exempting any group from the standards of civilized behavior is a net benefit to them or to society at large. Barbarism is hardly a gift to any community. Nor is an eventual violent backlash against barbarism. The history of intergroup backlashes— such as the Czech backlash against German civilians in

Czechoslovakia after World War II[119] or the atrocities and counter-atrocities between the Sinhalese and Tamils in Sri Lanka during the second half of the twentieth century[120]— is a history of horrors that no one should want to see repeated on American soil.

Letting organized racial attacks continue across the country, and perhaps escalate, may only delay a larger and more violent racial backlash and polarization, as knowledge of such things spreads, despite the mainstream media. But, in this as in many other things, political incentives are to postpone the day of reckoning, even if that means that the reckoning will be larger and more catastrophic. Moreover, too many people have too much of a vested interest— ideologically, if not materially or politically— in the welfare state vision to have to admit even the possibility that the negative behavioral consequences of the welfare state, and its accompanying non-judgmental vision, must be weighed against the material benefits extended so widely and often so unthinkingly.

Many Americans today may find it hard to imagine mobs of whites attacking blacks. But it is not necessary to imagine. This was precisely what a "race riot" meant in the United States a hundred years ago, especially in the first two decades of the twentieth century.[121] The first major race riot initiated by blacks took place in Harlem in 1935. Since the 1960s, the black-initiated riot has become the norm. But things were different before and can become different again. If so, the economic losses will be the least of the problems.

Chapter 6

IMPLICATIONS AND PROSPECTS

*You're entitled to your own opinion, but
you're not entitled to your own facts.*

Daniel Patrick Moynihan[1]

Q uestions about facts are obviously very different from questions
about values, goals or policies. We can put particular competing
explanations of economic disparities to factual tests and, perhaps
equally important, define our terms precisely enough so that we can
at least know what we disagree about. While differences of opinion on
issues may be inevitable, confusion on issues is not.

DIFFERENCES IN INCOME

AND WEALTH

What is the reason for differences in income and wealth among
individuals, races, nations or civilizations?

The simplest answer is that there is no such thing as "the" reason.
There are all sorts of factors— and many combinations and
permutations of those factors. Nor have we enumerated them all, and
it is by no means certain that anyone could do so. But what is clear

from the factors we have considered thus far is that the possibilities are too numerous to reasonably expect equal economic outcomes, either between nations or within nations, when the things that go into creating those outcomes vary so greatly. The all too familiar cliché about "the paradox of poverty in an affluent society" is a paradox only to those who start with (1) a preconception of an egalitarian world, in defiance of history, and (2) a disregard of the arbitrary nature of the government-defined word "poverty."

Much of the egalitarian thrust of contemporary redistributionists is directed toward the reduction or elimination of income or wealth "disparities" or "gaps" between various groups. But, as distinguished economic development economist Peter Bauer of the London School of Economics pointed out, "The promotion of economic equality and the alleviation of poverty are distinct and often conflicting."[2] If everyone's income doubles, that should certainly reduce poverty, but it would also widen income gaps and disparities. This applies to gaps and disparities both between nations and within nations. The welfare state can reduce, or perhaps even eliminate, poverty in any material sense, but it also reduces the need for many people to earn income— especially when earning income reduces eligibility for government-provided benefits— and therefore widens income gaps and disparities.

As regards economic differences among nations, all too often the question posed is much like that in a well-known study, *Why Nations Fail*: "Why is Egypt so much poorer than the United States? What are the constraints that keep Egyptians from becoming more prosperous?"[3] This implicitly treats what happens in the United States as a sort of norm, as what happens usually or more or less naturally, leaving the question as to why this usual, normal or natural development has been thwarted somehow in Egypt. But Egypt is much more typical of what has happened around the world, and over the centuries, than is the United States.

Given the many factors that go into the creation of wealth, and the wide variety of combinations and permutations of those factors, there is no more reason to expect those factors to come together in the same way in Egypt as in the United States than there is to expect that all the factors which come together to produce tornadoes would come together in Egypt as often as they come together in the United States— more so than in any other country, or all other countries combined.[4]

To pursue the analogy with tornadoes, there is nothing absolutely unique that strikes the eye about either the geography or the climate in the United States that cannot be found, as individual features, in many other places around the world. Wide level plains are among the things that facilitate the development of tornadoes, but wide level plains exist across much of Europe and in Argentina and India, among other places. What is unique about the United States is the *combination* of things that occur together— in the middle of the country rather than on the coasts, in particular seasons of the year, and in the afternoons more so than in the mornings or at night   that cause the vast majority of all the tornadoes in the world to occur in the United States.

We would not set out to discover why there are not more tornadoes in Egypt, if we were interested in knowing how tornadoes originate and behave. Similarly, there is not much reason to seek the causes of poverty in Egypt or in any other country. Poverty— genuine poverty— has been the lot of most of the human race for most of the existence of the species. However, a more reasonable question also appears in *Why Nations Fail*: "Was it historically— or geographically or culturally or ethnically— predetermined that Western Europe, the United States, and Japan would become so much richer than sub-Saharan Africa, Latin America, and China over the last two hundred years or so?"[5]

While nothing predestined particular nations or peoples to be more prosperous than others, many things facilitated or impeded the economic development of some nations and peoples more than others. It is hard to think of any fundamental development that advanced the human race coming out of isolated mountain communities, isolated islands or other places where geography impeded access to other peoples— Australia being for millennia the classic example of a continent isolated from other continents, with Australian aborigines being regarded as classic lagging peoples.

It may suggest something about human beings in general that no given individuals, or even small societies, have been capable of reaching the heights of human achievements, without access to the current and previous achievements of vastly larger numbers of other people. The invention of the rangefinder, used on naval ships and at one time on many cameras, drew upon mathematical principles developed in Greece more than two thousand years ago as the Pythagorean Theorem.

Without access to thoughts recorded in ancient times— and other information developed at other places and other times since then— to develop a rangefinder from scratch would be a far more formidable task. For more complex inventions, the task would be virtually impossible. Would an illiterate Einstein, growing up in a primitive tribe on an isolated island in the middle of the Pacific Ocean, have produced a theory of relativity? Even far less earth-shaking advances have built on the work of innumerable predecessors, scattered in many countries over many centuries, going all the way back to those who invented numbers and letters.

To ask "why nations fail" is to treat our conception of success as a norm, rather than the rare exception that it is in the long history of human beings. It may be an understandable human tendency for us to regard whatever we happen to be used to, immediately around us, as usual or natural. But that does not make it so. In pre-Civil War America, slavery was referred to as a "peculiar institution" because slavery was so inconsistent with the principles and practices in the rest of American society. But the tragic fact is that slavery was a pervasive institution, among innumerable peoples around the world, for thousands of years. It is *freedom* for ordinary people that has been a peculiar institution, of relatively recent vintage as history is measured— and still in jeopardy in many countries, even today, as well as being utterly suppressed in some other countries.

The real challenge in discussing wealth, poverty and politics is to try to understand what peculiar combination of circumstances has resulted in the level of prosperity found in such places as Japan and Western Europe, and in such offshoot nations of Western Europe as the United States or Australia. Nor have these particular combinations and permutations of factors been present from time immemorial, even in these particular countries. In ancient times, entirely different countries were on the frontiers of human economic and other advances.

Poverty occurs automatically. It is wealth that must be produced, and must be explained. That is why the approach here has been to examine such factors as geography, culture, demography and politics as influences on production. Income is a by-product of that production. This may all seem obvious, but its implications are apparently not obvious to many who wish to treat "income distribution" as a discrete issue, with virtually a life of its own, while production fades into the dim background— as if the patterns of incomes can be changed to suit our desires, without any repercussions on production, on which the standard of living of society as a whole depends. The attempt to treat poverty as a discrete "problem"— one that can be "solved" by an expansion of the welfare state, as in the American "war on poverty" launched in the 1960s— has had social repercussions that should be very sobering.

Because the most fundamental statistics on what is called "income distribution" are so widely misunderstood, we need to begin by clarifying what these data do and do not mean. After that, we can turn to a closer examination of some of the factors behind the differences in incomes that exist within nations and between nations.

Income Statistics

There are two fundamentally different kinds of statistics used to show income trends over time— *and these different kinds of statistics produce diametrically opposite conclusions.*

The people who appear in one kind of income statistics are a set of the same identical individuals, whose incomes are tabulated throughout the years covered by a given study. A very different kind of statistics— and the kind most often cited in the media, in politics and in academia— is based on tabulating the incomes of whatever mix of people happen to be in such categories as the top fifth, the bottom fifth and other brackets in between, in any given year. A series of such tabulations in a series of years then serves as the basis for conclusions about the incomes earned in each of the various brackets.

These latter kinds of statistics are often cited to assert that incomes of people in the top bracket ("the rich") are increasing relative to the incomes of people in the bottom bracket ("the poor") or relative to incomes of people in other brackets in between. Assertions that "the gap between rich and poor has widened in America" have appeared in the *New York Times*[6] and in innumerable other media outlets, including the *Washington Post*, where columnist E.J. Dionne described "the wealthy" as "people who have made almost all the income gains in recent years" and added that they are "undertaxed."[7] Books like *The Fair Society* by Peter Corning of Stanford University repeat the same theme, that "the income gap between the richest and the poorest members of our society has been growing rapidly."[8]

Although such statements, which abound throughout the media and are echoed in politics and in academia, are *phrased* as if they are comparing the incomes of specific sets of people over time— "the rich" and "the poor"— they are in fact comparing the incomes of particular income brackets *containing an ever-changing mix of people* over time, as individuals move massively from one bracket to another in the normal course of their careers, going from entry-level jobs to jobs that pay far more to successively more experienced people. Those who go into business or the professions likewise tend to acquire a larger clientele with the passing years, resulting in rising incomes there as well.

Studies which actually follow a given set of individuals over time reach not only different conclusions, but *opposite* conclusions from studies which follow income brackets containing ever-changing mixes of people, at very different stages of their individual careers. A study at the University of Michigan that followed specific individuals— working

Americans— from 1975 to 1991 found that those particular individuals who were initially in the bottom 20 percent in income had their real incomes rise over the years, not only at a higher rate but in a several times larger total amount, than the real incomes of those particular individuals whose incomes were initially in the top 20 percent.[9]

As a result of their rising incomes, 95 percent of those people who were initially in the bottom quintile in 1975 were no longer there in 1991. Twenty-nine percent of the people who were initially in the bottom quintile rose all the way to the top quintile, while just 5 percent remained behind in the bottom quintile where they began. Meanwhile, over that same span of time, those people who were initially in the top quintile in 1975 had the *smallest* increase in real income by 1991— smallest in both percentage terms and in absolute amount— of people in any of the quintiles. The amount by which the average income of people initially in the top quintile rose was less than half that in any of the other quintiles.[10]

However radically different this empirical pattern is from the many loudly proclaimed assertions that "the rich" have been getting richer and "the poor" getting poorer over time, there is nothing surprising about the mundane fact that people who start out at the bottom, in entry-level jobs, usually rise over the years to successively higher levels of work and pay. Meanwhile, those who have already reached middle age, where their productivity and earnings are highest, are unlikely to see any comparably large further increases in productivity and pay as time goes on.

A later study, using data from the Internal Revenue Service, found a very similar pattern. This study followed those specific individuals who filed income tax returns over the course of a decade, from 1996 through 2005. Those whose incomes were initially in the bottom 20 percent of this group saw their incomes rise by 91 percent during that decade— that is, their incomes nearly doubled. Those whose incomes were initially in the much-discussed "top one percent" saw their incomes actually *fall* by 26 percent during that same decade.[11] Again, the facts are the opposite of the loudly proclaimed assertions, based on statistics that measure what is happening over time to abstract categories— income brackets with changing mixes of people— which are then discussed as if they were statistics about what was happening over time to a given set of flesh-and-blood human beings.

A more recent study that followed specific individuals over time in Canada, from 1990 through 2009, found patterns very similar to the patterns found in studies of Americans. Those Canadians who were initially in the bottom 20 percent in income had their incomes increase at both a higher rate, and in a higher absolute amount, than those whose incomes were initially in higher brackets.[12] Yet again, what happened over time to a given set of human beings was the opposite of what happened over that same span of time in abstract categories with changing mixes of people. In Canada, as in the United States, the upper brackets' incomes were rising faster than the lower brackets' incomes— and, as in the United States, this was spoken of as if it represented what was happening to given sets of people.[13]

Unfortunately, statistical surveys that follow specific individuals over the years are more expensive than statistical surveys that simply compile data over the years in abstract categories, containing ever-changing mixtures of people at highly varying stages of their own individual life cycles. So it is not surprising that the U.S. Bureau of the Census and numerous other collectors of statistics turn out far more data on what is happening to abstract categories over time than data on what is happening to specific sets of people over time. Nevertheless, what happens in those abstract categories— income brackets— over time is then discussed just as if that is what is happening to specific sets of people over time, often called "the poor" and "the rich." Transients in the various income brackets are spoken of as if they were continuous residents in those brackets.

Understandable and commendable as it may be to be concerned about the fate of fellow human beings, that is very different from being obsessed with the fate of numbers in abstract categories. To say, as Professor Thomas Piketty does in his much acclaimed book, *Capital in the Twenty-First Century* that "the upper decile is truly a world unto

itself"[14] is to fly in the face of the fact that most American households—
56 percent— are in the top decile at some point in their lives,[15] usually
in their older years. For most Americans to envy or resent the top ten
percent would be to envy or resent *themselves*. This is not even "class
warfare," but confusion between social classes and age cohorts.

Statistics on income differences are almost universally and
automatically discussed as if these must be differences between social
classes, rather than differences among people of different ages.
Indeed, there is seldom even a mention of the *possibility* that these
numbers can refer to either social classes or age cohorts, much less
attempts in the popular media to determine to what extent they refer
to people of different ages, rather than people in different social
classes. The income and wealth statistics that are paraded with such
fervor can be perfectly accurate and yet completely misleading.

If infants have less income or wealth than their parents, who in
turn have less income or wealth than their grandparents, that is hardly
the same as if individuals are in wealth or poverty over the course of
their lives. Yet the latter is a common insinuation, garnished with
numbers. As statistics, infants can be the same as grandparents, but
only as statistics. Even if the data are limited to adults, younger adults
are the same as older adults only as statistics— and economic
disparities between people of different ages are not the same as
economic disparities between classes.*

Even the vaunted "top one percent," so often discussed in the
media, is a level reached by 12 percent of Americans at some point in
their lives.[16] What Professor Paul Krugman refers to as "the charmed
circle of the 1 percent"[17] must have a somewhat fleeting charm,
because most of the people in that circle in 1996 were no longer there
in 2005.[18] In Professor Piketty's vision, the top one percent in income

---

* Young adults can take years to raise their net wealth to *zero*, since people in these
age brackets are often in debt— for college loans, automobiles, home furnishings—
and these debts often exceed their savings. Meanwhile, people in their 60s have long
since passed that point, and have had decades in which to accumulate savings,
equity in a home and/or to have put money in a pension plan. These age disparities
in wealth can be large without necessarily being class disparities.

not only live in their own separate world but "stand out in society" and "exert a significant influence on both the social landscape and the political and economic order,"[19] according to Piketty, who says that they are atop the "hierarchy" and "structure of inequality"[20] he projects.

There is, however, a fundamental difference between a *structure* and a *process*. Piketty glosses over the process in which people's incomes change substantially over the course of their lives— or even in the course of just one decade. More than half of all taxpayers moved to a different income quintile between 1996 and 2005, and the same was true in the preceding decade.[21] Among people in the middle quintile, for example, 42 percent moved up to a higher income quintile, while 25 percent dropped to a lower quintile and only 33 percent remained in the middle quintile.[22]

Turnover is especially pronounced among those with the highest incomes. While less than half the people in the top one percent were still there at the end of a decade, only about one-quarter of those in the top one-hundredth of one percent in 1996 were still there in 2005.[23] More than half saw their incomes cut in half or more during that decade.[24] The turnover is even faster among those taxpayers with the 400 highest incomes in the country— incomes far higher than among the top one percent as a whole. Fewer than one-fourth of the income tax filers with the top 400 incomes in 1992 were in that same bracket more than once during the years ending in 2000— and only 13 percent were in that extremely high bracket more than twice during those nine years.[25] At very high income levels— whether the top one percent, one-hundredth of one percent or the top 400 incomes— that income is far more likely to come from investments, which are far more volatile than salaries.

In short, even more than most people in other income brackets, most of the people among the top 400 income recipients are transients— in this case, mostly people with a spike in income for just one year out of nine. Whether their one year at this level is due to receiving an inheritance or otherwise cashing in assets accumulated over the previous years, or is due to some other reason, the people who are fleeting residents in this income bracket are hardly credible candidates for the powerful and/or sinister roles assigned to them in much ideological and political rhetoric. This is not to say that there are no enduringly wealthy people who in fact have lives and lifestyles far removed from those in the rest of society. The question is whether they are the *same* people as those who happen to be in particular income brackets at particular times. Otherwise, what is the point of citing those statistics, based on ever-changing mixes of people, and talking about them as if they were data on a given set of human beings over time?

Piketty's crucial misstep is verbally converting a fluid process over time into a rigid structure, with a more or less permanent top one percent living isolated from the rest of society that is supposedly subjected to their control or influence. It is a vision divorced from demonstrable facts, however consonant it may be with prevailing preconceptions.

Much has been made of Piketty's voluminous statistics from various countries. But, as J.A. Schumpeter said long ago, "You can travel far and wide and yet wear blinkers wherever you go."[26] Testing the accuracy of Piketty's vast array of statistics would be a monumental task— and a task perhaps not worth the time and effort, since the real question is not about the accuracy of the numbers themselves, but about the accompanying misstatement of what the numbers are measuring. However, it may be worth noting in passing that Piketty's repeated statements that the top income tax bracket under President Herbert Hoover was taxed at 25 percent are contradicted by an official Internal Revenue Service document, showing that the top income tax bracket in 1932 was taxed at 63 percent.[27]

Another source of confusion in discussions of peoples' economic differences is a failure to distinguish income from wealth. Income and wealth are too fundamentally different from each other to make confident inferences about one from statistics about the other. Use of the term "the rich" to describe people in higher income brackets is just one sign of the confusion between income and wealth, since being rich means having an *accumulation* of wealth, rather than simply a high income in a given year. This is not just a matter of semantics. At a practical level, raising income tax rates to make "the rich" pay their undefined "fair share" is an exercise in futility, since *income taxes do not touch wealth*. It is a tax on people who may be trying to accumulate wealth, but people who *already* have accumulations of wealth, either personally earned or from inheritance, are exempt.

Praise for billionaires who say that they are in favor of higher income tax rates is completely misplaced, when those higher tax rates will not touch their billions, even if such tax rate increases are a serious burden to other people, who are trying to get ahead and accumulate something to leave for their families after they are gone.

Implicit in much discussion of "income distribution" statistics is the notion that certain income brackets receive not only a higher share of total income but do so *at the expense* of lower income brackets. That is, "the poor" are made poorer by "the rich" who become richer, according to this view. Some, such as *Washington Post* columnist Eugene Robinson, have made this claim explicit, as when he said, "The rich are getting richer at the expense not only of the poor but of the middle class as well." These non-"rich" are referred to as "long-suffering victims" of the "upper crust" who have been "waging an undeclared but devastating war" against them.[28]

Mr. Robinson has, however inadvertently, performed a real service by bringing to the surface a widespread undercurrent of confusion that cannot withstand scrutiny in the light of day. We can put aside for the moment his implicit assumption that trends in statistics about income brackets, with their ever-changing mixes of people, are the same as trends about what is happening to given sets of flesh-and-blood human beings called "the rich" and "the poor." We may, for the sake of argument, leave that particular confusion aside, in order to focus attention on the rest of his argument.

Even during periods when a higher share of total income goes to the top income bracket, that does not prevent the real income received in the bottom bracket from rising absolutely. During the period from 1985 through 2001, for example, the income share of the bottom 20 percent of American households declined from 4 percent of all incomes to 3.5 percent of all incomes, but the average real income of households in the bottom 20 percent *rose* by thousands of dollars.[29] This is not even taking into account the well-documented fact that most people initially in the bottom income quintile move up and out of that quintile over a span of years as long as that in this example. But even if they had all stayed put, the rising amount and share of income of "the rich" would still not have made them poorer, as the data show.

The rising absolute real income in the bottom quintile happened over the years, while the number of billionaires has been growing— and, according to people like Eugene Robinson, prospering at the expense of the poor, against whom the rich were "waging war." However, since most households in the bottom 20 percent in income have *no one* working,[30] it is not clear what "the rich" can be taking from those who are producing nothing.

The Randomness Assumption

With very few of the things that go into creating economic production being equally available to all— either among nations or within nations— it is hard to understand how the expectation of equality in economic outcomes has acquired such a hold on contemporary thinking that income inequalities— "disparities," "gaps" or "inequities"— are taken as being at least strange, if not sinister. But gross inequalities in outcomes are rampant in all kinds of human endeavors around the world— whether economic or otherwise— including those that can hardly be explained by discrimination, exploitation or the many other sins of human beings. Those sins are real, but their *moral* significance does not automatically make them *causal* factors of the same significance in economic outcomes. That is an important empirical question, though one seldom addressed by moral crusaders.

Because the implicit assumption that even or random outcomes are natural is so widespread, and so consequential in its moral, political and even legal implications, it is an assumption that needs to be examined at some length and confronted with many facts about many different kinds of human endeavors. As we have seen in earlier chapters, geographic, demographic and cultural factors are often grossly unequal. Moreover, people do not behave randomly but *purposefully*. They do not, for example, immigrate randomly, either in terms of the locations they come from in the country they leave or the locations where they settle in the countries they go to. They do not raise their children the same, as shown by the large differences in the number of words people at different socioeconomic levels speak to their children.

Purposeful human activities are seldom random in themselves or in their consequences. Nor are they the same among different groups, whether different by race, sex, religion, birth order or innumerable other variables.

Differences in achievements are drastic, not only in economic endeavors but in all sorts of other endeavors, from the most mundane to the most exalted. An international study of widely recognized European historic figures in the arts and sciences, from the beginning of the fifteenth century through the middle of the twentieth century, found their geographic origins highly concentrated in particular places. Thus "80 percent of all the European significant figures can be enclosed in an area that does *not* include Russia, Sweden, Norway, Finland, Spain, Portugal, the Balkans, Poland, Hungary, East and West Prussia, Ireland, Wales, most of Scotland, the lower quarter of Italy and about a third of France."[31]

In the United States, the same study found that about half of the significant American individuals in the arts and sciences, from the time of the founding of the republic to the middle of the twentieth century, were concentrated in an arc extending from Portland, Maine to the southern tip of New Jersey. The New England states plus New York, Pennsylvania and New Jersey produced more than *seven times* the number of significant American figures in the arts and sciences as did the states that had formed the Confederacy during the Civil War.

Most of those Southern states had none at all, with Virginia being a notable exception.[32]

Similar extreme disparities have been found in individual accomplishments in sports. Among professional golfers who had survived to the final two rounds of a Professional Golfers' Association (PGA) tournament, there was a rough approximation of a normal bell curve when it came to such individual aspects of golf as the average number of putts per round of play or driving distances off the tee.[33] But there was a radically skewed distribution of results when it came to the ultimate test of the *combinations* of the various golf skills, namely winning PGA tournaments.

Even among the above average group of professional golfers who had survived to the final two rounds of a PGA tournament, 53 percent never won a single PGA tournament in their entire careers. Among the 47 percent who did win a PGA tournament, almost all won just one, two or three.[34] But Arnold Palmer, Jack Nicklaus and Tiger Woods each won dozens of PGA tournaments, and more than 200 among the three of them.[35]

There have been similarly very skewed distributions among winners of Grand Slam titles in tennis, batting championships in baseball and winners of points in world chess championships.[36] Of the 100 top-ranked marathon runners in the world in 2012, 68 were Kenyans.[37] When two American boys whose ancestors came from India tied for first place in the U.S. National Spelling Bee in 2014, it was the seventh consecutive year in which the Spelling Bee was won by an Indian American. Indian Americans had also won twelve of the previous sixteen.[38] During the twentieth century, there were eight times when a major league baseball player stole 100 bases or more. All eight times, that player was black.[39]

The same skewed distribution is found among recipients of academic degrees. As of the early twenty-first century, every justice of the U.S. Supreme Court had a degree from one of the eight Ivy League institutions in the northeast, out of the thousands of American colleges and universities across the country. Among people who earned a

Bachelor's degree in the United States in academic year 2011–2012, nearly four-fifths of those with degrees in education were women and nearly four-fifths of those with degrees in engineering were men.[40]

Although blacks greatly outnumber Asians in the American population, and slightly outnumber them among recipients of Bachelor's degrees, Asians received more than twice as many Bachelor's degrees in engineering as blacks.[41] The disparity is even greater at the top engineering schools, where Asians have outnumbered blacks by three-to-one at M.I.T., ten-to-one at Harvey Mudd College and by forty-to-one at Cal Tech.[42] But even the extreme disparity at Cal Tech was not as great as the disparity between Chinese and Malays earning engineering degrees in Malaysia during the 1960s. During that decade, students from the Chinese minority earned just over a hundred times as many engineering degrees as students from the Malay majority[43]— in a country where the Malays control both the universities and the government that sets university policies.

Examples of such gross disparities in innumerable human endeavors could be extended almost indefinitely, just counting those where the circumstances virtually preclude discrimination, such as men being struck by lightning several times as often as women or dominant majorities being outperformed by subordinate minorities.[44]

Despite these and many other examples of outcomes in many different kinds of human endeavors that are remote from an even or random distribution, in situations where discrimination can be ruled out, the implicit assumption persists that uneven or non-random outcomes are strange and suspicious. Moreover, these are not just casual opinions. They are conclusions that have carried great weight in courts of law, in cases involving "disparate impact" statistics, which show demographic "under-representation" of particular groups that are very different from what would be expected by random chance. Among the intelligentsia in the media, or even in academia, such statistics are often treated as virtually iron-clad proof of discrimination. The implicit *assumption* of randomness thus trumps innumerable contrary *facts* showing grossly uneven and non-random outcomes from all sorts of purposeful human endeavors. Moreover, serious laws and policies are based on these assumptions in defiance of facts.

Redistributionists seldom, if ever, offer a principled criterion by which current inequalities might be judged. Few today are prepared to say that there should be absolute equality of income or wealth, but they seldom offer more than ad hoc pronouncements that current inequalities are "too much."

Perhaps the closest they come to some principle is that current inequalities are greater than the inequalities in some other time or place. But this offers no principle on which to choose a particular time or place to serve as a standard for judging other times and places. Moreover, the ignored production processes change over time, making different mixes of skills and talents more in demand than before and others less in demand than before, requiring different patterns of pay as incentives to attract people with the currently more valued qualifications.

An obvious example of such changes has been the reduced value of physical labor as machine power has in many cases replaced human muscle, thereby making the male worker's advantage in physical strength less relevant, reducing the pay gap between the sexes, even before there were equal pay laws.

To say that pay differences between people at the top and people at the bottom have increased over the years means something very different when these are differences between classes than when these are differences between people in different age brackets. Only 13 percent of American households headed by someone 25 years old have been in the top 20 percent of household incomes, while 73 percent of households headed by someone 60 years old have been.[45] Since every 60-year-old was once a 25-year-old, increased income differences between age brackets are hardly an injustice to Americans who live out a normal lifespan.

Increased income differences between those at the top and those at the bottom may in other situations reflect a greater demand for particular skills relative to unskilled and inexperienced labor, or a greater demand for financial expertise relative to personnel department experience, for example. Increased income disparities may also reflect the fact that an increasing proportion of the population can live without working, or with only sporadic or part-time work, thanks to the many benefits available from the welfare state. These benefits *are not counted* in income statistics, even though the value of these in-kind benefits— ranging from subsidized housing to medical care— greatly exceeds the recorded money income of people in the bottom 20 percent of income recipients.[46]

In short, income statistics greatly overstate differences in standards of living between income brackets, because income data are reported before taxes and before massive transfers of in-kind benefits, especially to those in the bottom income brackets.

Not all differences in income are due to age or welfare, of course, but whatever these differences are due to, the changing requirements of the production process imply that there is no reason why a particular pattern of income or wealth differences from a particular time or place should remain unchanged, or serve as a benchmark for people living in other times and places.

Even less is there any reason why intellectuals or politicians should acquire increased control over the lives of millions of fellow human beings as each imperfection of life is discovered or claimed. Not since the era of the "divine right of kings" has there been such an implicit assumption that some people are entitled to take away the right of other people to make their own decisions about their own lives. Often such powers are claimed on the basis of what is called "social justice."

"Social Justice"

Perhaps the best-known contemporary exposition of moral principles relevant to differences in income and wealth has been that in John Rawls' influential treatise *A Theory of Justice*. Professor Rawls' conception of "social justice" in the economy is that "those who are at the same level of talent and ability, and have the same willingness to use them, should have the same prospects of success regardless of their initial place in the social system, that is, irrespective of the income class into which they are born."[47]

Perhaps few Americans would object to this ideal, even if they might disagree as to how or whether it can be put into practice. However, that ideal is almost immediately modified by Rawls, with the proviso that "the advantages of persons with greater natural endowments are to be limited to those that further the good of the poorer sectors of society."[48] That is because "Justice is prior to efficiency," according to Rawls,[49] and differences in natural ability are as undeserved, and therefore as unjust, as being born an heir to a fortune.

To say, as Rawls does, that unjust rewards may be tolerated only to the extent necessary to benefit people in "the poorer sectors of society," raises both factual and moral issues. As we have seen, the poorer sectors of society, as defined by income, are a transient group disproportionately of the younger and less experienced, and no one remains younger for life. Among that small proportion— 5 percent— of those in the bottom income quintile who remain there over the years as most others move on up, it cannot be arbitrarily assumed that this unusual fate can have nothing to do with the way they have chosen to live their lives.

To say, as Rawls does, that morally nothing should be done to benefit the rest of society if it does not also help those at the bottom[50] can amount to enshrining a veto on progress, on behalf of those with a counterproductive lifestyle. Many conclusions that might make sense in a world of predestination do not make sense in a world of individual choices. That such choices may be influenced by past social conditions does not mean that they cannot also be influenced by current rewards or penalties for current conduct— including non-judgmental subsidies of counterproductive behavior.

Our survey of peoples and places around the world in earlier chapters, in search of reasons for disparities in income and wealth— whether between nations or within nations— has been, implicitly, a search for reasons behind differences in *productivity*. Others who are more interested in redistributing incomes and wealth often leave the *production* of these incomes and this wealth in the dim background. By pushing the production process off into the background, redistributionists avoid confronting the question whether income inequalities might be matched by corresponding inequalities in economic productivity.

What redistributionists seek to suggest, or to proclaim, is the injustice of existing rewards, given that so much of what a given individual receives originated in some windfall gain or windfall loss, of which "the accident of birth" is central. In short, redistributionists seek to judge merit, more so than productivity— or even in some cases to the exclusion of productivity, given the Rawlsian principle that justice is more important than economic efficiency.

We can use the criteria of "social justice" advocates, for the sake of argument. Imagine a man who was born to parents who were not merely poor but alcoholic, irresponsible and neglectful or abusive toward their children. For such an individual, born in such a family, to somehow have wrenched himself away from the culture of such an environment and become a very decent and hard-working man, acquiring a skill such as carpentry to support himself and his family, whom he treats far better than he was treated as a child, would certainly be a meritorious achievement.

Imagine now a different man born in very different circumstances, to loving and caring parents, raised in an affluent or wealthy home, with all the advantages that social position can confer, in terms of private education and wider cultural exposure. For such a man to go on to become a brain surgeon would certainly be commendable, but by no means necessarily more of a meritorious achievement than that of the carpenter.

In a world where rewards were based solely on merit, there would be no obvious reason to pay the brain surgeon any more than the carpenter was paid. But, in a world where *productivity* matters, this is no longer a question of the relative merits of individuals. What is far more important than merit-based "social justice" to particular income recipients is the well-being of all the people who stand to benefit from what they produce. Introducing *production* into the discussion makes a big difference. It is now a question of the relative urgency of brain surgery and carpentry, and of providing incentives for young people of high ability— however acquired— to choose the long and challenging preparation to become brain surgeons out of the many options they have, however unjust it may be that some people have so many more options than others have.

Instead of limiting ourselves to weighing the relative economic fates of particular individuals or groups as income recipients, a discussion of the goods and services *produced* by those individuals or groups weighs as well the fate of those other members of society who benefit from the goods and services produced by those who are the sole or primary focus of income redistributionists.

To call the fate of consumers of goods and services a matter of "efficiency," while calling the fate of those who receive incomes for producing those goods and services a matter of "social justice"— and then making "social justice" *categorically* more important than "efficiency," as Rawls does[51]— is to make a distinction without a difference. If income is redistributed in a way that reduces efficiency, which is what makes the distinction relevant, then the economic losses of some as consumers are simply arbitrarily declared to be less important than the economic gains of others from "social justice." But what is an injustice, if not an undeserved cost of some sort inflicted on people? It is hard to see how an undeserved cost inflicted on people in their role of consumers is morally different from an undeserved cost inflicted on people in their role of income recipients.

"Solutions"

The question must be raised as to the basis for arming intellectual coteries with the massive powers of government to forcibly undo economic transactions terms made by millions of people intimately familiar with their own individual circumstances and alternatives, in a way that distant intellectuals or government functionaries cannot possibly be familiar. Moreover, what if those millions of people do not share Rawls' notion that justice is more important than efficiency? Indeed, if any two things each have some value, one cannot be *categorically* more valuable than the other, as Rawls claims.[52] A diamond may be worth much more than a penny, but enough pennies will be worth more than any diamond.

Comfortable academics on ivy-covered campuses may be able to afford a preoccupation with statistical patterns and a preference for income numbers that fit their preconceptions. But that is very different from saying that people mired in poverty— genuine poverty, perhaps in the Third World— are wrong to welcome some billionaire investor who wants to set up a factory near them that will provide jobs enabling them to give their families things they have never been able to afford before,* just because that billionaire's investment will also make him richer than before, to the discomfort of those reading statistics on distant campuses or in distant editorial offices.

Those among the intelligentsia and other "social justice" advocates may prefer a statistically more equal society to a more prosperous society, even one that is better able to subsidize the poor. But, while that is the right of those who hold such views, it is also the right of others, including low-income people, to prefer a more prosperous society. If the aversion of the intelligentsia to the level of inequality in the United States were shared by the poor in other countries, it would be hard to account for the long-standing, massive and sometimes desperate efforts of poor immigrants from around the world to reach America.

The very idea that millions of fellow human beings must be forced to arrange themselves in a tableau pleasing to a relative handful of intellectuals or politicians is not only grotesque in itself, but still more

---

* Multinational corporations typically pay higher wages than local employers in the Third World.

amazing as part of a claim of higher morality, equality or humanitarianism under the name of "social justice." Nor does the actual track record of intellectuals in many other aspects of life inspire confidence in either their assumptions or their conclusions.*

One of the reasons for paying people for their productivity, rather than their merits, is that productivity is far easier to determine than merit. This is especially so in a market economy, where the value of what is produced is judged by whoever chooses to buy it and use it. Few can have anything approaching a comparable knowledge or understanding of someone else's merit, especially when they have not "walked in his shoes."

This, of course, does not mean that nothing whatever should be done to widen the options of those born into less fortunate circumstances, and who consequently have had fewer options for developing their productivity. Indeed, there has never been a time in the entire history of the United States when nothing whatever was being done for such people. American society is one where major voluntary philanthropy has been going on for centuries. The United States has been, and is, unique in the extent to which private philanthropy has created schools, libraries, scholarships, colleges, foundations, hospitals and other civic institutions that are elsewhere provided by government or by religious organizations.

Nor have all contributions been in money. Vast amounts of time have been donated to many civic causes, including those aimed at extending the options available to the less fortunate. The thousands of whites from the North who went into the South after the Civil War,

---

* It was, after all, not the unwashed masses but exquisitely educated intellectuals who urged Western democracies to disarm in the 1930s, while Hitler was building a massive war machine in Germany and while imperial Japan was doing the same in Asia. And it was the triumph of the intellectuals' social vision in America during the 1960s that was followed by sharp reversals of long downward trends in murder rates and rates of venereal diseases and teenage pregnancy in the population at large, as well as the disintegration of two-parent black families, which was the norm a hundred years after slavery but not after 30 years following the expanded welfare state of the 1960s.

to teach the children of newly freed slaves in private institutions established by philanthropists, were a classic example.

These teachers, usually young women, braved nearly impossible conditions, including the hostility of Southern white society, from which they were often ostracized and sometimes threatened, and many utterly unprepared black students, handicapped both by the experience of slavery and by the general Southern culture in which education was by no means a high priority. W.E.B. Du Bois called the work of these white volunteers from the North the "finest thing in American history."[53]

Much of such philanthropic activity as this is ignored by those who largely ignore productivity in general, whether economically or socially motivated productivity. But such voluntary civic-minded activities cannot be taken as given, natural or something that just happens *somehow*. It differs as greatly as the economic production that is so often also treated as something that just happens *somehow*, in disregard of how very differently it happens in different places and times, with correspondingly different effects on people's standards of living. But such civic-minded activities do *not* occur equally in all societies around the world, or even to the same extent throughout Western civilization.

Nineteenth century French visitor Alexis de Tocqueville was struck by the extent of voluntary civic activities among Americans, as he reported in his classic, *Democracy in America*.[54] But distinguished American scholar Edward C. Banfield found no such widespread attitudes or practices in the Italian mountain village where he stayed in the middle of the twentieth century, where "some find the idea of public-spiritedness unintelligible." No one will "lift a finger to assist a nun carrying a heavy burden to the orphanage at the top of the mountain," and though the local monastery is crumbling, "none of the many half-employed stone masons has ever given a day's work to its repair."[55]

A twenty-first century study of Russian society likewise found very little civic-mindedness, or even organized voluntary social activities in general, as compared to the United States. This study of "non-governmental associations" in 60 countries found that "Russia's best ranking was in sports and recreation, where the country rose as far as 9th from the very bottom." In that category, "nearly 4% of the adults surveyed said they were involved in a sports club or some other athletic voluntary association." But less than 2 percent were involved in voluntary social welfare activities to help others.

Among Americans, the study found that "participation is roughly ten times higher in sports and social welfare organizations; roughly twenty times higher in environmental, religious, and professional organizations; roughly thirty times higher in cultural/educational and women's organizations, and roughly fifty times higher in human rights organizations."[56]

The limiting factor in the success of efforts to raise the educational and economic levels of those born into less fortunate circumstances is the degree of *receptivity* of many of the people born and raised in a culture that does not provide them with the desire, habits or discipline required to make the most of expanded opportunities. Here the leadership of lagging groups is often a major impediment to those groups' advancement, since such leaders have every incentive to promote a vision in which the group's problems are caused primarily, if not exclusively, by the sins of other people. What incentive is that to engage in the arduous process of trying to change oneself?

This is a leadership pattern that has appeared on every inhabited continent, so there is no reason to expect a different pattern in America, or in any other country, except for highly exceptional leaders here and there. The great eighteenth century philosopher David Hume could urge his fellow Scots to learn English precisely because his career was *not* that of an ethnic leader. When you want to help people, you tell them the truth. When you want to help yourself, you tell them what they want to hear. People with careers as ethnic leaders usually tell their followers what they want to hear.

Those who have promoted the prevailing vision, in which lags, gaps or disparities to the detriment of black people are the fault of other people, are trapped in the corollary that these lags, gaps or disparities should disappear, once those other people are constrained by civil rights laws and policies. But nothing of the sort has happened in the wake of the civil rights revolution of the 1960s.* However dramatic the increase of black political representation at local and national levels, there were no correspondingly dramatic reductions in economic disparities. Economic progress continued, but the rise out of poverty was not at as fast a pace as in the years *preceding* the civil rights revolution of the 1960s.[57]

This leaves those who cling to the prevailing vision little alternative but to claim that even an absence of concrete evidence that continuing black lags, gaps or disparities can be traced to what others are doing only shows that the continuing gaps must be due to the diabolical cleverness with which "covert" or "institutional" racism has been concealed. When an absence of tangible evidence is assumed to prove a proposition that tangible evidence would also prove, that is essentially an arbitrary heads-I-win-and-tails-you-lose argument. But, given the initial premises of those who are driven to this desperate expedient, genetic determinism might seem to loom in the background. Hence the fierce but strained and unconvincing attempts to come up with alternative explanations.

A more realistic set of initial assumptions, rather than the prevailing civil rights vision, could have spared such apologists from having painted themselves into a corner, where they have to resort to such questionable claims. The economic gap between Eastern Europeans and Western Europeans is greater than the economic gap between blacks and whites in America[58]— and has persisted for centuries, even though Western Europeans have been in no position to thwart the economic rise of Eastern Europeans. Yet those who

---

* However dramatic the *political* changes in the wake of the civil rights laws, the economic improvements in the wake of these laws have shown no sustained upward movement over and above the upward trend line of economic improvements among blacks that began in the decades preceding the civil rights revolution of the 1960s.

expected blacks to rise to parity with whites in a few decades had obviously left many things out of their calculations.

Given the specific historical circumstances of American blacks, their record has by no means been something calling for some esoteric apologetics or blame-shifting. As a white Southern scholar observed in the early twentieth century, "no race has come further against greater handicaps." A race "peremptorily shorn of its cultural heritage, became in three generations" a group "substantially comparable to the peasant classes of our western culture." The failure to advance further at that time "may be due mainly to contacts restricted by inescapable physical stigmata"— that is, social isolation based on color. Though "limited in cultural opportunities, encircled by race prejudice as by a barrier of fire, the Negro's rise to partial land ownership, to industrial position, and to a modicum of success in the arts and sciences is frankly a notable achievement for any race."[59]

This was said at a time when most black adults had only an elementary school education, and in inferior Southern schools at that. Whatever may be said about the pace of black progress in the first hundred years after slavery, that progress was not marked by the kinds of stark retrogressions in behavior that set in among lower-class blacks in the 1960s and then spread to others. The unwillingness to acknowledge these retrogressions, much less try to deal with them, makes the further reduction of economic gaps between blacks and whites needlessly more difficult.

International Differences in Wealth

For different nations around the world to all have even approximately similar incomes or wealth, despite their great differences in geography, culture, history, political systems, religious beliefs and the demographic makeups of their respective populations, would require virtually a miracle. Nevertheless, the status quo is by no means predestination, and the histories of particular very poor and very backward nations of the past that have moved to the forefront of human achievement and prosperity show what can be done. The dramatic rise of Scotland in the eighteenth century, Japan in the nineteenth century, and Singapore, Hong Kong and South Korea in the twentieth century all show what can be done— and, to some extent, how.

None of these heartening examples of dramatic economic rises was due to the international transfers of wealth known as "foreign aid." Nor were these economic rises due to "nation-building" by outsiders, whether foreign governments or various experts supplied by international agencies such as the World Bank or the International Monetary Fund. Despite the many attempts to blame the poverty of some nations on exploitation by other nations or by foreign investors, it would be hard to find nations that rose from poverty to prosperity by ridding themselves of colonial overlords— however desirable that might be on other grounds— or by confiscating the property of foreign investors. Indeed, impressive lists of the failures, or even counterproductive consequences, of such approaches can be, and have been, compiled.[60]

Still less often can nations be found that rose from poverty to prosperity by expelling, or by driving out through oppression or mob violence, various minorities widely described as "exploiters" or "parasites"— such as the Jews in Eastern Europe, the Chettiars in Burma, the Asians in East Africa, or others in various other parts of the world and in different periods of history.

Often the nations that drove out such groups were worse off economically after they were gone, and the nations that welcomed them were better off. The United States has benefitted from the arrival of millions of Jews from Europe, who not only provided disproportionate numbers of people in many professions, but also included world class scientists who were disproportionately represented among those who created the first nuclear bomb, on which America's international position as a superpower rested.

The descendants of great conquering nations and peoples often have little to show economically from the historic feats of their ancestors, whether the hordes of Genghis Khan, the Spanish conquistadors, the Ottoman Turks or others. Some conquests have left behind prosperous progeny among the descendants of the conquerors but these were usually conquests by nations that were already prosperous, such as the British who conquered and settled Australia and most of North America, displacing the indigenous populations in both places. The even larger conquests of Spain in the Western Hemisphere usually led to nations in Latin America that have seldom been as prosperous as the former British colonies in North America or Australia, even when the Latin American countries have had fertile soil and rich natural resources.

If there is any common thread in these widely varying outcomes, it seems to be human capital. This can be seen by comparisons of nations and by comparisons of groups within given nations.

Argentina, for example, has been described as "among the world's most richly endowed countries" with "extraordinarily fertile" land, in which the roots of some plants go down 15 feet in soil unencumbered by rocks.[61] Unlike some other Latin American countries, Argentina's population is predominantly of European ancestry. Yet Barbados, whose population is predominantly of sub-Saharan African ancestry— that is, this population originated in a region of the world much poorer than Europe— has a 40 percent higher per capita Gross Domestic Product than that of Argentina.[62]

Although the Barbadians arrived in the Western Hemisphere as slaves and the Spaniards arrived as conquerors, the Barbadians absorbed the British culture, in which they lived longer than the peoples of sub-Saharan Africa from which they came, and the British culture was very different from the culture of Spain, as regards the values attached to work, education, and entrepreneurship, among other cultural factors that the British promoted and the Spaniards disdained. Cultural differences among groups within Argentina reinforce the conclusion that the inherited culture from Spain was no more economically productive in the Western Hemisphere than it was in Western Europe, where Spain has long been one of the poorer countries.

Immigrants to Argentina from other parts of Europe than Spain have been much more economically successful than the native

Argentines, even when these immigrants were initially very poor on arrival. This was especially true of immigrants from Italy, who were the largest number of immigrants to Argentina in the nineteenth and early twentieth centuries. Italian immigrants were 40 percent of all immigrants to Argentina as early as 1864 and remained nearly 40 percent half a century later, in 1914.[63]

Two of the most striking ways in which Italians in Argentina differed from the Argentines was in the Italians' willingness to take on the hardest work, and to save, even out of low incomes. Seasonal migrants from Italy were in great demand as agricultural laborers, and have been credited with contributing to the vast expansion of agriculture in nineteenth century Argentina.[64] In addition to these agricultural laborers, who were called *golondrinas* or swallows because they came and went with the seasons, there were other Italian farm workers who remained as permanent residents. These latter Italians often began as peons and then saved over the years until they could become sharecroppers and then eventually landowners.[65]

Despite the unusual fertility of Argentine land, the country imported wheat, until foreign farmers— notably Italians, but also including Germans from Russia, among others— arrived and transformed Argentina into one of the world's great wheat-exporting nations.[66] But the fact that the land was always capable of growing wheat meant nothing before Argentina acquired people who were prepared to do what was required to be successful wheat farmers. Yet again, geography is not predestination.

In the cities, as in the farmlands, Argentines were outperformed by immigrants. As of 1914, foreigners— who were about 30 percent of the Argentine population— owned 72 percent of the commercial businesses in Argentina, and 82 percent in Buenos Aires.[67] Italian entrepreneurs in Buenos Aires predominated in the production of alcoholic beverages— except beer, where the Germans were pre-eminent.[68]

Argentines were not noted for saving, and were in fact called "the spendthrift of the world."[69] In 1887, the Banco de la Provincia de

Buenos Aires had twice as many depositors who were citizens of Italy as there were who were citizens of Argentina.[70] During that era, most of the Italian immigrants were laborers but, at the same time, most of Argentina's masons, seamen, tradespeople, architects, importers, engineers and restaurant and hotel owners were also Italian.[71]

The Argentine government itself recognized differences between immigrants from different countries in Europe, and sought to attract people from outside the Spanish culture prevailing in Argentina. They deliberately sought at first to attract immigrants from Britain, Germany and Scandinavia, but without much success, so they then welcomed immigrants from Italy and Spain— preferably *Northern* Italians and *Basques* from Spain, people with very different cultures from those in southern Italy or in the rest of Spain— Basques, for example, being noted for being "thrifty and hard workers."[72] The Argentine government also sent agents to Europe to recruit Germans there.[73] Volga Germans settled in what then became Argentina's wheat belt.[74]

While people from outside the prevailing Spanish culture of Argentina dominated much of that country's economy, Argentines dominated its political institutions. In the early twentieth century, Argentina was one of the world's most prosperous nations— ranking above France and Germany, for example.[75] But, by the middle of the twentieth century, disastrous political policies dropped Argentina out of the front ranks of nations economically. Despite its rich soil and other natural advantages, including a location that spared it from being devastated by two World Wars like nations in Europe, Argentina's political culture destroyed the prosperity that the country's economy had once enjoyed. Messianic political demagoguery and class warfare rhetoric and policies, epitomized by Juan Peron and his wife Evita— patroness of "the shirtless ones"— were part of an economically counterproductive pattern that began before them and continued long after their time, nullifying both the advantages provided by nature and the human capital supplied largely by foreigners, whether immigrants or international investors and entrepreneurs.

Argentina was by no means the only country in Latin America whose economic advancement was heavily dependent on foreigners— especially those from countries other than the founding nations of Spain or Portugal— to develop its economy. As late as the mid-twentieth-century, in Brazil's most industrialized states— São Paulo, Rio Grande do Sul and Santa Catarina— most of the industrialists were recent European immigrants or their children. In São Paulo "521 enterprises out of 714 were owned by men in these categories." In Rio Grande do Sul and in Santa Catarina, nearly four-fifths of the industries were developed by people of similar description.[76] Germans and Italians were especially prominent. In the state of Rio Grande do Sul, Germans in the early twentieth century were the sole producers of metal furniture, trunks, stoves, paper, hats, neckties, leather, soap, glass, matches, beer, confections, and carriages, as well as the sole owners of foundries and carpentry shops.[77]

Not only in industry, but also in agriculture, immigrants were sought from outside the Iberian peninsula. The government of Brazil, like the government of Argentina, deliberately recruited Germans in Europe,[78] to be immigrants who would not be reluctant to do the hard physical labor of pioneering in the wilderness, nor were disdainful of it, like people from the Portuguese culture of Brazil and the Spanish culture of Argentina. The state of São Paulo subsidized the immigration of Italian peasants.[79] The governments of Chile and Paraguay likewise deliberately sought European immigrants from outside the Iberian peninsula for the hard work and severe living conditions that went with pioneering in opening up virgin wildernesses in these countries.[80]

In short, these governments recognized cultural differences in the work habits, skills and values required to develop their countries, whether in agriculture or in industry and commerce, despite however much the recognition of such differences may be taboo in many places today. In the words of distinguished French historian Fernand Braudel, it was immigrants who "created modern Brazil, modern Argentina, modern Chile."[81]

Not all these immigrants were from Europe. Japanese immigrants played a significant role in the economies of Brazil and Peru. Although the Japanese were only 2 to 3 percent of the population in Brazil's state of São Paulo, and owned less than 2 percent of its land, they produced nearly 30 percent of the state's agricultural output in the early 1930s— including 46 percent of the cotton, 57 percent of the silk, and 75 percent of the tea. A substantial proportion of the banana plantations were also in Japanese hands.[82]

Peru was another Latin American nation in which a small number of Japanese immigrants played a disproportionate role in the economy. Beginning in the late nineteenth and early twentieth centuries as agricultural laborers, working under conditions that led to high death rates,[83] the Japanese in Peru soon moved into urban communities, where they began working in occupations ranging from domestic servants to small business owners.[84] Eventually, the Japanese owned three-quarters of all the barbershops and 200 grocery stores in Peru's capital city, Lima. Even as agricultural laborers, the Japanese work habits made them more in demand than Peruvian workers, and the Japanese laborers were paid more.[85]

The Japanese acquired a reputation not only for hard work, but also for reliability and honesty.[86] They also took more interest than Peruvians in the education of their children. The illiteracy rate in Peru was 79 percent in 1876 and, though it declined over the generations, 58 percent of the population was still illiterate in 1940.[87] Manufacturing firms in Peru during this era were usually controlled either by foreigners or by recent immigrants.

Like other minority groups who have been more successful than members of the majority population in other times and places, the Japanese were resented in Peru. These resentments were expressed in editorial criticisms and in boycotts of Japanese-owned businesses, though these boycotts failed because the Japanese usually charged lower prices than others.[88] However, political measures against the Japanese were more effective. These included a law requiring at least

80 percent of all employees to be Peruvians,[89] and immigration from Japan was severely restricted in the mid-1930s.[90]

In Chile, foreigners in general played a disproportionate role in the development of the country's economy. As late as the middle of the twentieth century, most of the industrial enterprises in Santiago, Chile, were controlled by either immigrants or the children of immigrants.[91] Nor was this an unusual pattern in Latin America, where there has often been an over-representation— sometimes an absolute predominance— of non-Hispanic, non-Portuguese, immigrants and their children among the leading commercial and industrial figures of various countries.[92]

Disdain for commerce and industry at the higher social levels of Hispanic and Portuguese societies— whether in Europe or among their Western Hemisphere offshoots— has been paralleled by an aversion to manual labor and hard work at the lower social levels. What has been involved in such attitudes has not been simple laziness, but what a scholar writing about seventeenth-century Spain characterized as "pride in indolence," reflecting an aversion to the "stigma" associated with manual work in that culture.[93]

Centuries later, Paraguayans were bewildered by the unrelenting work of people in Japanese agricultural colonies in their country,[94] and Honduran farmers complained that it was unfair for them to have to compete with German farmers in their country, since the latter were considered to be working too hard.[95]

Latin America has by no means been unique on the world stage in not simply failing to reach the standards of productivity set by others, but in positively rejecting, resenting and restricting those who were more productive— and explaining away their own lags by blaming "exploitation" by others at home and abroad. Latin American intellectuals led the way in developing "dependency theory," blaming the lags of South Americans on North Americans and others. Eventually, the striking success of Asian countries that opened their economies to foreign trade, foreign investors and foreign technology eroded the foundations of dependency theory in Latin America. But not before whole generations had paid the price of this self-indulgence.

When considering cultural or other factors, timing must be considered among the reasons for particular outcomes. Finally abandoning dependency theory offered the possibility for more economic progress but the negative effects of all the years when that theory was an obstacle to economic growth were not negated. Similarly, a nation whose population remained illiterate, while literacy became widespread among other nations, will of course benefit from finally bringing literacy to its own people, but that will not put its people on a par with people in countries where literacy has been the norm for generations, or for centuries.

Timing is important in another sense. It has long been observed that a transplanted culture is less subject to change than the culture in its country of origin. Thus, many words and phrases in the French spoken in Quebec and in the Spanish spoken in Mexico have become archaic in France and Spain. Some of the counterproductive attitudes that Latin America inherited from Spain have been said to have begun to change in Spain itself, more so than in Latin America.[96]

It is hard to escape the fact that former British colonies proper— that is, countries founded by a transplanted British population— have generally done better economically than former Spanish or Portuguese colonies. Nor can this be due to the British Empire's having made better initial choices as to places to settle, because the Spanish Empire was established first, giving Spain the first choices. Spaniards conquered lands and peoples in both North America and South America in the 16th century, before the first permanent British settlement in America was established, tenuously, at Jamestown in the 17th century.

FACING THE FACTS— AND THE FUTURE

In dealing with the social and economic problems involving wealth, poverty and politics, specific policy prescriptions are not necessarily the most urgent need. Blueprints for Utopia are available in abundance. What are not nearly so abundant are prerequisites for rational thinking about current problems and future alternatives. The most important of these prerequisites is the *truth*. Whatever destination we are seeking, either literally or figuratively, we can only get there from where we are. This means that we must first know the truth about where we are, in order to advance toward our destination.

If our physical destination is Hawaii, then we must first know whether we are currently east, west, north or south of Hawaii. Otherwise we are likely to head in the wrong direction to get there. If the destination we wish to reach is figurative and social, rather than geographic, the same principle applies. If we wish to promote the economic or other advancement of black Americans, for example, we need to know the truth about where black Americans are now— not where we might wish they were, or where some blacks might prefer to believe they are, or to have others believe they are, but where they are in fact, in *truth*. Wrong premises seldom lead to correct conclusions.

What are the obstacles to knowing the truth?

Unfortunately, these obstacles are all too plain and all too numerous. They include things you cannot say, even with a mountain of empirical evidence behind you, and other things you can shout from the rooftops, without a speck of evidence behind you, and in defiance of whatever evidence exists to the contrary. This is nowhere more true than on college and university campuses, where either a student or a professor publicly speaking unpalatable truths about any minority group currently in favor risks adverse reactions, ranging from becoming an instant social pariah to punishment under campus "speech codes" to physical harassment and threats of violence.

Meanwhile, there are other things that can be said, no matter how demonstrably false, with little risk of even criticism, much less discrediting.

Unfortunately, arbitrary premises that are demonstrably false and misleading abound in all too many settings, whether in academia, the media or in government. One of the most pervasive of these false premises is one that we have already noted— the assumption that disparities in economic outcomes among nations or among groups within nations are symptoms of malign actions by others. This implicit assumption of equal outcomes in the absence of malice flies in the face of evidence from around the world that geographic, demographic, cultural and other factors influencing outcomes are not even approximately equal. Nor are performances in purely individual endeavors that can be objectively measured, such as individual performances in sports, chess or spelling bees— all of which show highly skewed distributions of success.

Given the many things that go into economic productivity, and the many differences among people in their likelihood of having those things, there is a major difference between *equal opportunity* and *equal chances* of achieving a given outcome— a difference often ignored or blurred.

Even a Nobel Prizewinning economist like Joseph Stiglitz says that one way of "looking at equality of opportunity is to ask to what extent the life chances of a child are dependent on the education and income of his parents." More specifically, he asks, "Is it just as likely that a child of poor or poorly educated parents gets a good education and rises to the middle class as someone born to middle-class parents with college degrees?" As evidence of unequal opportunities, he says, "Latinos and African-Americans still get paid less than whites, and women still get paid less than men." According to Professor Stiglitz, "Americans are coming to realize that their cherished narrative of social and economic mobility is a myth."[97]

If equal *opportunity* and equal *probability* of success are used interchangeably, what does that accomplish? It finesses aside the question whether some people make better use of their opportunities than other people do. When Asian students outnumber white students by more than two-to-one in each of New York City's three elite public high schools— Stuyvesant, Bronx Science and Brooklyn Tech[98]— are we to say that whites are being denied equal opportunity?

Are we to say that this must mean that Asians have higher incomes and more education than whites, even when we know that Chinese immigrants from Fujian province have neither? Are we to equate equal opportunity with equal chances, even when we know that the children of black doctors and lawyers in affluent Shaker Heights neglect their studies?[99]

Words matter. So does the slippery use of words, which can insinuate what they cannot substantiate. To people who are seeking the truth, it is a crucial question whether, or to what extent, those groups who are less successful are being thwarted by external barriers— that is, by less *opportunity*— or instead are less successful because of their own internal deficiencies in knowledge, discipline, values or other things that affect their *life chances*. But to people who are seeking ideological victory, that is precisely the question to be kept off the agenda.

If Joseph Stiglitz prefers to make life chances his issue, that is his prerogative. But to claim that he has refuted *other people's* belief in social mobility as a "myth" is to impute his conception of social mobility to those other people. And to cite as evidence income differences between blacks and whites, or between women and men, is to add to the confusion, when many— if not most— Americans would take that to mean that external discrimination must be the reason.

Yet innumerable empirical studies have shown that blacks and whites, as groups, do *not* have the same job qualifications and that women and men likewise differ in many of the things that go into economic advancement, beginning with the simple fact that women average fewer hours of employment per year and fewer years of continuous employment— *among many other consequential differences*.[100]

As far back as 1971, those single women who had worked continuously from high school into their thirties were earning slightly *more* than men of the same description,[101] even though women as a group were not earning as much as men as a group were earning. As far back as academic year 1972–73, while black academics as a group earned less than white academics as a group, nevertheless those black academics with Ph.D.s from equally high-ranked universities as whites, and with equal numbers of articles published, earned *more* than white academics of the same description.[102]

The approach of Professor Stiglitz is by no means unique. Redefining words is a major part of the ideological arsenal of income redistributionists in general, whether discussing the less successful or the more successful members of society. When discussing the latter, the very concept of achievement is often replaced by the concept of privilege. For example, another writer has argued that income statistics show "unambiguously" that "persons of Irish-Catholic ethnicity were the second most privileged group in U.S. society, adjudged on the basis of annual income, educational level and occupational prestige," with Jews being "the most privileged."[103]

What makes this statement grotesque is that Irish and Jewish immigrants were among the most desperately poor of the immigrants who arrived in the United States in the nineteenth century, and lived in a poverty and squalor unseen today and virtually inconceivable today.

That the Irish and the Jews rose from such painful beginnings to prosperity in the next century is an *achievement*, not a privilege. That they did so in the face of once common employers' notices that said "No Irish Need Apply," and in the face of quota limits on how many Jewish students would be admitted to Harvard and other elite universities, and even smaller limits— usually zero— on how many Jewish professors would be appointed during the pre-World War II era, makes their achievements more striking, even as others now try to make those achievements vanish by the verbal magic of calling them "privileges." Even middle-class blacks have been described as "privileged,"[104] though their ancestors were by no means brought to America as doctors, lawyers or teachers.

The same word games are played in discussions of group differences in outcomes in foreign countries— and not simply by politicians or journalists, but in serious academic publications. Thus Malays in Malaysia, for example, have been referred to as "deprived"[105] and non–Malays as having "privilege,"[106] despite pervasive government-mandated preferences for Malays in both public and private institutions. Similarly, Canadians of Japanese ancestry in Toronto have been described as "privileged," because they have achieved higher incomes than others in that city[107]— despite a prior history of severe anti-Japanese discrimination in Canada, climaxed by internment during the Second World War for longer than Japanese Americans were interned.[108]

In short, the achievements of these and other groups, after long and hard struggles upward, are made to vanish from discussion by a simple substitution of the word "privilege" for the word "achievement"— even though privilege refers to a condition that exists *ex ante* and achievement refers to a condition that exists *ex post*. More fundamentally, these tactics remove behavior and productivity from discussions of intergroup economic disparities. So too does the tactic of arbitrarily dismissing any negative information about particular groups as "stereotypes." Such verbal virtuosity is an obstacle to truth, simply by corrupting the words that might otherwise convey unwelcome truths that redistributionists avoid.

Moreover, by focusing on the *rewards* received for achievements, such statements ignore the benefits of those achievements for *others*, which is the very reason that those others— whether employers, patients, customers, or other recipients of the goods or services that people with these achievements produce— are willing to pay their own money to receive those benefits. As in many other contexts, *productivity* vanishes into thin air by verbal sleight of hand, when discussing the "income distribution" that results from that productivity. It is as if all that matters is the income difference between *A* and *B*, ignoring the benefits of their respective achievements for *C*, *D*, *E* and many others.

Preoccupation with the differential benefits to those with various achievements too often obscures the benefits of those achievements to society as a whole. Back in prehistoric times, whoever invented the wheel, or whoever first figured out how to start a fire, may well have acquired an "advantage" over others, but surely what is most important is that these things were major additions to the human capital of mankind in its infancy. It might well have been even better if everyone, all over the world, had acquired these advances at the same time. But surely what is far more important than this theoretical possibility is that these fundamental advances were in fact made in the real world, as the human race began its long advance toward civilization.

When some children today are raised in ways that make it easier for them to become doctors, scientists or engineers, that is not simply a *differential advantage* over other children who are raised in ways that make it more likely that they will become welfare recipients or criminals. These are differences that affect the well-being of the whole society. Yet there are academics who deplore college admissions decisions based on the academic qualifications of individual applicants because, in their view, this is simply rewarding those who have already been "privileged." The consequences *for society* of different admissions criteria are considerations that simply vanish into thin air, just as with the group activist in Nigeria who deplored "the tyranny of skills."[109]

In a sense, there is indeed a tyranny of skills, though it exists independently of a given institution or a given society, because of inherent realities beyond our control. The presence or absence of medical skills, for example, can be the difference between life and death for millions of people. That is an inherent reality— or tyranny— we cannot escape. All that a given institution or society can do is recognize the value of skills— or else subordinate skills to social preconceptions or political expediency. Skills confer benefits, even on those who do not have skills. When a graduate of a selective public high school and a selective city college in New York created a polio vaccine, that was a boon to people of every income level and every race, color, creed and nationality around the world.

Frequent expressions of astonishment at how large the differences in rewards are between individuals, groups or nations seldom lead to questions as to whether what is produced by those who receive these rewards differs correspondingly. It is not so much that redistributionists give different answers to that question than others give. More fundamentally, that question is seldom asked, much less answered. Here again, production usually remains somewhere in the dim background, as something that just happens *somehow*.

Studies of people who became genuinely rich, with huge fortunes, like that of John D. Rockefeller, may abound with assertions about their "greed." But those who use such characterizations seldom pose the most basic question: What did Rockefeller supply to others that caused so many of those others to turn their own individually modest sums of money over to him, adding up to his vast fortune?

Despite the frequency with which "greed" is invoked in this context, it explains absolutely nothing— unless you believe that an insatiable desire for money will itself cause others to pay you that money. But regardless of how often this causally meaningless explanation— greed— has passed muster among the intelligentsia, a more old-fashioned expression conveys a more fundamental truth: "If wishes were horses, beggars would ride." Greed may or may not be an accurate characterization of any given individual, but wishes cannot explain why others provide the money to satisfy those wishes.

Nor is the amount of wealth received even a barometer of greed: A small-time criminal who robs a little mom-and-pop store and kills the owner, to keep from being identified, is surely greedy, even if the money received from the robbery is trivial compared to what an engineer or a surgeon earns honestly in a month.

In the case of John D. Rockefeller, his fortune began in the nineteenth century, with his reducing the price of kerosene to a fraction of what it was before his innovations in production and distribution greatly reduced the cost of producing and delivering this product to consumers.[110] For example, the units in which we measure oil today are barrels, even though oil is no longer actually shipped in barrels but in tankers, due to Rockefeller's cost-saving shift to railroad tanker cars.

As of the time when this happened, light bulbs had not yet been invented, so the ancient saying, "The night cometh when no man can work" still applied to all who could not afford to use candles or oil-burning sources of light for hours at a time each night. Many working class people had few options besides going to bed when nightfall came. Only after Rockefeller's innovations in production and distribution cut the cost of kerosene to a fraction of what it had been before, were ordinary people able to afford to stay up for hours after dark, using kerosene lamps.

What such people were purchasing were hundreds of hours of additional light per year. It is hardly surprising that millions of people were willing to pay to enlarge their lives in this way.

We take so many of the benefits of today's world for granted that it is hard to conceive of how different life was in the world of earlier times— much less grasp the full impact of landmark advances that enabled people to transcend the severe limitations of those times.

It has been estimated, for example, that most Americans in the early nineteenth century lived out their entire lives and died within a fifty-mile radius of where they were born.[111] The railroad and the automobile expanded their world to vastly larger dimensions, especially in the early twentieth century, after Henry Ford's mass-production methods drastically reduced the cost of producing an automobile. This changed cars from being luxuries of the rich to being accessible to the masses.

The fortune made by Henry Ford was an incidental by-product of this historic expansion of productivity that expanded the lives of millions. Why third parties should imagine themselves entitled to intervene in such processes, to which they contributed nothing, and to preempt the decisions of others— decisions for which the interventionists pay no price when they are wrong— is one of the many mysteries of our time.

Many fortunes of historic dimensions came from producing a new product or making an old product either better or cheaper, or both. In less spectacular ways as well, other people who have acquired other skills are paid for what those skills add to the lives of other people, whether these are the skills of doctors curing diseases or the skills of pilots transporting hundreds of people thousands of miles. Acquiring valuable skills to do these and other things is an *achievement* that benefits others, rather than a "privilege" that benefits only themselves at the expense of others. The difference is fundamental, regardless of how much verbal cleverness goes into obscuring that difference.

Redistributionists may demand proof that all fortunes, or all high incomes, are earned that way, but this is putting the burden of proof on others, instead of putting the burden of proof on those who seek to restrict the freedom of their fellow human beings to live their own lives and make their own economic decisions as they see fit. There is no reason why the divine right of kings, from earlier centuries, should be inherited by today's intelligentsia or politicians.

Are there imperfections in a market economy? Yes! There are imperfections in all things human, including alternatives to the market economy. As a distinguished scholar put it: "The study of human institutions is always a search for the most tolerable imperfections."[112]

None of this means that the status quo must be maintained. It cannot be and has not been. Even leading conservative figures, ranging from Edmund Burke in the eighteenth century to Milton Friedman in the twentieth century, have advocated major social changes.* The fact that they opposed some other changes does not mean that they opposed change as such. But the word "change" is not a blank check for self-indulgence— least of all self-indulgence in the notion that disparities imply villainy, which in turn implies a crusade on the side of the angels against the forces of evil, despite how self-flattering such a vision of the world might be.

---

* In addition to devoting years to the impeachment of the British viceroy of India, on grounds that he oppressed the native peoples, Burke advocated the abolition of slavery at a time when that was a distinctly minority view in Western civilization and virtually a non-existent view in non-Western societies. Burke even drew up plans for preparing slaves for freedom and providing them with property with which to begin their lives as free people. Milton Friedman proposed sweeping changes in public schools and in the Federal Reserve System, as well as a negative income tax to transfer money to low-income people. Burke said, "A state without the means of some change is without the means of its conservation" and Milton Friedman wrote a book titled *The Tyranny of the Status Quo*.

An even more dangerous illusion is that the undoubted unfairness of life chances is a reason to give politicians ever more control of a nation's resources and ever more power over our individual lives. The track record of that approach is— at the very least— sobering, when even most socialist and communist governments had been forced by counterproductive consequences to abandon economic central planning by the end of the twentieth century, and when the material benefits of an expansive welfare state to some in England and the United States have been accompanied by painful social retrogressions to the detriment of each society as a whole.

Most important of all, whatever changes are made must begin with the truth about our current situation, whether that truth is palatable or unpalatable, if "change" is to mean progress. To the extent that this book has offered at least a slice of that truth, it has achieved its purpose. Drawing up policy blueprints is a task for which there has never been a shortage of eager candidates. We can only hope that those policies will be based on hard facts about the real world, rather than on rhetoric or preconceptions.

EPILOGUE

Few subjects provoke such strong emotions as differences in income and wealth, especially when these are differences between groups into which individuals are born and usually remain for life, such as races, castes, tribes or nations— in descending order of permanence. People can change nationality by immigrating but changing race is an option available to a relatively few people of hybrid ancestry— and not without psychic costs to those few, including costs which such people have often refused to pay, which would have been the consequence of abandoning the race into which they were born.*

People born into groups defined by religion, such as Jews or Mormons, all have an option to re-designate themselves, but likewise usually do not. Therefore concerns and resentments over group differences in income and wealth engage the emotions of many individuals who may be doing quite well economically themselves, but who belong to groups that are not. Indeed, even where both the individual and the group to which that individual belongs are prospering more so than the rest of society, there are moral issues raised

---

* Among black Americans, such historic figures as Homer Plessy, of *Plessy v. Ferguson* fame, and Walter White, the mid-twentieth century head of the National Association for the Advancement of Colored People, were physically indistinguishable from white men, but remained socially "black" by choice. The landmark Supreme Court case of *Plessy v. Ferguson* was made possible only because Plessy's attorney gave prior notice to the railroad company involved that a man classified as black would challenge racial segregation by traveling in a railroad car legally designated as for whites only. Had Plessy simply seated himself in that car without explicitly proclaiming his racial classification, there is little reason to believe that he would have been questioned, much less prosecuted, but the whole point was to have a legal case to pursue, in order to challenge racial segregation laws in the courts.

about whether the less fortunate are receiving not only enough for a decent life but also "social justice," however that term might be defined.

The strong emotions surrounding issues of income and wealth make careful— and honest— uses of words especially important, if our goal is truth, and not simply ideological victory in a contest of fencing with words. Among the careful distinctions we need to make is the distinction between causation and blame, and between the general unfairness of life and the question of specific unfairness in particular institutions or in particular societies.

CAUSATION

Both moral and causal arguments are important, but amalgamating the two, even implicitly, is a formula for confusion, perhaps exemplified in the catch phrase, "blaming the victim." Whether particular individuals, groups or nations with poorer outcomes are in fact victims of others is precisely the question that is preempted by this phrase. There is no question that for an individual to be born blind or crippled is a tragic misfortune but that in itself does not mean that someone has victimized that individual. There are, after all, causes besides humans— various geographic features being obvious examples. For a group, a race or a nation to be located in a geographic setting that affords far less promising prospects of either prosperity or progress can be a major, fundamental misfortune, but that in itself does not mean that some other people have victimized them.

Determining where some disadvantage to particular individuals or groups originated is often no easy matter. Because data collected at a given institution may *convey* a certain negative outcome does not mean that the institution where those data were collected *caused* that outcome. Some hospitals have significantly higher death rates than others precisely because they have the most highly skilled doctors and the most advanced medical technology— and therefore treat patients with the most difficult, life-threatening medical problems that some other hospitals are simply not equipped to handle. A hospital that treats mostly people with routine medical conditions such as child birth or broken legs may well have a lower death rate than a hospital which performs operations like brain surgery or heart transplants. Higher death rates at more advanced hospitals *convey* a reality that these hospitals did not *cause*. That reality in this case is that its patients have more severe afflictions, for which neither they nor the hospital are to blame.

Similarly with outcomes in economic and social institutions, where negative outcomes at particular institutions are often more or less automatically taken to mean that it was these institutions which *caused* negative results that the data collected there *conveyed*. When, for example, statistics on the employment, pay and promotion of people from different ethnic backgrounds are collected at a particular business, differences in these respects from one group to another do not mean that the *cause* of such differences must have originated at those businesses where data *conveying* these differences originated.

Often other data, or just common observations, show children being raised differently in different groups, and behaving and performing differently in schools or in society as they grew up, years before they reached a particular employer. Yet courts of law have accepted "disparate impact" statistics collected at particular businesses as evidence of discrimination by those particular businesses. In the same vein, group differences in results on particular tests are often taken to mean that these tests are "biased," when the scores on these tests *convey* differences among the participants which these tests are accused of *causing* by asking questions geared to a white culture, for example— even when Asian Americans in fact score higher than whites on these tests.

Individuals, groups, races and nations may be handicapped by their cultural settings, as they have been handicapped by their geographic settings. In either case, their misfortunes do not necessarily mean victimhood, which requires people who are victimizing others. While cultures are man-made, they were usually made jointly by people long dead before the present generation was born, and these cultures were certainly not made with malice against future descendants. In short, misfortunes cannot automatically be transmuted into victimhood by a catch phrase, not if one is serious about the truth, rather than fencing with words. To suggest that there can be cultural patterns inconsistent with progress in the world as it has evolved is not to "blame the victim," except for those who are satisfied with trying to verbally turn the tables on people who speak unwelcome truths.

The Localization of Blame

People who seek blame, rather than causation, often also seek a *localized* source of evil to blame. Professor Paul Krugman, for example, refers to slavery as "America's original sin"[1] when in fact slavery was a virtually universal evil around the world, for thousands of years of recorded history. Would anyone refer to cancer as "America's horrible disease"? No doubt cancer has been a dreadful affliction for many Americans but it is not a *localized* affliction. What was different about Americans was not that they suffered the ravages of cancer, but that American doctors and medical researchers led the fight against cancer, resulting in Americans having the world's highest rate of survival against various forms of cancer.[2]

In parallel fashion, slavery was not peculiar to the United States, to white society or to Western civilization. What was peculiar to Western civilization was not that it had slavery, like non-Western civilizations around the world, but that Western civilization was where the drive to destroy slavery began— a drive that lasted more than a century, fought on many fronts and succeeded over the opposition of non-Western societies.[3] Only the military dominance of the West in the nineteenth and early twentieth centuries allowed the West to impose the abolition of slavery on the countries it conquered or threatened, along with many other things— good, bad or mixed— imposed during the era of Western imperialism.

Referring to slavery as "America's original sin" was not a verbal slip peculiar to Professor Krugman. Many intellectuals and others act as if enslavement of fellow human beings was peculiar to the white race, or gross economic inequalities peculiar to capitalism, or imperialism, despite a vast historical record to the contrary, and despite other economic and social systems, and other races and religions, leaving a trail of horrors matching or exceeding anything in the West or under capitalism or imperialism.

Evils common to human beings around the world, and across thousands of years of recorded history, do not provide as promising a target for ideological crusades as evils attributable to an identifiable, localized source of evil that can be removed and replaced by whatever one puts one's faith in. But universal evils or failings of human beings can mean that even the most sweeping, devastating and bloody victory over those currently in power may produce only a change in the cast of characters, without changing the tragedy itself. The tyranny and carnage that followed the French Revolution was at least as horrible as the horrors of the old regime it replaced. In the twentieth century, the replacement of oppressive, monarchical dynasties by Communist, Fascist and Nazi dictatorships was a major change for the worse.

The false narrative of "America's original sin" has led to other false narratives, including "the legacy of slavery" as a blanket explanation of various forms of social pathology in today's black ghettos. With both false narratives, sheer repetition has substituted for empirical verification. The question is seldom asked, much less answered, as to whether today's levels of one-parent families or murder rates among blacks have existed since the time of slavery or have escalated to present levels largely since the 1960s. As of 1960, most black children were still being raised in two-parent families, which have become the exception, rather than the rule, *after the 1960s.*

Nor was the level of violence in black communities in general, or in housing projects in particular, at the levels of today. While it is true, historically, that rates of both broken families and violence were higher in black communities than in the American population at large, that was not uncommon among other low-income groups, whether in the United States or in other countries, and whether or not the low-income groups had been enslaved. But neither one-parent families nor violent crime was as high among black Americans in the middle of the twentieth century as today. Homicide rates among black males were in fact *declining* substantially during the much lamented 1950s, but this trend abruptly reversed during the much celebrated 1960s and rose sharply to significantly higher levels than in either 1950 or 1960.[4] Labor force participation rates were higher among blacks than among whites in every census from 1890 to 1970, but the reverse has been true for every year since 1972.[5] This reversal occurred in the wake of the expansion of the welfare state, not in the wake of slavery.

The fundamental problem is not that some people were not familiar with these facts. The fundamental problem was that they chose to make sweeping assertions without bothering to check the facts— and that their sweeping assertions have been widely accepted, and repeated, in the absence of supporting facts and in defiance of readily available contrary facts.

Multiple Causation

The fact that the human species achieved nothing that we today would consider to be civilization, until well within the last 10 percent of its existence, has weighty implications for our times. Even races and nations that are today considered the most backward are more advanced than any race was during most of the existence of the human species. Were all the races of the world genetically inferior for all those scores of millennia? Or was some other factor or factors holding them back?

The most obvious factor was isolation in prehistoric times, as in later times. Hunter-gatherers could travel only so far, and could interact with only so many other hunter-gatherers in ancient times. How could a hunter-gatherer in Scandinavia even suspect the existence of other hunter-gatherers in Asia or even Southern Europe, much less interchange goods or thoughts with them across continents, and certainly not interchange genes? Even today, we look in vain for breakthroughs on the frontiers of knowledge from people living on isolated islands or in remote mountain villages, or from people living anywhere who are isolated by illiteracy. Such people may have all they can do to survive, much less try to keep up with what other people in more advanced settings are doing.

At a minimum, this suggests that the truly isolated human being, denied even vicarious contact with the rest of his species through reading about them, is incapable of achieving even a small fraction of what his potential might be if immersed in the knowledge created by his contemporaries and heir to the knowledge of the many generations that went before him. Indeed, even a hundred, or a thousand, isolated human beings, knowing only each other, and nothing about other contemporaries or predecessors, have seldom, if ever, produced anything the world has bothered to notice.

Yet there is no evidence that human genes changed drastically within the last 5 or 10 percent of human existence. Nor is there any hard evidence that the specific races that made the first world-changing advances in agriculture— in the Middle East, on the Indian subcontinent or in ancient China— were genetically superior then or now. These are certainly not the most prosperous, or the most advanced, regions today.

What seems far more likely, in this context as in many others, is that a large number of factors had to come together and interact, in order to produce a particular outcome, such as civilization. Most of those factors might well have been present for millennia, but impotent without the other factor or factors needed to complete the prerequisites for civilization. Yet, once agriculture was established, on a scale sufficient to permit or promote urbanization, there began many advances, within the last few millennia of recorded history, across a wide sweep of human endeavors, by descendants of people who previously did not even know how to plant seeds to grow food. Yet this development of civilization led ultimately to people who can now travel to the moon and send complex scientific instruments throughout the solar system and beyond into outer space. This enormous disparity of achievements between different eras of human existence dwarfs disparities between rich and poor contemporaries in the world of today. Yet this vast disparity between the achievements of different eras hardly seems explicable by either victimhood or genetics.

This scenario of progress has yet to be played out fully in the Amazon jungles or in other isolated places around the world, even though people in such places have benefitted as consumers of products created by fellow human beings in more fortunate settings.

If a number of factors have to come together, in order to produce a given outcome— whether tornadoes or economic advances— then it is possible that a number of those factors may come together in a number of places, while all of the factors come together in very few places, or even in only one. If there are ten factors required for success in a particular endeavor, individuals or groups with nine of those factors will not necessarily do 90 percent as well. They may be utter failures. The net result can be a very skewed distribution of outcomes, whether the particular outcome is most of the world's tornadoes occurring in just one country or a trio of professional golfers winning more than 200 PGA tournaments while most professional golfers never win even a single PGA tournament in their entire careers.

Most notable economic, scientific or intellectual achievements involve many factors— beginning with a desire to succeed in the particular endeavor, without which all the ability and opportunity mean nothing, just as the desire and the opportunity mean nothing without the ability. What this implies, among other things, is that an individual, a people, or a nation may have some, many or most of the prerequisites for a given achievement without having any real success in producing that achievement. And yet that individual, that people or that nation may suddenly burst upon the scene with spectacular success when whatever the missing factor or factors are finally get added to the mix.

Poor and backward nations that suddenly moved to the forefront of human achievements include Scotland in the nineteenth century and Japan in the twentieth century. But there have been other social phenomena pointing in the same direction, as examples of multiple causation.

We have become so used to seeing numerous world-class performances by Jewish intellectual figures that it is necessary to reflect that this has been a phenomenon that burst upon the world in the nineteenth and twentieth centuries. There were individual Jewish intellectuals of international stature here and there in earlier centuries, but the proliferation of Jewish Nobel Prize winners across numerous fields in the twentieth century was a new and unpredictable phenomenon. Since Jews existed as a separate people for thousands of years before, and had a long tradition of reverence for learning, most of the factors required for their breakout in the nineteenth century may already have been present. But, for centuries, Jews were denied the rights of Christians in Europe or the rights of Muslims in the Middle East— and these included access to universities.

The first Christian nation in which Jews had the same rights as other people was the United States, late in the eighteenth century, when the American Constitution simply forbad religious distinctions in the law. After the French Revolution in 1789, France also granted equal rights to Jews. As restrictions against Jews began to erode in Europe, Jews began to flow, and then to flood, into universities. The missing ingredient had apparently been added.

Conversely, when a given individual, group, institution or nation has already had a highly successful combination of factors for many years, either internal changes in just one of those factors, or changes in external circumstances, can suddenly drop that institution, that people or that nation out of the top ranks in the particular endeavor. Thus the Eastman Kodak Company's global dominance in photographic equipment and supplies for more than a century came to a sudden end in the early twenty-first century, including a decline into bankruptcy, when the worldwide shift to digital cameras made film, film cameras and the chemicals and equipment for developing film obsolete.*

China's historic decline, over the centuries, from an advanced nation in the forefront of human progress, to a Third World country, prey to more powerful nations in many ways, began with a decision by its fifteenth century rulers to isolate China from the outside world. Loss of just one prerequisite— rulers rational enough to avoid irreparably self-destructive policies— was enough to negate all the other positive qualities that had for centuries given China historic achievements.

Just as a combination of prerequisites for success in a particular endeavor may deny success to individuals, groups, institutions or nations that may have most of those prerequisites, but not all, so may variations in the number or kind of prerequisites from one endeavor to another let individuals or groups seriously lagging in some or most other endeavors nevertheless be not merely competent but outstanding or even dominant in particular endeavors that do not require the particular qualities or circumstances that they do not have, even if there is fierce competition within the particular endeavor in which they compete.

Thus, during the era when Irish American immigrants and their offspring were over-represented among unskilled laborers and domestic servants, they were also among the leading performers in such sports as boxing and baseball, and among popular entertainers.

Sports and entertainment are highly competitive fields, with many trying but few succeeding. Yet the crucial qualities, skills and talents tend to be individual, and do not require an elaborate infrastructure of formal education or long years of training by specialists, which few poor people can afford. Other low-income Americans, lacking in educational traditions or high-level industrial or commercial

---

* The irony in all this is that Eastman Kodak could hardly have been caught by surprise by the emergence of digital cameras, since the digital camera was *invented* within Eastman Kodak. As in many other contexts, having facts is not the same as seeing the implications of those facts.

experience, have followed in the footsteps of Irish Americans, not only in sports and entertainment in general, but even in many of the very same kinds of sports and entertainment in which Irish Americans once excelled so strikingly— that is, boxing and baseball rather than polo or golf, popular music rather than symphonic music, vaudeville performers rather than ballet dancers or Shakespearean actors.

However demanding the skills or talents, and however rare the individuals able to reach the peaks, when the prerequisites for particular endeavors did not include an elaborate formal infrastructure, such as that required to become a scientist, a surgeon or an engineer, economically and educationally lagging groups have often been over-represented not only numerically but especially among the star performers.

A whole succession of Irish American boxing champions in the nineteenth and early twentieth centuries, from the era of John L. Sullivan to that of Gene Tunney, was followed by a succession of black American boxing champions, beginning in the 1930s with the legendary Joe Louis,* who still holds the record for one-round knockouts in heavyweight championship fights. Decades later, the era of black boxing champions was succeeded by an era of Hispanic American boxing champions. Similarly in baseball where, despite a ban on black players in the major leagues until 1947— which is to say, more than half a century after major league baseball began— there were seven consecutive years when no white man won the National League's Most Valuable Player award,[6] and now 5 of the top 10 players who hit the most home runs in their careers are black.[7] Here too, the era of black dominance among baseball stars was followed by

---

* There was an isolated black heavyweight champion— Jack Johnson— beginning in 1908, but the succession of black champions began with Joe Louis.

an era when a wholly disproportionate number of baseball stars were Hispanic.*

It was not only among some ethnic groups, but also among white Southerners, that a lagging group, in economic and educational terms, produced many stars in sports and entertainment. Although white Southerners have long been no more than one-third of the white population of the country, in baseball four of the top five highest lifetime batting averages were by white players born in the South— Ty Cobb (.367) in Georgia, Rogers Hornsby (.358) in Texas, Shoeless Joe Jackson (.356) in South Carolina and Tris Speaker (.345) in Texas.

The lone non-Southerner among the top five, Ed Delahanty, had a lifetime batting average of .346.[8] His career began earlier, in the late nineteenth century and continued into the early twentieth century, encompassing an era with such other Irish baseball stars as Wee Willie Keeler (.343 lifetime batting average), Eddie Collins (.333), John J. McGraw (.333), James Edward (Tip) O'Neill (.326), Roger Connor (.317), Jim O'Rourke (.310) and Michael (King) Kelly (.308) who, at his peak, led the National League in batting with .354 in 1884 and .388 in 1886.[9] Among the Irish pitching stars of that era was "Iron Man" McGinnity, who led the National League in games pitched in six different seasons, was a 35-game winner with an earned run average of 1.61 in 1904, and became renowned for sometimes pitching both games of a double-header.[10]

While some might imagine that sports involve only physical skills, it is harder to believe that when it comes to entertainers, and especially musicians and musical composers. Here again, there has been a fault line between the kinds of entertainment requiring a formal infrastructure of education and training, such as ballet and classical music versus popular music and dance, where individual talents and creativity are key. Among musical instruments, the violin

---

* In 1990, 17 percent of major league baseball players were black and 13 percent were Hispanic. By 2014, however, only 8.2 percent of major league baseball players were black and 28.4 percent were Hispanic. "The History of Latinos in America's Pastime Isn't Black and White," *The Game We Love: The Sporting News and 125 Years of Baseball*, 2015, p. 27.

requires formal training, while the piano can be self-taught, even though becoming a top popular pianist has been a rare triumph. Here black American musicians have not merely held their own but excelled and created musical genres that became popular across America and even internationally. Black composers emerged early in the twentieth century, with Scot Joplin and W.C. Handy, followed later by a new, more sophisticated musical genre created by Duke Ellington and others.

Here again, with entertainment as with sports, what blacks achieved was preceded by similar achievements by the Irish before them, Hispanics after them and by white Southerners. A whole line of famous Irish American singers in the early twentieth century was climaxed by Bing Crosby as the leading entertainer in the first half of the twentieth century and, in 1947, he was named "Most Popular Living Person" in a radio poll.[11] It was said that, through his recordings, radio broadcasts and movies, his voice was heard by more people around the world than the voice of any other human being at that time. Later there were famous Hispanic entertainers, and white Southern entertainers went from being regionally prominent to being nationally famous, with Elvis Presley becoming an international icon. *Billboard* magazine's 2010 rankings of the "Top 100 Artists 1955–2009" had Elvis Presley first, with a large lead over The Beatles in second place.[12]

Even within sports, there are areas where the skills required for success are clearly and unmistakably *not* physical. These would include baseball broadcasters whose renown put them in the Baseball Hall of Fame, such as Red Barber, Mel Allen, Russ Hodges and Ernie Harwell— all four of whom were from the 1940s and 1950s heyday of radio sportscasters, and all of them white Southerners.[13] What is especially remarkable is that these broadcasters became famous in an era when there was not one major league baseball team in the entire South. To become major league broadcasters, they had to move to other regions of the country and compete with people living there, in order to get a job, and then to become renowned in their field.

Despite the poverty and backwardness of many mountain peoples on every inhabited continent, there have been areas in which they too excelled. A sweeping spectrum of elegant handicrafts have for centuries poured out of mountain communities around the world. Among the mountain handicraft products in demand internationally have been shawls from Kashmir and watches and clocks from Switzerland, France and the Black Forest region of southern Germany.[14] Because of high transportation costs from mountains to the outside world, only articles with a high value concentrated in a small physical size could find a market in the lowlands, and be sold successfully in competition with products produced in the lowlands. At one time, in centuries past, villages in the Pindus Mountains of Greece developed high skills in metalworking and wool processing, producing "fine handiwork in gold and silver" and "exquisitely embroidered woolens," which found markets from Istanbul to Vienna. Silk handicrafts flourished for a time in the mountains of Greece, Italy and Morocco, though these eventually succumbed to competition from Asia, where silk originated.[15]

In the Andes, weaving techniques were adapted to the hair of the llamas.[16] From the mountains of Tibet came many high quality handicraft products based on the same social circumstances as in other mountains around the world— namely, great amounts of free time in the winters, spent indoors, where special skills could be developed and practiced. From the deposits of silver and gold in that region, Tibetans made jewelry, and from local woods various artistic objects were designed and carved. In other parts of the world, other mountain and highland peoples also used local resources to produce various local specialties such as dolls, rugs, lace and violin strings. As a distinguished geographer once said: "Most of these mountain industries merely supplement the scant agricultural resources; they represent the efforts of industrious but hard pressed people to eke out their meager subsistence."[17] In the process, many became skilled weavers, potters, dye makers, wood carvers, stone carvers, and jewelers.[18]

No matter how lagging, poor or backward particular peoples may be at particular times, or even for centuries, it is hard to find large groups of human beings so lacking in skills or talents as to be fit only to be the proverbial "hewers of wood and drawers of water," though some welfare state policies and practices have reduced some people to a level where they cannot, or will not, come up to even that modest level of productivity.

While it may be readily understandable that lagging groups can find some niche in which they can hold their own, what is striking is that such groups often do not merely hold their own, but are especially successful in reaching the peaks, more so than the population at large, including other groups who greatly outperform them in many other kinds of endeavors. This pattern, however, seems consistent with lagging groups and advanced groups being innately not very different, if different at all, but different primarily in whether they have or do not have the full ensemble of factors required for success in various fields, even if the lagging group has most of these factors but lacks part of the ensemble that comes from either internal culture or external circumstances.

If so, then it is not surprising that a backlog, as it were, of innate potential unable to come to fruition in other fields would be concentrated in the fields where the prerequisites are met, and therefore make groups lagging elsewhere be among the top performers in the fields accessible to them. What is also consistent with this hypothesis is that when groups rise out of the status of lagging groups— Irish Americans being a classic example— and become part of the mainstream of American achievements in a variety of fields, they tend also to forfeit their predominance among the stars in sports and entertainment.

Against this background, many current assumptions and beliefs are hard to sustain. One of these current notions is that lagging groups require a lowering of existing standards, so that more of their members can advance via various forms of "affirmative action." Yet the fields in which many lagging minorities have had their greatest success— especially sports and entertainment— are fields notorious for severe competition, in which even star performers whose performances begin to decline are ruthlessly cast aside. In short, lagging minorities have flourished in endeavors whose conditions are the direct opposite of those of affirmative action. They have had real achievements against unsparing competition, rather than make-believe achievements based on affirmative action quotas.

Advocates of affirmative action who imagine that they can simply tack on whatever factors may be needed for individuals from lagging groups to succeed usually see this as something that can be done in the later stages of education, at the college or university level, when in fact it is seldom possible to make up for many years of substandard education or ingrained habits with negative consequences. On the contrary, affirmative action has too often taken minority students with all the prerequisites of success and turned them into artificial failures by mismatching them with institutions where most members of the general population would also fail. Thus when black students were admitted to M.I.T. with mathematics scores at the 90th percentile, this left them in the bottom 10 percent at M.I.T., where the other students were at the 99th percentile. More than one-fifth of these black students dropped out, while most of those who remained performed below the level of their white classmates.[19]

In other words, black students with qualifications that would have made them candidates for honors at most colleges and universities were artificially turned into failures at M.I.T. Conversely, when affirmative action was banned in the University of California system, the proportion of black and Hispanic students who graduated increased substantially, as did their grades and their graduation rates in challenging fields like mathematics, science and engineering.

Another popular notion of our time is an expectation of equal economic outcomes for groups in the absence of malign treatment by others. Neither more fortunate nor less fortunate groups are randomly distributed. Instead, different kinds of groups have very different patterns of distribution in different kinds of endeavors. In the bitter battles between those who ascribe different results to external barriers and those who ascribe them to internal deficiencies, both often ignore the possibility that what people *want* to do, or *do not* want to do is a factor not to be overlooked. These culturally shaped preferences can make the ability-versus-barriers dichotomy irrelevant in particular cases. With all the innate ability in the world, and with all the doors of opportunity wide open, people who have no desire to do *X* have very little likelihood of doing *X*, either well or badly.

Given multiple factors required for success in many endeavors, including some in which people with most, or perhaps almost all, of these factors may nevertheless be complete failures, there is no reason to expect either even or random patterns of success. Nor is there any basis for expecting a persistence of a given uneven pattern of success over time— especially when the particular prerequisites can change over time. Nor can a general presumption of malign actions by others being behind the fate of the less fortunate be sustained with logic, much less evidence, despite how common that assumption has become in American courts of law, under the "disparate impact" theory of discrimination, or how common that same presumption has been in other nations as well.

The presumption of equal outcomes in the absence of malign actions can lead to incorrect— and disastrous— conclusions in other circumstances as well. When Dr. Marcus Whitman treated both indigenous American Indians and white Americans for measles in the Pacific northwest in 1847, the estimated death rate among the Indians was 50 percent and among the whites was 15 percent at most. Other Indians did not regard this pattern, which involved the deaths of their loved ones, as just a matter of random chance. Blaming their deaths on some malign action by Dr. Whitman, they killed him and his wife, among other whites massacred or enslaved.[20] However, the whites and the Indians who were ill differed in one crucial factor, the greater exposure of people of European origin to many diseases with which the Indians had historically had no contact, and therefore had developed no biological resistance.

Something similar sometimes happened in medieval Europe, when epidemics struck. When the rate of infection and death was noticeably lower among Jews than among Gentiles, demagogues were able to convince some people that Jews must somehow be behind the epidemic and were sparing themselves. Where enough people believed this story, it could lead to mass violence against Jews. What no one knew at the time was that unseen microorganisms were the cause of these epidemics. Because Jewish religious practices required them to pray before every meal and, since they could not go before God with dirty hands, they also had to wash their hands before every meal. Neither Jews nor Gentiles knew about germs at this point but their cultural differences had serious consequences in their susceptibility to communicable diseases.

These were neither the first nor the last times when statistical disparities led people to jump to conclusions about villainy being the cause. False assumptions are more than intellectual errors, and their consequences go far beyond economic losses.

GOALS

While goals are in principle quite different from facts— we may all agree on the facts and yet desire to pursue very different goals— many goals are based on a particular set of beliefs about what the existing facts are. If the less fortunate peoples of the world are less fortunate primarily because they are victims of the more fortunate, then the goal to pursue in trying to make things right can be very different from what the goal would be if the less fortunate are seen as people lacking the geographic, cultural and other advantages enjoyed by others, largely through no fault of theirs or of others. Not only may goals differ between people with these very different conceptions of the facts, so may the criteria by which progress is measured.

Some might regard the spread of prosperity to human beings in general as the prime criterion of economic success. Others, especially those who believe that the poor are poor because the rich are getting rich at their expense, may be more likely to see the prime criterion as being a reduction or elimination of economic "gaps" and "disparities," which are equated with "inequities." Many people may be in favor of both these things, and think of them as complementary goals, when in fact beyond some point there are inescapable trade-offs that can make the two goals incompatible in practice, however desirable they may seem together in theory. If everyone's income doubles, for example, that will almost certainly reduce poverty but it will also increase economic "gaps," "disparities" and "inequities." Some nations have in fact had their real per capita income double, over varying periods of time.

Obviously, some people may value the spread of prosperity more than the reduction of inequality, while others prefer the opposite. When China, after the death of Mao, abandoned the original Communist emphasis on economic egalitarianism and adopted more market-oriented reforms under Deng Xiaoping— who said, "Let some people get rich first"[21]— the economic growth rate hit new highs and literally hundreds of millions of people rose out of poverty.[22] That a country historically plagued by famines, including a famine under Mao in which tens of millions died, became a country in which about one-fourth of the adult population is now overweight, is one measure of the change. But such market-driven rises in per capita real income have not been evenly spread in China, any more than in other places and times, whether within nations or between nations.

When prosperity is widespread, even if not equalized, that may be of more significance to those released from the worst deprivations of grinding poverty than would reductions in the statistical gaps between the poor and the rich. A low-income mother whose sick baby's chances of dying in infancy have been cut in half, as a result of rising prosperity, is unlikely to think of this as inconsequential, much less a grievance, even if she learns that a rich mother's baby's smaller chances of dying in infancy have also been cut in half or by more than half.

Preoccupation with "disparities," "gaps" and "inequities" has largely been the hallmark of the intelligentsia, the media and politicians. Yet the people whose lives have been most changed by rising levels of prosperity around the world have often been those who were most lacking in basic things before. Thus even a redistributionist has noted that the population growth in low-income countries has increased at a higher rate than in more affluent countries.[23] This has largely been due to growing economic prosperity and advances in medical knowledge originating in more affluent countries.

If the desperately poor people in the Italian mountain village described by Edward C. Banfield in the mid-twentieth century were later enabled to add some meat to their diet— even if only hamburgers or frankfurters— that might be a more meaningful benefit to them than if people in a more affluent society could afford more steak or lobster.* Being able to afford motor scooters might add more to the range of the mountain villagers' mobility than if a rich family bought a second Rolls Royce. In their book *Free to Choose*, Rose and Milton Friedman pointed out such patterns more generally:

> Industrial progress, mechanical improvement, all of the great wonders of the modern era have meant relatively little to the wealthy. The rich in Ancient Greece would have benefited hardly at all from modern plumbing: running servants replaced running water. Television and radio— the patricians of Rome could enjoy the leading musicians and actors in their home, could have the leading artists as domestic retainers. Ready-to-wear clothing, supermarkets— all these and many other modern developments would have added little to their life. They would have welcomed the improvements in transportation and in medicine, but for the rest, the great achievements of Western capitalism have redounded primarily to the benefit of the ordinary person.[24]

---

* On a personal note, at a dire time in my life as a young man, I pawned my one suit, in order to get money to be able to eat. After emerging from a pawn shop on the Lower East Side of New York, which was a predominantly Jewish neighborhood at that time, I went into a nearby eating place and ordered a knish and an orange soda. Many years later, I would eat at the Waldorf Astoria, in Parisian restaurants and in the White House. But no meal ever topped that knish and orange soda.

Back in 1836, Nathan Rothschild— one of the richest men in the world, and perhaps *the* richest— died from an infection that defied the efforts of leading doctors summoned to his side.[25] Today, the poorest child of a welfare mother in America is unlikely to die from that same infection because economic and medical advances present routine cures for such things. This happened not because governments intervened to prevent people from becoming as rich as Nathan Rothschild, but because people in some countries remained free to work out their own lives and make their own mutual accommodations on such terms as they could with their fellow human beings— and it was largely from such countries that the technological and medical advances came.

Emphasis on "income distribution"— and especially *redistribution*— to the neglect of *production* downplays the benefits to society at large, and to the poor especially, from what is produced in the course of earning higher incomes.* As new, better and often cheaper products spread throughout societies around the world, much of this output benefits people of all sorts, which is the very reason why millions of people are willing to pay for it, and thus create fortunes such as that of Bill Gates and others.

Since the reduction of poverty and the closing of economic gaps are competing goals, on what basis can we choose between them? One basis might be what is actually achievable and at what cost. There is a serious question as to whether economic equality— even approximate equality— can be achieved at all, since economic achievements depend on things largely beyond any government's control, such as geography, or totally beyond anyone's control, such as the past. That does not mean that we can do nothing, but it does suggest that we cannot do everything that strikes us as desirable.

Even leaving aside all practical issues arising from conflicts between the goal of increasing prosperity and the goal of reducing gaps, the

---

* It is not that money income "trickles down" to the poor— a proposition advocated by no one, but used as a straw man by many. See my monograph, *"Trickle-Down" Theory and "Tax Cuts for the Rich"*.

achievement of equal incomes can be literally impossible, when equality in one sense is inherently incompatible with equality in another sense.

To take the most extreme case, even if every American man, woman and child had equal individual incomes, that would still leave substantial inequalities in *household* incomes, because households that are in the top 20 percent of income recipients today contain millions more people than households in the bottom 20 percent. Such households would remain in higher income brackets if incomes were made equal among all individuals. If we restrict income equality to adults, there would be even more inequality between households, since households consisting of a single mother with multiple children would not have as much income per person as households consisting of two parents and their children, even if welfare paid the single mother as much as other adults received for working.

Putting aside the case of literal equality between every individual or every individual adult, if by some miracle it were possible to have all individuals in all groups attain both the same quantitative levels of education, as measured by number of years in school, and also the same qualitative levels as measured by mastery of subjects of the same difficulty and economic rewards, that would still leave intractable differences in age, which would mean inescapable differences in experience since, when the age of adulthood is eighteen, a forty-year-old worker has more than ten times as much work experience as a twenty-year-old worker.

In these circumstances, even if every twenty-year-old Puerto Rican in the United States had identical incomes with every twenty-year-old Japanese American, and similar equality at every other age, that would still leave a major income inequality between these two groups, since the average Japanese American is more than twenty years older than the average Puerto Rican. In short, even extraordinary and unprecedented equalizations among individuals could still leave major statistical inequalities among groups. This raises a crucial question: What are the consequences of choosing and fervently proclaiming an unreachable goal?

Theoretically, everyone could get together and agree on which particular definition of equality they would use, so that it would then at least be *possible* to have equality. But what incentive would there be to do that, in an atmosphere where every disparity or gap is seen as an intolerable grievance, redeemable by various benefits to be supplied by others? Whatever the merits of any particular definition of equality of outcomes, what must be faced are the consequences of perpetually promoting a fervent crusade, perpetually frustrated by its own internal contradictions— but whose frustration is instead blamed on some human enemies of a sacred cause.

Those who are in the business of protesting grievances are not going to stop protesting, or taking disruptive or violent action, because equality has been achieved by one definition, when equality by one definition precludes equality by some other definitions. In this context, such phrases as "No justice, no peace" are a declaration of unending internal strife, since justice by one definition is injustice by another. But no society has inexhaustible patience with unending turmoil. If history is any guide, it is only a matter of time before patience is exhausted and severe repressive measures are imposed, to the ultimate detriment of the whole society.

Again, if history is any guide, no amount of progress toward an unreachable goal can satisfy fiercely promoted aspirations seen as sacred, so that all remaining unfulfilled hopes are seen as intolerable impositions of injustice. Some have argued from history that major social upheavals have often occurred when social problems were in fact lessening, but not at a pace comparable to rising expectations. If so, it may be more than coincidence that the wave of ghetto riots that swept across the United States in the 1960s began just days after passage of the Voting Rights Act of 1965, the capstone of historic civil rights legislation that had preceded.

Preoccupation with income differences, and with political crusades against them, have not seized the minds and emotions of the general public to anything like the degree to which such preoccupations have dominated the thinking of the intelligentsia. The obsession of the intelligentsia with economic "gaps" and "disparities" has not usually been shared by the public at large.

This has been true even in many countries with the most poisonous form of this obsession, resentment and hatred of ethnic minorities who are more productive, and therefore more prosperous, than the population at large. A scholarly study of Romania between the two World Wars, for example, found that the "anti-Jewish mood proved most rampant among the middle and upper classes and among the intellectuals."[26] It was much the same story of hostile reactions to other minority businessmen and professionals in other countries around the world.

An international treatise on ethnic conflicts found that "the supposed economic resentments of businessmen by their customers often do not exist."[27] Malays often preferred dealing with Chinese shopkeepers, for example.[28] Maharashtrians preferred shopping at businesses run by non-Maharashtrians in Bombay (now Mumbai) in the late twentieth century.[29] In Indonesia and Burma, indigenous farmers often preferred dealing with Arab money-lenders (in Indonesia) and Indian money-lenders (in Burma) to dealing with government money-lenders of their own ethnicity, even though the latter offered lower interest rates.[30] Boycotts of Indian businesses in Uganda in 1959–1960 and of Japanese businesses in Peru in 1930 lacked public support.[31] But such boycotts and other actions against minority businesses have been supported by indigenous business rivals in these and other countries, as an obvious matter of self-interests— and by the respective intelligentsia, on ideological grounds.

African university students have been hostile toward Indian businessmen in Uganda; Lebanese businessmen in Nigeria, Ghana and Senegal; Armenian businessmen in Ethiopia.[32] The Third World intelligentsia have seldom had any business experience, and greatly prefer government jobs to working in the private sector.[33] Similar hostility to business has long been common among intellectuals in more prosperous industrial societies as well. It is not surprising that the goal of reducing economic inequalities has often permeated their advocacies and actions. With sufficient time, persistence and fervor, the obsessions of the intelligentsia can of course spread to the public at large, but that is seldom where such zeal originates.

More generally, the crucial question in economic and social issues is whether the success of whatever goal is being pursued is measured by its tangible effects on human happiness or unhappiness, or is instead measured by abstract numbers or other indicators of approaching a preconceived tableau. Despite all the horrors under totalitarian Communist governments in the twentieth century, it should not be forgotten that the Communist movements which led to such governments included people dedicated to equality, to "ending exploitation" and to other humane goals. Many in such movements were willing to risk or sacrifice their livelihoods, or if necessary their lives, in pursuit of these goals. The willingness of many to also sacrifice their own integrity and the truth, in order to forward the cause, was a key factor in the political success of ruthless Communist leaders in imposing horrors with impunity.

This was not unique to Communist movements. Similar phenomena have existed in smaller messianic movements, such as that which led to the Jonestown massacre in 1978. But the Communist movement was the largest and most thoroughly documented example of a movement's implacable pursuit of an unachievable ideal, and the demonizing of all who got in the way, while lionizing ruthless leaders with unbridled powers, including the power to make a mockery of the ideals of the movement itself and exterminate any of its members he chose.

Communists are of course an extreme example. But, under any movement or set of collective beliefs, being on the side of the angels can be a dangerous self-indulgence in a heedless willfulness sometimes called idealism. This kind of idealism can seduce thinking into feeling, replace realities with preconceptions, and make the over-riding goal the victory of some abstract vision, in defiance of reality or in disregard of the truth and the fate of fellow human beings.

ACKNOWLEDGEMENTS

One of the most general acknowledgements that needs to be made, more often than it is, is that we all stand on the shoulders of giants. I am especially awed and indebted to those who have obviously invested great amounts of time and wisdom writing monumental treatises, from *The Chinese in Southeast Asia* by Victor Purcell to *Human Accomplishment* by Charles Murray, *America in Black and White* by Stephan Thernstrom and Abigail Thernstrom, *Influences of Geographic Environment* by Ellen Churchill Semple, *Ethnic Groups in Conflict* by Donald L. Horowitz and a whole series of insightful and enlightening scholarly books on Europe's history and geography by N.J.G. Pounds.

Other books more notable for their very high quality than for their physical size would include *Life at the Bottom* by Theodore Dalrymple, Charles A. Price's *Southern Europeans in Australia* and David S. Landes' *The Wealth and Poverty of Nations*. No doubt the infirmities of memory mean that this brief list leaves out some equally worthy works among the hundreds of other publications consulted and/or cited in this book. But the list is offered as suggestive, rather than definitive.

There would of course be no point standing on the shoulders of these and other giants if we saw only what they saw and simply repeated what they had already said, often quite well. But we can at least look in different directions from the vantage point they give us.

Then there are the many wrong-headed publications, including specious Supreme Court decisions, which have spurred my examination of issues that I might not have noticed otherwise. But the authors of these wrong-headed notions might not fully appreciate my expressions of gratitude to them by name in this context.

Closer to home, it would be hard to exaggerate how much I owe to my research assistants of many years, Na Liu and Elizabeth Costa. They have not simply gotten research material that I asked for but have participated more actively by seeking out and evaluating other material on their own initiative. In addition, Ms. Costa has done the painstaking copy-editing and fact-checking, while Ms. Liu has created the Quark computer files from which the finished manuscript can be printed directly into books.

All of this takes place with the support, and under the auspices, of the Hoover Institution, utilizing the vast library resources of Stanford University. My wife Mary and my friend of many years, Joseph Charney, both gave critiques of the original version of Chapter 1 that caused it to be drastically revised and improved.

All conclusions, and whatever errors there may be, are solely my responsibility.

Thomas Sowell
The Hoover Institution
Stanford University

NOTES

Chapter 1: Issues

1. See, for example, N.J.G. Pounds, *An Historical Geography of Europe* (Cambridge: Cambridge University Press, 1990), p. 21.

2. Ibid., p. 27. The advanced state of ancient civilizations in Egypt and China during the same era has been covered in many books and articles by many authors, including Margaret Oliphant, *The Atlas of the Ancient World: Charting the Great Civilizations of the Past* (New York: Simon & Schuster, 1992), pp. 38–41, 162–165.

3. Charles O. Hucker, *China's Imperial Past: An Introduction to Chinese History and Culture* (Stanford: Stanford University Press, 1975), p. 65; Jacques Gernet, *A History of Chinese Civilization*, second edition, translated by J.R. Foster and Charles Hartman (New York: Cambridge University Press, 1996), pp. 69, 138, 140.

4. David S. Landes, *The Wealth and Poverty of Nations: Why Some Are So Rich and Some So Poor* (New York: W.W. Norton & Company, 1998), pp. 93–95.

5. Charles Murray, *Human Accomplishment: The Pursuit of Excellence in the Arts and Sciences, 800 B.C. to 1950* (New York: Harper Collins, 2003), pp. 355–361.

6. Ellen Churchill Semple, *Influences of Geographic Environment* (New York: Henry Holt and Company, 1911), p. 20.

7. Fernand Braudel, *The Mediterranean and the Mediterranean World in the Age of Philip II*, translated by Siân Reynolds (Berkeley: University of California Press, 1995), Vol. I, p. 35.

8. *The World Almanac and Book of Facts: 2014* (New York: World Almanac Books, 2014), pp. 748, 771, 779–780, 821, 831, 839, 846.

9. Ibid., pp. 764, 786, 793.

10. The Economist, *Pocket World in Figures: 2013 edition* (London: Profile Books, 2012), p. 25.

11. Herbert Heaton, *Economic History of Europe* (New York: Harper & Brothers, 1936), p. 246; Saskia Sassen, *Territory, Authority, Rights: From Medieval to Global Assemblages* (Princeton: Princeton University Press, 2006), p. 83.

12. Jaime Vicens Vives, "The Decline of Spain in the Seventeenth Century," *The Economic Decline of Empires*, edited by Carlo M. Cipolla (London: Methuen & Co., 1970), p. 147; Carlo M. Cipolla, *Before the Industrial Revolution:*

European Society and Economy, 1000–1700, second edition (New York: W.W. Norton, 1980), p. 252.

13. David S. Landes, *The Wealth and Poverty of Nations*, p. 250.

14. U. S. Bureau of the Census, *Historical Statistics of the United States: Colonial Times to 1970* (Washington: Government Printing Office, 1975), Part 1, p. 382.

15. The Economist, *Pocket World in Figures: 2003 edition* (London: Profile Books, 2002), p. 26; U.S. Census Bureau, "Money Income in the United States: 2000," *Current Population Reports*, P60–213 (Washington: U.S. Bureau of the Census, 2001), p. 2.

16. The phrase "income distribution" leads some people to reason as if there is some pre-existing block of income or wealth— created "somehow"— that is then divided up among individuals or groups. In reality, it is the process of creating wealth that leads to individual incomes being received in exchange for individual productivity in that process. These individual incomes may later be added up by others into a verbally collectivized "national income," which is then spoken of as being "distributed" to individuals or groups. Sometimes the same way of thinking is applied internationally, leading to laments about such things as how Americans, for example, consume a disproportionate share of "the world's output." But there is no one named "World" who produces all output, or indeed any output at all. Americans essentially consume what Americans produce, using a portion of what they produce to exchange for an equivalent amount of imported goods from others. In a purely figurative statistical sense, income can be said to be "distributed" in the same sense in which there is a statistical "distribution" of heights in a population, without anyone imagining that these heights exist collectively and are then sent out to individuals. Those who believe that income or wealth *should* be collectivized in reality, and then be shared out, are of course free to advocate such an economic system explicitly, but that is very different from insinuating such a process with words that have more than one meaning.

17. Henry Hazlitt, *The Wisdom of Henry Hazlitt* (Irvington-on-Hudson, New York: The Foundation for Economic Education, 1993), p. 224.

18. Darrel Hess, *McKnight's Physical Geography: A Landscape Appreciation*, eleventh edition (Upper Saddle River, New Jersey: Pearson Education, 2014), pp. 100–101; E.A. Pearce and C.G. Smith, *The Times Books World Weather Guide* (New York: Times Books, 1984), pp. 129, 130, 131, 132, 142, 376.

19. E.A. Pearce and C. G. Smith, *The Times Books World Weather Guide*, pp. 132, 376.

20. Daron Acemoglu and James A. Robinson, *Why Nations Fail: The Origins of Power, Prosperity, and Poverty* (New York: Crown Business, 2012), p. 62.

21. Richard Lynn, *The Global Bell Curve: Race, IQ, and Inequality Worldwide* (Augusta, Georgia: Washington Summit Publishers, 2008).

22. As complained by Richard Lynn, *The Global Bell Curve*, p. 5.

23. Attributed to John Maynard Keynes, without specific citation. A very similar statement appeared earlier in Carveth Read, *Logic: Deductive and Inductive*, third edition (London: Alexander Moring, Limited, The De La More Press, 1909), p. 320.

Chapter 2: Geographic Factors

1. David S. Landes, *The Wealth and Poverty of Nations: Why Some Are So Rich and Some So Poor* (New York: W.W. Norton & Company, 1998), p. 6.

2. Darrell Hess, *McKnight's Physical Geography: A Landscape Appreciation*, eleventh edition (Upper Saddle River, New Jersey: Pearson Education, Inc., 2014), p. 200.

3. T. Scott Bryan, *The Geysers of Yellowstone*, fourth edition (Boulder: University of Colorado Press, 2008), pp. 9–10.

4. Alan H. Strahler, *Introducing Physical Geography*, sixth edition (Hoboken, New Jersey: Wiley, 2013), pp. 402–403.

5. Frederick R. Troeh and Louis M. Thompson, *Soils and Soil Fertility*, sixth edition (Ames, Iowa: Blackwell, 2005), p. 330; Xiaobing Liu, et al., "Overview of Mollisols in the World: Distribution, Land Use and Management," *Canadian Journal of Soil Science*, Vol. 92 (2012), pp. 383–402.

6. Ellen Churchill Semple, *Influences of Geographic Environment* (New York: Henry Holt and Company, 1911), p. 69.

7. William S. Maltby, *The Rise and Fall of the Spanish Empire* (New York: Palgrave Macmillan, 2009), p. 18; Peter Pierson, *The History of Spain* (Westport, Connecticut: Greenwood Press, 1999), pp. 7–8.

8. John H. Chambers, *A Traveller's History of Australia* (New York: Interlink Books, 1999), p. 35.

9.   Ellen Churchill Semple, *Influences of Geographic Environment*, pp. 442–443; Don Funnell and Romola Parish, *Mountain Environments and Communities* (London: Routledge, 2001), p. 115.

10.   The total area of all 50 states is 3,678,190 square miles. Subtracting the area of Alaska (590,693 square miles) and Hawaii (6,468 square miles) leaves 3,081,029 square miles as the area of the remaining 48 contiguous states. The area of the Sahara Desert is 3,320,000 square miles or approximately 8 percent larger than the 48 contiguous states. *Time Almanac: 2013* (Chicago: Encyclopedia Britannica, 2012), pp. 173, 466, 582–583, 587.

11.   Fernand Braudel, *A History of Civilizations*, translated by Richard Mayne (New York: The Penguin Group, 1994), p. 124. Likewise, a geographer said: "Enlightenment filtering in here was sadly dimmed as it spread." Ellen Churchill Semple, *Influences of Geographic Environment*, p. 392.

12.   William H. McNeill, *History of Western Civilization: A Handbook*, sixth edition (Chicago: University of Chicago Press, 1986), p. 247.

13.   Charles Murray, *Human Accomplishment: The Pursuit of Excellence in the Arts and Sciences, 800 B.C. to 1950* (New York: Harper Collins, 2003), pp. 355–361.

14.   N.J.G. Pounds, *An Historical Geography of Europe* (Cambridge: Cambridge University Press, 1990), p. 1.

15.   Ellen Churchill Semple, *Influences of Geographic Environment*, pp. 29, 131.

16.   Ibid., p. 25.

17.   Oscar Handlin, "Introduction," *The Positive Contributions by Immigrants*, edited by Oscar Handlin (Paris: United Nations Educational, Scientific and Cultural Organization, 1955), p. 13.

18.   Ulrich Bonnell Phillips, *The Slave Economy of the Old South: Selected Essays in Economic and Social History* (Baton Rouge: Louisiana State University Press, 1968), p. 269.

19.   Ellen Churchill Semple, *Influences of Geographic Environment*, p. 84.

20.   Jeffry A. Frieden, *Global Capitalism: Its Fall and Rise in the Twentieth Century* (New York: W.W. Norton, 2006), p. 5.

21.   Daniel Yergin, *The Prize: The Epic Quest for Oil, Money, and Power* (New York: Simon & Schuster, 1991), p. 60.

22.   Jack Chen, *The Chinese of America* (San Francisco: Harper & Row, Publishers, 1980), pp. 65–66.

23. William A. Hance, *The Geography of Modern Africa* (New York: Columbia University Press, 1964), p. 5.

24. Jocelyn Murray, editor, *Cultural Atlas of Africa* (New York: Facts on File Publications, 1981), p. 10.

25. Robert Stock, *Africa South of the Sahara: A Geographical Interpretation*, third edition (New York: The Guilford Press, 2013), p. 29; Robert O. Collins and James M. Burns, *A History of Sub-Saharan Africa*, second edition (New York: Cambridge University Press, 2014), p. 17.

26. Robert Stock, *Africa South of the Sahara*, third edition, p. 129.

27. Jacques Gernet, *A History of Chinese Civilization*, second edition, translated by J.R. Foster and Charles Hartman (New York: Cambridge University Press, 1996), p. 321.

28. Ellen Churchill Semple, *Influences of Geographic Environment*, p. 260.

29. William Howarth, "The St. Lawrence: A River of Boundaries," National Geographic Society, *Great Rivers of the World*, edited by Margaret Sedeen (Washington: National Geographic Society, 1984), pp. 415–416, 420; Ronald Stagg, *The Golden Dream: A History of the St. Lawrence Seaway* (Toronto: Dundurn Press, 2010), p. 233.

30. U.S. Navy Hydrographic Office, *Africa Pilot*, Vol. II: *South and East Coasts of Africa from Cape of Good Hope to Ras Hafun* (Washington: Government Printing Office, 1916), p. 248.

31. William A. Hance, *The Geography of Modern Africa*, second edition (New York: Columbia University Press, 1975), pp. 497–498.

32. Virginia Thompson and Richard Adloff, *French West Africa* (Stanford: Stanford University Press, 1957), p. 305.

33. Edwin O. Reischauer and John K. Fairbank, *A History of East Asian Civilization*, Volume I: *East Asia: The Great Tradition* (London: George Allen & Unwin, Ltd., 1960), pp. 20–21.

34. Ellen Churchill Semple, *Influences of Geographic Environment*, p. 341.

35. William H. McNeill, *History of Western Civilization*, sixth edition, p. 247.

36. Jocelyn Murray, editor, *Cultural Atlas of Africa*, p. 13.

37. F. J. Pedler, *Economic Geography of West Africa* (London: Longmans, Green and Co., 1955), p. 118.

38. Jean W. Sedlar, *East Central Europe in the Middle Ages, 1000–1500* (Seattle: University of Washington Press, 1994), p. 335.

39. David S. Landes, *The Wealth and Poverty of Nations*, p. 295.

40. Nicholas Wollaston, "The Zaire," *Great Rivers of the World*, edited by Alexander Frater (Boston: Little, Brown and Company, 1984), p. 80.

41. Rupert B. Vance, *Human Geography of the South: A Study in Regional Resources and Human Adequacy* (Chapel Hill: University of North Carolina Press, 1932), p. 261.

42. Robert E. Gabler, et al., *Physical Geography*, ninth edition (Belmont, California: Brooks/Cole Cengage Learning, 2009), p. 470.

43. Ellen Churchill Semple, *Influences of Geographic Environment*, p. 343.

44. Ellen Churchill Semple, *The Geography of the Mediterranean Region: Its Relation to Ancient History* (New York: Henry Holt and Company, 1931), p. 579.

45. Ellen Churchill Semple, *Influences of Geographic Environment*, p. 330.

46. Ibid., p. 331.

47. Ibid.

48. Fernand Braudel, *The Mediterranean and the Mediterranean World in the Age of Philip II*, translated by Siân Reynolds (Berkeley: University of California Press, 1995), Vol. I, pp. 95, 144.

49. William H. McNeill, *History of Western Civilization*, sixth edition, p. 246.

50. Don Hinrichsen, *Coastal Waters of the World: Trends, Threats, and Strategies* (Washington: Island Press, 1998), p. 75.

51. Fernand Braudel, *The Mediterranean and the Mediterranean World in the Age of Philip II*, translated by Siân Reynolds, Vol. I, p. 138.

52. Ibid.

53. Ibid.

54. Darrell Hess, *McKnight's Physical Geography*, eleventh edition, p. 271.

55. James S. Gardner, et al., "People in the Mountains," *Mountain Geography: Physical and Human Dimensions*, edited by Martin F. Price, et al (Berkeley: University of California Press, 2013), pp. 268, 269.

56. See, for example, J.R. McNeill, *The Mountains of the Mediterranean World: An Environmental History* (New York: Cambridge University Press, 1992), pp. 27, 44–46, 104, 142–143; Ellen Churchill Semple, *Influences of Geographic Environment*, pp. 530, 531, 599, 600; Fernand Braudel, *The Mediterranean*

and the Mediterranean World in the Age of Philip II, translated by Siân Reynolds, Vol. I, pp. 38, 57, 97; Rupert B. Vance, *Human Geography of the South*, pp. 242, 246–247.

57. Rupert B. Vance, *Human Geography of the South*, p. 242.

58. "Each settlement. . . constitutes a world within itself, for it is insulated from its neighbors by one or two thousand feet of steep wooded ridge." Rupert B. Vance, *Human Geography of the South*, p. 242. See also Ibid., pp. 243, 246.

59. Jean W. Sedlar, *East Central Europe in the Middle Ages, 1000–1500*, p. 335.

60. Fernand Braudel, *The Mediterranean and the Mediterranean World in the Age of Philip II*, translated by Siân Reynolds, Vol. I, p. 283.

61. J.R. McNeill, *The Mountains of the Mediterranean World*, p. 44.

62. James S. Gardner, et al., "People in the Mountains," *Mountain Geography*, edited by Martin F. Price, et al., p. 269.

63. Douglas W. Freshfield, "The Great Passes of the Western and Central Alps," *The Geographical Journal*, Vol. 49, No. 1 (Jan. 1917), pp. 2–22; James S. Gardner, et al., "People in the Mountains," *Mountain Geography*, edited by Martin F. Price, et al., p. 288.

64. J. R. McNeill, *The Mountains of the Mediterranean World*, p. 143.

65. Ibid., pp. 27, 54.

66. Ibid., p. 27.

67. Alton C. Byers, et al., "An Introduction to Mountains," *Mountain Geography*, edited by Martin F. Price, et al., p. 6.

68. James S. Gardner, et al., "People in the Mountains," Ibid., p. 267.

69. Martin F. Price and Thomas Kohler, "Sustainable Mountain Development," Ibid., p. 336.

70. Edward C. Banfield, *The Moral Basis of a Backward Society* (New York: The Free Press, 1958), pp. 10, 17, 35, 46.

71. Ibid., pp. 46–47.

72. J. R. McNeill, *The Mountains of the Mediterranean World*, p. 47.

73. Ibid., p. 29.

74. Alton C. Byers, et al., "An Introduction to Mountains," *Mountain Geography*, edited by Martin F. Price, et al., p. 2.

75. See for example, Don Funnell and Romola Parish, *Mountain Environments and Communities*, p. 99; James S. Gardner, et al., "People in the Mountains,"

Mountain Geography, edited by Martin F. Price, et al., pp. 276, 306; Ellen Churchill Semple, *Influences of Geographic Environment*, pp. 595–596.

76. J. R. McNeill, *The Mountains of the Mediterranean World*, p. 206; William H. McNeill, *The Age of Gunpowder Empires: 1450–1800* (Washington: The American Historical Association, 1989), p. 38.

77. Ellen Churchill Semple, *Influences of Geographic Environment*, pp. 586–588; J.R. McNeill, *The Mountains of the Mediterranean World*, pp. 118–119, 228–229, 268.

78. Edward C. Banfield, *The Moral Basis of a Backward Society*, p. 35.

79. Peter Levi, *Atlas of the Greek World* (New York: Facts on File, Inc., 1980), p. 13.

80. J.R. McNeill, *The Mountains of the Mediterranean World*, pp. 126, 127, 129.

81. Ibid., p. 133.

82. Fernand Braudel, *The Mediterranean and the Mediterranean World in the Age of Philip II*, translated by Siân Reynolds, Vol. I, p. 42.

83. Don Funnell and Romola Parish, *Mountain Environments and Communities*, p. 206.

84. Rupert B. Vance, *Human Geography of the South*, p. 247.

85. Amy Chua and Jed Rubenfeld, *The Triple Package: How Three Unlikely Traits Explain the Rise and Fall of Cultural Groups in America* (New York: The Penguin Press, 2014), p. 169.

86. Kevin D. Williamson, "Left Behind," *National Review*, December 16, 2013, p. 26.

87. Martin F. Price and Thomas Kohler, "Sustainable Mountain Development," *Mountain Geography*, edited by Martin F. Price, et al., p. 339.

88. J.R. McNeill, *The Mountains of the Mediterranean World*, pp. 116, 117, 139.

89. See, for example, Ibid., p. 144.

90. Josip Roglič, "The Geographical Setting of Medieval Dubrovnik," *Geographical Essays on Eastern Europe*, edited by Norman J.G. Pounds (Bloomington: Indiana University Press, 1961), p. 150.

91. Fernand Braudel, *The Mediterranean and the Mediterranean World in the Age of Philip II*, translated by Siân Reynolds, Vol. I, p. 46; Don Funnell and Romola Parish, *Mountain Environments and Communities*, pp. 225, 227; J.R. McNeill, *The Mountains of the Mediterranean World*, p. 110.

92. James N. Gregory, *The Southern Diaspora: How The Great Migrations of Black and White Southerners Transformed America* (Chapel Hill: University of North Carolina Press, 2005), p. 76.

93. Mandel Sherman and Cora B. Key, "The Intelligence of Isolated Mountain Children," *Child Development*, Vol. 3, No. 4 (1932), pp. 279–290. A similar pattern among black youngsters was found in Otto Klineberg, "Mental Testing of Racial and National Groups," *Scientific Aspects of the Race Problem*, edited by H.S. Jennings, et al (Washington: Catholic University Press, 1941), p. 280.

94. Lester R. Wheeler, "A Comparative Study of the Intelligence of East Tennessee Mountain Children," *Journal of Educational Psychology*, Vol. XXXIII, No. 5 (May 1942), pp. 322, 324.

95. Rupert B. Vance, *Human Geography of the South*, p. 256.

96. Ibid., p. 243.

97. Fernand Braudel, *The Mediterranean and the Mediterranean World in the Age of Philip II*, translated by Siân Reynolds, Vol. I, p. 44.

98. Martin F. Price and Thomas Kohler, "Sustainable Mountain Development," *Mountain Geography*, edited by Martin F. Price, et al., p. 340; Don Funnell and Romola Parish, *Mountain Environments and Communities*, pp. 111, 217; James N. Gregory, *The Southern Diaspora*, p. 36.

99. James S. Gardner, et al., "People in the Mountains," *Mountain Geography*, edited by Martin F. Price, et al., pp. 272, 273; Stephen F. Cunha and Larry W. Price, "Agricultural Settlement and Land Use in Mountains," Ibid., pp. 304–305; Don Funnell and Romola Parish, *Mountain Environments and Communities*, p. 213; Ellen Churchill Semple, *Influences of Geographic Environment*, pp. 579–580.

100. See, for example, Don Funnell and Romola Parish, *Mountain Environments and Communities*, p. 215; James S. Gardner, et al., "People in the Mountains," *Mountain Geography*, edited by Martin F. Price, et al., p. 268; Stephen F. Cunha and Larry W. Price, "Agricultural Settlement and Land Use in Mountains," Ibid., p. 304; J.R. McNeill, *The Mountains of the Mediterranean World*, pp. 54, 107, 134, 175, 213.

101. Don Funnell and Romola Parish, *Mountain Environments and Communities*, pp. 223–224; J.R. McNeill, *The Mountains of the Mediterranean World*,

pp. 119, 213; James S. Gardner, et al., "People in the Mountains," *Mountain Geography*, edited by Martin F. Price, et al., p. 272.

102. J.R. McNeill, *The Mountains of the Mediterranean World*, p. 213; N.J.G. Pounds, *An Historical Geography of Europe*, p. 264.

103. Alton C. Byers, et al., "An Introduction to Mountains," *Mountain Geography*, edited by Martin F. Price, et al., p. 1.

104. J. R. McNeill, *The Mountains of the Mediterranean World*, pp. 20, 35, 41.

105. Monica and Robert Beckinsale, *Southern Europe: The Mediterranean and Alpine Lands* (London: University of London Press, 1975), pp. 42, 43, 228.

106. John K. Fairbank and Edwin O. Reischauer, *China: Tradition & Transformation* (Boston: Houghton Mifflin, 1978), p. 17.

107. Frederick R. Troeh and Louis M. Thompson, *Soils and Soil Fertility*, sixth edition, p. 330; Xiaobing Liu, et al., "Overview of Mollisols in the World: Distribution, Land Use and Management," *Canadian Journal of Soil Science*, Vol. 92 (2012), pp. 383–402.

108. Uzo Mokwunye, "Do African Soils Only Sustain Subsistence Agriculture?" *Villages in the Future: Crops, Jobs and Livelihood*, edited by Detlef Virchow and Joachim von Braun (New York: Springer, 2001), p. 175.

109. World Bank Independent Evaluation Group, *World Bank Assistance to Agriculture in Sub-Saharan Africa* (Washington: The World Bank, 2007), p. 14.

110. Rattan Lal, "Managing the Soils of Sub-Saharan Africa," *Science*, May 29, 1987, p. 1069.

111. *The World Almanac and Book of Facts: 2013* (New York: World Almanac Books, 2013), p. 335.

112. E.A. Pearce and C. G. Smith, *The Times Books World Weather Guide* (New York: Times Books, 1984), p. 19.

113. Ibid., pp. 149, 188, 279, 380, 413.

114. Ibid., pp. 26, 41, 47, 54, 57.

115. Ibid., pp. 130, 199, 357.

116. George W. Hoffman, "Changes in the Agricultural Geography of Yugoslavia," *Geographical Essays on Eastern Europe*, edited by Norman J.G. Pounds, p. 114.

117. Andrew J. Bach and Larry W. Price, "Mountain Climate," *Mountain Geography*, edited by Martin F. Price, et al., p. 41.

118. Ellen Churchill Semple, *Influences of Geographic Environment*, p. 27.

119. E.A. Pearce and C. G. Smith, *The Times Books World Weather Guide*, p. 199.

120. Don Funnell and Romola Parish, *Mountain Environments and Communities*, pp. 145–146.

121. *The World Almanac and Book of Facts: 2014* (New York: World Almanac Books, 2014), p. 733; Barbara F. Grimes, editor, *Ethnologue: Languages of the World* (Dallas: SIL International, 2000), Volume I, p. 846.

122. Gordon F. McEwan, *The Incas: New Perspectives* (Santa Barbara, California: ABC-CLIO, 2006), p. 89.

123. National Geographic Society, *Great Rivers of the World*, edited by Margaret Sedeen, p. 278.

124. Ellen Churchill Semple, *Influences of Geographic Environment*, p. 434.

125. Ibid.

126. William S. Maltby, *The Rise and Fall of the Spanish Empire*, p. 18.

127. Ellen Churchill Semple, *Influences of Geographic Environment*, p. 144.

128. Ibid.

129. "The Indigenous People," *The Australian People: An Encyclopedia of the Nation, Its People and Their Origins*, edited by James Jupp (Cambridge: Cambridge University Press, 2001), p. 4.

130. Darrell Hess, *McKnight's Physical Geography*, eleventh edition, p. 324.

131. Nicholas Wade, *A Troublesome Inheritance: Genes, Race and Human History* (New York: The Penguin Press, 2014), p. 93.

132. Alfred W. Crosby, "An Ecohistory of the Canary Islands: A Precursor of European Colonialization in the New World and Australasia," *Environmental Review*, Vol. 8, No. 3 (Autumn 1984), p. 217.

133. Donald P. Whitaker, et al., *Area Handbook for Australia* (Washington: Government Printing Office, 1974), pp. 46, 361–362.

134. J.M. Roberts, *A History of Europe* (New York: The Penguin Press, 1997), p. 139.

135. Burr Cartwright Brundage, *Empire of the Inca* (Norman: University of Oklahoma Press, 1963), pp. 261–262.

136. Francis Jennings, *The Invasion of America: Indians, Colonialism, and the Cant of Conquest* (Chapel Hill: University of North Carolina Press, 1976), p. 22.

137. Caroline Golab, *Immigrant Destinations* (Philadelphia: Temple University Press, 1977), p. 102.

138. Donald L. Horowitz, *Ethnic Groups in Conflict* (Berkeley: University of California Press, 1985), p. 663.

Chapter 3: Cultural Factors

1. David S. Landes, "Culture Makes Almost All the Difference," *Culture Matters: How Values Shape Human Progress*, edited by Lawrence E. Harrison and Samuel P. Huntington (New York: Basic Books, 2000), p. 2.

2. "Africa's Testing Ground," *The Economist*, August 23, 2014, p. 59.

3. See, for example, Richard Lynn and Tatu Vanhanen, *IQ and Global Inequality* (Augusta, Georgia: Washington Summit Publishers, 2006).

4. Victor Wolfgang von Hagen, *The Germanic People in America* (Norman: University of Oklahoma Press, 1976), p. 326; Alfred Dolge, *Pianos and Their Makers* (Covina, California: Covina Publishing Company, 1911), pp. 172, 264; Edwin M. Good, *Giraffes, Black Dragons, and Other Pianos: A Technological History from Cristofori to the Modern Concert Grand* (Stanford: Stanford University Press, 1982), p. 137n; W. D. Borrie, "Australia," *The Positive Contribution by Immigrants*, edited by Oscar Handlin (Paris: United Nations Educational, Scientific and Cultural Organization, 1955), p. 94.

5. Adam Giesinger, *From Catherine to Khrushchev: The Story of Russia's Germans* (Lincoln, Nebraska: American Historical Society of Germans from Russia, 1974), pp. 143–144.

6. Larry V. Thompson, Book Review, *Journal of Latin American Studies*, Vol. 8, No. 1 (May 1976), p. 159. See also Victor Wolfgang von Hagen, *The Germanic People in America*, pp. 242–243; Ronald C. Newton, *German Buenos Aires, 1900–1933: Social Change and Cultural Crisis* (Austin: University of Texas Press, 1977), pp. 7–8, 22.

7. T. N. Dupuy, *A Genius for War: The German Army and General Staff, 1807–1945* (Englewood Cliffs, New Jersey: Prentice-Hall, Inc., 1977), p. 4.

8. Carlo M. Cipolla, *Literacy and Development in the West* (Baltimore: Penguin Books, 1969), pp. 24, 28, 30–31, 70.

9. Richard Sallet, *Russian-German Settlements in the United States*, translated by Lavern J. Rippley and Armand Bauer (Fargo: North Dakota Institute for Regional Studies, 1974), p. 14.

10. T. Lynn Smith, *Brazil: People and Institutions*, revised edition (Baton Rouge: Louisiana State University Press, 1963), p. 134.

11. Thomas W. Merrick and Douglas H. Graham, *Population and Economic Development in Brazil: 1800 to the Present* (Baltimore: The Johns Hopkins University Press, 1979), p. 111.

12. Carlo M. Cipolla, *Literacy and Development in the West*, p. 17.

13. Irina Livezeanu, *Cultural Politics in Greater Romania: Regionalism, Nation Building, & Ethnic Struggle, 1918–1930* (Ithaca: Cornell University Press, 1995), pp. 230, 231.

14. Hain Tankler and Algo Rämmer, *Tartu University and Latvia: With an Emphasis on Relations in the 1920s and 1930s* (Tartu: Tartu Ülikool, 2004), pp. 23–24; F.W. Pick, "Tartu: The History of an Estonian University," *American Slavic and East European Review*, Vol. 5, No. 3/4 (November 1946), p. 159.

15. Anders Henriksson, *The Tsar's Loyal Germans: The Riga German Community: Social Change and the Nationality Question, 1855–1905* (New York: Columbia University Press, 1983), pp. 6–7; Ingeborg Fleischhauer and Benjamin Pinkus, *The Soviet Germans: Past and Present* (London: C. Hurst & Company, 1986), p. 16.

16. Victor Purcell, *The Chinese in Southeast Asia*, second edition (London: Oxford University Press, 1965); Jack Chen, *The Chinese of America* (San Francisco: Harper & Row, Publishers, 1980); Duvon Clough Corbitt, *A Study of the Chinese in Cuba, 1847–1947* (Wilmore, Kentucky: Asbury College, 1971); Watt Stewart, *Chinese Bondage in Peru: A History of the Chinese Coolie in Peru, 1849–1874* (Durham: Duke University Press, 1951); Cecil Clementi, *The Chinese in British Guiana* (Georgetown, British Guiana: "The Argosy" Company, Ltd., 1915); David Lowenthal, *West Indian Societies* (New York: Oxford University Press, 1972), pp. 202–208.

17. *The Lebanese in the World: A Century of Emigration*, edited by Albert Hourani and Nadim Shehadi (London: The Centre for Lebanese Studies, 1992).

18. Paul Johnson, *A History of the Jews* (New York: Harper & Row, 1987); Jonathan I. Israel, *European Jewry in the Age of Mercantilism: 1550–1750* (Oxford: Clarendon Press, 1985); Ezra Mendelsohn, *The Jews of East Central Europe between the World Wars* (Bloomington: Indiana University Press, 1983); Bernard Lewis, *The Jews of Islam* (Princeton: Princeton University Press,

1984); Moses Rischin, *The Promised City: New York's Jews, 1870–1914* (Cambridge, Massachusetts: Harvard University Press, 1962); Louis Wirth, *The Ghetto* (Chicago: University of Chicago Press, 1956); Irving Howe, *World of Our Fathers* (New York: Harcourt Brace Jovanovich, 1976); Hilary L. Rubinstein, *Chosen: The Jews in Australia* (Sydney: Allen & Unwin, 1987); Daniel J. Elazar and Peter Medding, *Jewish Communities in Frontier Societies: Argentina, Australia, and South Africa* (New York: Holmes & Meier, 1983).

19. Hugh Tinker, *The Banyan Tree: Overseas Emigrants from India, Pakistan, and Bangladesh* (Oxford: Oxford University Press, 1977).

20. Victor Purcell, *The Chinese in Southeast Asia,* second edition, pp. 277–279.

21. Stanford M. Lyman, *Chinese Americans* (New York: Random House, 1974), Chapter 4; Betty Lee Sung, *The Chinese in America* (New York: Macmillan Publishing, 1972), Chapter 3.

22. Watt Stewart, *Chinese Bondage in Peru,* p. 98.

23. Duvon Clough Corbitt, *A Study of the Chinese in Cuba, 1847–1947,* pp. 79–80; United States House of Representatives, "Coolie Trade," Report No. 443, 36th Congress, 1st Session, April 16, 1860, p. 10.

24. Duvon Clough Corbitt, *A Study of the Chinese in Cuba, 1847–1947,* p. 80.

25. Ibid.

26. Stanford M. Lyman, *Chinese Americans,* p. 152.

27. Kay S. Hymowitz, "Brooklyn's Chinese Pioneers," *City Journal,* Spring 2014, pp. 21, 23.

28. Ibid., pp. 26, 27.

29. Jacob Riis, *How the Other Half Lives: Studies Among the Tenements of New York* (New York: Charles Scribner's Sons, 1914), p. 125.

30. Simon Kuznets, "Immigration of Russian Jews to the United States: Background and Structure," *Perspectives in American History,* Vol. IX (1975), pp. 115–116.

31. Reports of the Immigration Commission, *The Children of Immigrants in Schools* (Washington: Government Printing Office, 1911), Vol. I, p. 110.

32. Carl C. Brigham, *A Study of American Intelligence* (Princeton: Princeton University Press, 1923), p. 190.

33. Charles Murray, *Human Accomplishment: The Pursuit of Excellence in the Arts and Sciences, 800 B.C. to 1950* (New York: Harper Collins, 2003), pp. 291–292.

34. Carl C. Brigham, "Intelligence Tests of Immigrant Groups," *Psychological Review*, Vol. 37, Issue 2 (March 1930), p. 165.

35. Clark S. Knowlton, "The Social and Spatial Mobility of the Syrian and Lebanese Community in Sao Paulo, Brazil," *The Lebanese in the World*, edited by Albert Hourani and Nadim Shehadi, p. 298.

36. Luz Maria Martinez Montiel, "The Lebanese Community in Mexico: Its Meaning, Importance and the History of Its Communities," Ibid., pp. 380, 385.

37. Trevor Batrouney, "The Lebanese in Australia, 1880–1989," Ibid., p. 419.

38. H. Laurens van der Laan, "A Bibliography on the Lebanese in West Africa, and an Appraisal of the Literature Consulted," *Kroniek van Afrika*, 1975/3, No. 6, p. 285.

39. H. L. van der Laan, *The Lebanese Traders in Sierra Leone* (The Hague: Mouton & Co, 1975), p. 249.

40. Ibid., p. 236.

41. Ibid., pp. 237–240.

42. Ibid., pp. 41, 105; Albert Hourani, "Introduction," *The Lebanese in the World*, edited by Albert Hourani and Nadim Shehadi, p. 7; Charles Issawi, "The Historical Background of Lebanese Emigration, 1800–1914," Ibid., p. 31; Alixa Naff, "Lebanese Immigration into the United States: 1880 to the Present," Ibid., p. 145; Trevor Batrouney, "The Lebanese in Australia, 1880–1989," Ibid., p. 421.

43. Albert Hourani, "Introduction," *The Lebanese in the World*, edited by Albert Hourani and Nadim Shehadi, p. 7.

44. Alixa Naff, "Lebanese Immigration into the United States: 1880 to the Present," Ibid., pp. 144, 145, 147.

45. Ibid., p. 148.

46. H. L. van der Laan, *The Lebanese Traders in Sierra Leone*, p. 112.

47. Milton & Rose D. Friedman, *Two Lucky People: Memoirs* (Chicago: University of Chicago Press, 1998), pp. 20–21.

48. Alixa Naff, "Lebanese Immigration into the United States: 1880 to the Present," *The Lebanese in the World*, edited by Albert Hourani and Nadim Shehadi, p. 157.

49. Ignacio Klich, "Criollos and Arabic Speakers in Argentina: An Uneasy *Pas de Deux*, 1888–1914," Ibid., p. 265.

50. Trevor Batrouney, "The Lebanese in Australia, 1880–1989," Ibid., p. 421.

51. H. L. van der Laan, *The Lebanese Traders in Sierra Leone*, pp. 106–109.

52. David Nicholls, "Lebanese of the Antilles: Haiti, Dominican Republic, Jamaica, and Trinidad," *The Lebanese in the World*, edited by Albert Hourani and Nadim Shehadi, pp. 345, 351, 352, 355.

53. Alixa Naff, "Lebanese Immigration into the United States: 1880 to the Present," Ibid., pp. 141–165.

54. H.L. van der Laan, *The Lebanese Traders in Sierra Leone*, pp. 210, 240, 276; Albert Hourani, "Introduction," *The Lebanese in the World*, edited by Albert Hourani and Nadim Shehadi, p. 4; Clark S. Knowlton, "The Social and Spatial Mobility of the Syrian and Lebanese Community in Sao Paulo, Brazil," Ibid., pp. 300, 304, 305; Boutros Labaki, "Lebanese Emigration During the War (1975–1989)," Ibid., p. 625; Marwan Maaouia, "Lebanese Emigration to the Gulf and Saudi Arabia," Ibid., p. 655.

55. Amy Chua and Jed Rubenfeld, *The Triple Package: How Three Unlikely Traits Explain the Rise and Fall of Cultural Groups in America* (New York: The Penguin Press, 2014), p. 6.

56. Ibid., pp. 38–39.

57. Ibid., pp. 39, 40.

58. Andrew Tanzer, "The Bamboo Network," *Forbes*, July 8, 1994, pp. 138–144; "China: Seeds of Subversion," *The Economist*, May 28, 1994, p. 32.

59. Robert Bartlett, *The Making of Europe: Conquest, Colonization and Cultural Change, 950–1350* (New York: The Penguin Press, 1993), pp. 60, 70–84, 281, 283; Paul Robert Magocsi, *Historical Atlas of Central Europe*, revised and expanded edition (Seattle: University of Washington Press, 2002), pp. 54–55; Jean W. Sedlar, *East Central Europe in the Middle Ages, 1000–1500* (Seattle: University of Washington Press, 1994), p. 116; N.J.G. Pounds, *An Historical Geography of Europe: 1800–1914* (Cambridge: Cambridge University Press, 1985), pp. 75, 449–458; Walter Nugent, *Crossings: The Great Transatlantic Migrations, 1870–1914* (Bloomington: Indiana University Press, 1992), p. 84; Roy E.H. Mellor and E. Alistair Smith, *Europe: A Geographical Survey of the Continent* (New York: Columbia University Press, 1979), p. 92; *The Oxford Encyclopedia of Economic History*, edited by Joel Mokyr (Oxford: Oxford University Press, 2003), Vol. 2, pp. 247–248.

60. Glenn T. Trewartha, *Japan: A Geography* (Madison: University of Wisconsin Press, 1965), pp. 78–79.

61. Edwin O. Reischauer, *The Japanese* (Cambridge, Massachusetts: Harvard University Press, 1980), p. 5.

62. Ibid., p. 8.

63. Ibid., p. 9.

64. Tetsuro Nakaoka, "The Transfer of Cotton Manufacturing Technology from Britain to Japan," *International Technology Transfer: Europe, Japan and the USA, 1700–1914*, edited by David J. Jeremy (Aldershot, Hants, England: Edward Elgar, 1991), p. 184.

65. John K. Fairbank, Edwin O. Reischauer and Albert M. Craig, *East Asia: Tradition & Transformation*, revised edition (Boston: Houghton-Mifflin Company, 1989), p. 410.

66. Irokawa Daikichi, *The Culture of the Meiji Period*, translated and edited by Marius B. Jansen (Princeton: Princeton University Press, 1985), p. 7.

67. Yasuo Wakatsuki, "Japanese Emigration to the United States, 1866–1924: A Monograph," *Perspectives in American History*, Vol. XII (1979), p. 431. See also p. 434.

68. Ibid., pp. 414, 415.

69. John K. Fairbank, Edwin O. Reischauer and Albert M. Craig, *East Asia*, revised edition, p. 532.

70. Ibid., p. 530.

71. Sydney and Olive Checkland, *Industry and Ethos: Scotland 1832–1914* (Edinburgh: Edinburgh University Press, 1989), p. 147; William R. Brock, *Scotus Americanus: A Survey of the Sources for Links between Scotland and America in the Eighteenth Century* (Edinburgh: Edinburgh University Press, 1982), p. 114.

72. T. C. Smout, *A History of the Scottish People, 1560–1830* (New York: Charles Scribner's Sons, 1969), pp. 480–489; Alexander Bain, *James Mill: A Biography* (London: Longmans, Green, and Co., 1882), Chapter 1; Michael St. John Packe, *The Life of John Stuart Mill* (London: Secker and Warburg, 1954), p. 9n.

73. Henry Thomas Buckle, *On Scotland and the Scotch Intellect* (Chicago: University of Chicago Press, 1970), p. 154.

74. "The Tragedy of the Arabs," *The Economist*, July 5, 2014, p. 9.

75. Edward Nawotka, "Translating Books into Arabic," *Los Angeles Times*, January 4, 2008, p. E24.

76. United Nations Development Programme, *Arab Human Development Report 2003* (New York: United Nations Development Programme, 2003), p. 67.

77. "Self-doomed to Failure," *The Economist*, July 6, 2002, pp. 24–26.

78. Freeman Dyson, "The Case for Blunders," *New York Review of Books*, March 6, 2014, p. 6.

79. Niall Ferguson, *Civilization: The West and the Rest* (New York: The Penguin Press, 2011), p. 47.

80. Jürgen Osterhammel, *The Transformation of the World: A Global History of the Nineteenth Century*, translated by Patrick Camiller (Princeton: Princeton University Press, 2014), p. 786.

81. Toivo U. Raun, *Estonia and the Estonians*, second edition (Stanford: Hoover Institution Press, 1991), pp. 55, 56.

82. Derek Sayer, *The Coasts of Bohemia: A Czech History* (Princeton: Princeton University Press, 1998), p. 77.

83. Ibid., p. 90.

84. Paul Robert Magocsi, *Historical Atlas of Central Europe*, revised and expanded edition, pp. 37–41; Sidney Pollard, *Marginal Europe: The Contribution of Marginal Lands Since the Middle Ages* (Oxford: Oxford University Press, 1997), p. 153; Robert Bartlett, *The Making of Europe*, pp. 128–132; Péter Gunst, "Agrarian Systems of Central and Eastern Europe," *The Origins of Backwardness in Eastern Europe: Economics and Politics from the Middle Ages Until the Early Twentieth Century*, edited by Daniel Chirot (Berkeley: University of California Press, 1989), p. 64.

85. Anders Henriksson, *The Tsar's Loyal Germans*, p. 15.

86. Thomas Sowell, *Migrations and Cultures: A World View* (New York: Basic Books, 1996), pp. 181–213.

87. Myron Weiner, *Sons of the Soil: Migration and Ethnic Conflict in India* (Princeton: Princeton University Press, 1978), p. 250.

88. A.A. Ayoade, "Ethnic Management in the 1979 Nigerian Constitution," *Canadian Review of Studies in Nationalism*, Spring 1987, p. 127.

89. *Encyclopedia of Human Rights*, edited by David P. Forsythe (Oxford: Oxford University Press, 2009), Volume 1, p. 58.

90. Cacilie Rohwedder, "Germans, Czechs Are Hobbled by History as Europe Moves Toward United Future," *Wall Street Journal*, November 25, 1996, p. A15.

91. J.H. Elliott, *Spain and Its World, 1500–1700: Selected Essays* (New Haven: Yale University Press, 1989), pp. 225–226.

92. Solomon Grayzel, *A History of the Jews: From the Babylonian Exile to the End of World War II* (Philadelphia: The Jewish Publication Society of America, 1947), pp. 355–356, 386–393; Jonathan I. Israel, *European Jewry in the Age of Mercantilism*, pp. 5, 6.

93. W. Cunningham, *Alien Immigrants to England* (London: Frank Cass & Co., Ltd., 1969), Chapter 6.

94. Simon Kuznets, "Immigration of Russian Jews to the United States: Background and Structure," *Perspectives in American History*, Vol. IX (1975), p. 39.

95. Donald L. Horowitz, *Ethnic Groups in Conflict* (Berkeley: University of California Press, 1985), pp. 176–177.

96. Hugh LeCaine Agnew, *Origins of the Czech National Renascence* (Pittsburgh: University of Pittsburgh Press, 1993), p. 51.

97. Derek Sayer, *The Coasts of Bohemia*, p. 50.

98. Gary B. Cohen, *The Politics of Ethnic Survival: Germans in Prague, 1861–1914*, second edition (West Lafayette: Purdue University Press, 2006), pp. 87, 91.

99. Donald L. Horowitz, *Ethnic Groups in Conflict*, p. 176.

100. Camille Laurin, "Principles for a Language Policy," *Cultural Diversity and Canadian Education: Issues and Innovations*, edited by John R. Mallea and Jonathan C. Young (Ottawa: Carleton University Press, 1990), pp. 186, 189.

101. Donald L. Horowitz, *Ethnic Groups in Conflict*, pp. 176–177.

102. Will Pavia, "French Zealots Just Don't Fancy an Italian," *The Times* (London), February 22, 2013, p. 28; Jeremy King, *Budweisers Into Czechs and Germans: A Local History of Bohemian Politics, 1848–1948* (Princeton: Princeton University Press, 2002), pp. 4, 128.

103. See, for example, Stuart Buck, *Acting White: The Ironic Legacy of Desegregation* (New Haven: Yale University Press, 2010).

104. Donald L. Horowitz, *Ethnic Groups in Conflict*, p. 153.

105. Archie Brown, Michael Kaser, and Gerald S. Smith, *The Cambridge Encyclopedia of Russia and the Former Soviet Union*, second edition (Cambridge: Cambridge University Press, 1994), p. 5.

106. Ibid., pp. 17–18.

107. Jonathan P. Stern, "Soviet Natural Gas in the World Economy," *Soviet Natural Resources in the World Economy*, edited by Robert G. Jensen, et al (Chicago: University of Chicago Press, 1983), p. 372.

108. Russell B. Adams, "Nickel and Platinum in the Soviet Union," Ibid., p. 536.

109. Theodore Shabad, "The Soviet Potential in Natural Resources: An Overview," Ibid., p. 269.

110. Nikolai Shmelev and Vladimir Popov, *The Turning Point: Revitalizing the Soviet Economy* (New York: Doubleday, 1989), pp. 128–129.

111. John Stuart Mill, *The Collected Works of John Stuart Mill*, Volume III: *Principles of Political Economy with Some of Their Applications to Social Philosophy* (Toronto: University of Toronto Press, 1965), p. 882.

112. John P. McKay, *Pioneers for Profit: Foreign Entrepreneurship and Russian Industrialization 1885–1913* (Chicago: University of Chicago Press, 1970), pp. 176, 187.

113. Karl Stumpp, *The German-Russians: Two Centuries of Pioneering* (Bonn: Edition Atlantic-Forum, 1971), p. 68.

114. Alec Nove, *The Soviet Economic System* (London: George Allen & Unwin, Ltd., 1977), pp. 100–101; Linda M. Randall, *Reluctant Capitalists: Russia's Journey Through Market Transition* (New York: Routledge, 2001), pp. 56–57.

115. Raghuram G. Rajan and Luigi Zingales, *Saving Capitalism from the Capitalists* (New York: Crown Business, 2003), p. 57.

116. Bryon MacWilliams, "Reports of Bribe-Taking at Russian Universities Have Increased, Authorities Say," *The Chronicle of Higher Education*, April 18, 2002 (online).

117. Renée Rose Shield, *Diamond Stories: Enduring Change on 47th Street* (Ithaca: Cornell University Press, 2002), p. 94.

118. Susan Wolcott, "An Examination of the Supply of Financial Credit to Entrepreneurs in Colonial India," *The Invention of Enterprise: Entrepreneurship from Ancient Mesopotamia to Modern Times*, edited by David S. Landes, et al (Princeton: Princeton University Press, 2010), p. 458.

119. S. Gordon Redding, *The Spirit of Chinese Capitalism* (Berlin: Walter de Gruyter, 1990), p. 213.

120. H.L. van der Laan, *The Lebanese Traders in Sierra Leone*, pp. 42–43, 190, 191–192.

121. "The World's Least Honest Cities," *The Telegraph.UK*, September 25, 2013.

122. "Scandinavians Prove Their Honesty in European Lost-Wallet Experiment," *Deseret News*, June 20, 1996; Eric Felten, "Finders Keepers?" *Reader's Digest*, April 2001, pp. 102–107; "The World's Least Honest Cities," *The Telegraph.UK*, September 25, 2013; "So Whom Can You Trust?" *The Economist*, June 22, 1996, p. 51.

123. See Raymond Fisman and Edward Miguel, "Cultures of Corruption: Evidence from Diplomatic Parking Tickets," Working Paper 12312, National Bureau of Economic Research, June 2006, Table 1.

124. Transparency International, *Transparency International Corruption Perceptions Index 2013* (Berlin: Transparency International Secretariat, 2013).

125. Nicholas Eberstadt, *Russia's Peacetime Demographic Crisis: Dimensions, Causes, Implications* (Seattle: National Bureau of Asian Research, 2010), p. 282.

126. Ibid., pp. 232, 233.

127. Donald L. Horowitz, *Ethnic Groups in Conflict*, p. 663.

128. Feroz Ahmad, "Unionist Relations with the Greek, Armenian, and Jewish Communities of the Ottoman Empire, 1908–1914," *Christians and Jews in the Ottoman Empire: The Functioning of a Plural Society*, Volume I: *The Central Lands*, edited by Benjamin Braude and Bernard Lewis (New York: Holmes & Meier, 1982), pp. 411, 412.

129. Mohamed Suffian bin Hashim, "Problems and Issues of Higher Education Development in Malaysia," *Development of Higher Education in Southeast Asia: Problems and Issues*, edited by Yip Yat Hoong (Singapore: Regional Institute of Higher Education and Development, 1973), Table 8, pp. 70–71.

130. Sarah Gordon, *Hitler, Germans and the "Jewish Question"* (Princeton: Princeton University Press, 1984), p. 13; Peter Pulzer, *The Rise of Political Anti-Semitism in Germany & Austria*, revised edition (Cambridge, Massachusetts: Harvard University Press, 1988), pp. 10–13.

131. Leon Volovici, *Nationalist Ideology and Antisemitism: The Case of Romanian Intellectuals in the 1930s*, translated by Charles Kormos (Oxford: Pergamon Press, 1991), p. 60; Irina Livezeanu, *Cultural Politics in Greater Romania*, pp. 63, 115; Howard M. Sachar, *Diaspora: An Inquiry into the Contemporary Jewish World* (New York: Harper & Row, 1985), pp. 297, 299; Australian

Government Commission of Inquiry into Poverty, *Welfare of Migrants* (Canberra: Australian Government Publishing Service, 1975), p. 107.

132. Jason L. Riley, *Please Stop Helping Us: How Liberals Make It Harder for Blacks to Succeed* (New York: Encounter Books, 2014), p. 49.

133. Gary B. Cohen, *The Politics of Ethnic Survival*, p. 28.

134. See, for example, Gunnar Myrdal, *Asian Drama: An Inquiry Into the Poverty of Nations* (New York: Pantheon, 1968), Vol. III, p. 1642; Myron Weiner and Mary Fainsod Katzenstein, *India's Preferential Policies: Migrants, the Middle Classes, and Ethnic Equality* (Chicago: University of Chicago Press, 1981), p. 99.

135. Leon Volovici, *Nationalist Ideology and Antisemitism*, translated by Charles Kormos, p. 60.

136. Mary Fainsod Katzenstein, *Ethnicity and Equality: The Shiv Sena Party and Preferential Policies in Bombay* (Ithaca: Cornell University Press, 1979), pp. 48–49; Myron Weiner and Mary Fainsod Katzenstein, *India's Preferential Policies*, pp. 10–11, 44–46.

137. Ezra Mendelsohn, *The Jews of East Central Europe between the World Wars*, pp. 98–99, 106.

138. Larry Diamond, "Class, Ethnicity, and the Democratic State: Nigeria, 1950–1966," *Comparative Studies in Society and History*, Vol. 25, No. 3 (July 1983), pp. 462, 473; Donald L. Horowitz, *Ethnic Groups in Conflict*, p. 225.

139. Anatoly M. Khazanov, "The Ethnic Problems of Contemporary Kazakhstan," *Central Asian Survey*, Vol. 14, No. 2 (1995), pp. 244, 257.

140. Leon Volovici, *Nationalist Ideology and Antisemitism*, translated by Charles Kormos, *passim*; Joseph Rothschild, *East Central Europe between the Two World Wars* (Seattle: University of Washington Press, 1992), p. 293; Irina Livezeanu, *Cultural Politics in Greater Romania*, *passim*.

141. Gunnar Myrdal, *Asian Drama*, Vol. I, p. 348; Donald L. Horowitz, *Ethnic Groups in Conflict*, p. 133; Donald L. Horowitz, *The Deadly Ethnic Riot* (Berkeley: University of California Press, 2001), pp. 144–145.

142. Conrad Black, "Canada's Continuing Identity Crisis," *Foreign Affairs*, March/April 1995, p. 100.

143. See, for example, Gary B. Cohen, *The Politics of Ethnic Survival*, pp. 26–28, 32, 133, 236–237; Ezra Mendelsohn, *The Jews of East Central Europe between*

the World Wars, p. 167; Hugh LeCaine Agnew, *Origins of the Czech National Renascence, passim.*

144. Some examples can be found, among other places, in John H. Bunzel, *Race Relations on Campus: Stanford Students Speak* (Stanford: Stanford Alumni Association, 1992).

145. Philip Nobile, "Uncovering *Roots,*" *Village Voice*, February 23, 1993, p. 34. Another devastating critique of *Roots* is that of Gary B. and Elizabeth Shown Mills, "'*Roots*' and the New 'Faction': A Legitimate Tool for Clio?" *The Virginia Magazine of History and Biography*, Vol. 89, No. 1 (January 1981), pp. 3–26.

146. Donald L. Horowitz, *Ethnic Groups in Conflict*, p. 72; See also Keith Windschuttle, "The Fabrication of Aboriginal History," *The New Criterion*, Vol. 20, No. 1 (September 2001), pp. 41–49.

147. Nathan Glazer and Daniel Patrick Moynihan, *Beyond the Melting Pot: The Negroes, Puerto Ricans, Jews, Italians, and Irish of New York City*, second edition (Cambridge, Massachusetts: MIT Press, 1970), p. 241.

148. Joseph Rothschild, *East Central Europe between the Two World Wars*, p. 385.

149. Chandra Richard de Silva, "Sinhala-Tamil Relations and Education in Sri Lanka: The University Admissions Issue— The First Phase, 1971–7," *From Independence to Statehood: Managing Ethnic Conflict in Five African and Asian States*, edited by Robert B. Goldmann and A. Jeyaratnam Wilson (London: Frances Pinter, Ltd. 1984), p. 126.

150. Donald L. Horowitz, *Ethnic Groups in Conflict*, p. 225.

151. Robert A. Kann and Zdeněk V. David, *The Peoples of the Eastern Habsburg Lands, 1526–1918* (Seattle: University of Washington Press, 1984), p. 201.

152. Gary B. Cohen, *The Politics of Ethnic Survival*, p. 148. See also Derek Sayer, *The Coasts of Bohemia*, p. 101.

153. Jeremy King, *Budweisers Into Czechs and Germans*, p. 4.

154. Philip Authier, "Camille Laurin, Father of Bill 101, Dies," *The Gazette* (Montreal, Quebec), March 12, 1999, p. A1; Guy Dumas, "Quebec's Language Policy: Perceptions and Realities," *Language and Governance*, edited by Colin Williams (Cardiff: University of Wales Press, 2007), pp. 250–262.

155. Robert Bothwell, et al., *Canada Since 1945: Power, Politics, and Provincialism*, revised edition (Toronto: University of Toronto Press, 1989), pp. 375–376;

Graham Fraser, *Sorry, I Don't Speak French: Confronting the Canadian Crisis That Won't Go Away* (Toronto: McClelland & Stewart, 2006), pp. 121–122.

156. Grady McWhiney, *Cracker Culture: Celtic Ways in the Old South* (Tuscaloosa: University of Alabama Press, 1988), pp. 45–47, 49; David Hackett Fischer, *Albion's Seed: Four British Folkways in America* (New York: Oxford University Press, 1989), pp. 365–366, 740–743; Lewis Cecil Gray, *History of Agriculture in the Southern United States to 1860* (Washington: Carnegie Institution of Washington, 1933), Vol. I, p. 484; Frederick Law Olmsted, *The Cotton Kingdom: A Traveller's Observations on Cotton and Slavery in the American Slave States* (New York: Alfred A. Knopf, 1953), pp. 12, 65, 147, 527; Alexis de Tocqueville, *Democracy in America* (New York: Alfred A. Knopf, 1989), Vol. I, pp. 363, 369; Forrest McDonald, "Cultural Continuity and the Shaping of the American South," *Geographic Perspectives in History,* edited by Eugene D. Genovese and Leonard Hochberg (London: Basil Blackwell, Ltd., 1989), pp. 231–232; Lewis M. Killian, *White Southerners,* revised edition (Amherst: University of Massachusetts Press, 1985), pp. 108–109.

157. Robert E. Lee, *Lee's Dispatches: Unpublished Letters of General Robert E. Lee, C.S.A. to Jefferson Davis and the War Department of the Confederate States of America, 1862–65,* edited by Douglas Southall Freeman, New Edition (New York: G. P. Putnam's Sons, 1957), p. 8.

158. Ulrich Bonnell Phillips, *The Slave Economy of the Old South: Selected Essays in Economic and Social History,* edited by Eugene D. Genovese (Baton Rouge: Louisiana State University Press, 1968), p. 107.

159. Grady McWhiney, *Cracker Culture,* p. 19; Virginia Brainard Kunz, *The Germans in America* (Minneapolis: Lerner Publications Co., 1966), pp. 11–12.

160. Lewis Cecil Gray, *History of Agriculture in the Southern United States to 1860,* Vol. II, p. 831.

161. Rupert B. Vance, *Human Geography of the South: A Study in Regional Resources and Human Adequacy* (Chapel Hill: University of North Carolina Press, 1932), p. 168. See also Grady McWhiney, *Cracker Culture,* p. 83.

162. P.T. Bauer, *Reality and Rhetoric: Studies in the Economics of Development* (London: Weidenfeld and Nicolson, 1984), p. 7.

163. G.M. Trevelyan, *English Social History: A Survey of Six Centuries, Chaucer to Queen Victoria* (Middlesex, England: Penguin Books, 1986), pp. 140–141.

164. William H. McNeill, *History of Western Civilization: A Handbook*, sixth edition (Chicago: University of Chicago Press, 1986), p. 252.

165. W. A. Armstrong, "The Countryside," *The Cambridge Social History of Britain: 1750–1950*, Vol. 1: *Regions and Communities*, edited by F. M. L. Thompson (Cambridge: Cambridge University Press, 1993), p. 87.

166. G. M. Trevelyan, *English Social History*, pp. 243, 271–272, 315, 325, 335, 386–387, 393n, 409, 414, 419–420, 492–493.

167. Carl K. Eicher, "Facing Up to Africa's Food Crisis," *Foreign Affairs*, Fall 1982, p. 166.

168. Ibid., p. 170.

169. Gunnar Myrdal, *Asian Drama: An Inquiry Into the Poverty of Nations*, abridged edition (New York: Pantheon, 1972), p. 296.

170. Daniel J. Boorstin, *The Americans*, Vol. II: *The National Experience* (New York: Random House, 1965), p. 176.

171. Grady McWhiney, *Cracker Culture*, p. 253. As of 1860, the total population of the South was 39 percent of the total population of the United States. Since slaves were about one-third of the population of the South, and were usually in no position to invent, that leaves white Southerners as 26 percent of the total population of the country and approximately one-third of the white population. For population statistics, see Lewis Cecil Gray, *History of Agriculture in the Southern United States to 1860*, pp. 656, 811.

172. Paul Johnson, *A History of the American People* (New York: Harper Collins, 1998), p. 462.

173. Rupert B. Vance, *Human Geography of the South*, pp. 301–303.

174. Ibid., pp. 304–305.

175. Ibid., pp. 112–116, 127–128.

176. Ibid., p. 292.

177. David S. Landes, *The Wealth and Poverty of Nations: Why Some Are So Rich And Some So Poor* (New York: W.W. Norton, 1998), pp. 516–517.

Chapter 4: Social Factors

1. Thomas Robert Malthus, *An Essay on the Principle of Population* (London: J. Johnson, 1798), p. 14; Thomas Robert Malthus, *Population: The First Essay*

(Ann Arbor: University of Michigan Press, 1959), p. 5; Thomas Robert Malthus, "An Essay on the Principle of Population, As It Affects the Future Improvement of Society with Remarks on the Speculations of Mr. Godwin, M. Condorcet and Other Writers," *On Population*, edited by Gertrude Himmelfarb (New York: The Modern Library, 1960), p. 9.

2.   Eduardo Porter, "Old Forecast of Famine May Yet Come True," *New York Times*, April 2, 2014, p. B1.

3.   American Petroleum Institute, *Basic Petroleum Data Book*, Volume XX, No. 2 (Washington: American Petroleum Institute, 2000), Section II, Table 1.

4.   See my *Basic Economics: A Common Sense Guide to the Economy*, fifth edition (New York: Basic Books, 2014), pp. 294–301.

5.   See my *On Classical Economics* (New Haven: Yale University Press, 2006), pp. 57–63, 120–122.

6.   *Geography of Sub-Saharan Africa*, third edition, edited by Samuel Aryeetey Attoh (New York: Prentice Hall, 2010), p. 182; *The World Almanac and Book of Facts: 2013* (New York: World Almanac Books, 2013), p. 793.

7.   P.T. Bauer, *Equality, the Third World and Economic Delusion* (Cambridge, Massachusetts: Harvard University Press, 1981), p. 43.

8.   Paul Robert Magosci, *A History of Ukraine* (Seattle: University of Washington Press, 1996), p. 6; Norman Davies, *Europe at War, 1939–1945: No Simple Victory* (London: Macmillan, 2006), p. 32; Tony Judt, *Postwar: A History of Europe Since 1945* (New York: Penguin Books, 2006), p. 648.

9.   Shirley S. Wang, "Obesity in China Becoming More Common," *Wall Street Journal*, July 8, 2008, p. A18.

10.   The Economist, *Pocket World in Figures: 2014 edition* (London: Profile Books, 2013), p. 18.

11.

GROUPS	MEDIAN AGE
BLACK	32.9
CAMBODIAN	31.0
CHINESE	38.0
CUBAN	39.8
JAPANESE	49.5
MEXICAN	26.0
PUERTO RICAN	28.4
WHITE	40.2
TOTAL	37.4

SOURCE: U.S. Census Bureau, 2012 American Community Survey 1-Year Estimates

12. W. Michael Cox and Richard Alm, "By Our Own Bootstraps: Economic Opportunity & the Dynamics of Income Distribution," *Annual Report 1995*, Federal Reserve Bank of Dallas, p. 16.

13. "Choose Your Parents Wisely," *The Economist*, July 26, 2014, p. 22.

14. Ibid.

15. Ibid.

16. Charles A. Price, *Southern Europeans in Australia* (Melbourne: Oxford University Press, 1963), p. 276; Charles A. Price, *The Methods and Statistics of 'Southern Europeans in Australia'* (Canberra: The Australian National University, 1963), p. 21.

17. Charles A. Price, *Southern Europeans in Australia*, p. 162.

18. Philip Taylor, *The Distant Magnet: European Emigration to the USA* (New York: Harper & Row, 1971), pp. 210, 211; Jonathan Gill, *Harlem: The Four Hundred Year History from Dutch Village to Capital of Black America* (New York: Grove Press, 2011), p. 139; Robert F. Foerster, *The Italian Emigration of Our Times* (New York: Arno Press, 1969), p. 393; Dino Cinel, *From Italy to San Francisco: The Immigrant Experience* (Stanford: Stanford University Press, 1982), p. 28.

19. Samuel L. Baily, "The Adjustment of Italian Immigrants in Buenos Aires and New York, 1870–1914," *American Historical Review*, April 1983, p. 291; John E. Zucchi, *Italians in Toronto: Development of a National Identity, 1875–1935* (Kingston, Ontario: McGill-Queen's University Press, 1988), pp. 41, 53–55, 58.

20. Louise L'Estrange Fawcett, "Lebanese, Palestinians and Syrians in Colombia," *The Lebanese in the World: A Century of Emigration*, edited by Albert Hourani and Nadim Shehadi (London: The Centre for Lebanese Studies, 1992), p. 368.

21. Kay S. Hymowitz, "Brooklyn's Chinese Pioneers," *City Journal*, Spring 2014, pp. 20–29.

22. Theodore Huebener, *The Germans in America* (Philadelphia: Chilton Company, 1962), p. 84.

23. Hildegard Binder Johnson, "The Location of German Immigrants in the Middle West," *Annals of the Association of American Geographers*, edited by Henry Madison Kendall, Volume XLI (1951), pp. 24–25.

24. LaVern J. Rippley, "Germans from Russia," *Harvard Encyclopedia of American Ethnic Groups*, edited by Stephan Thernstrom, et al (Cambridge, Massachusetts: Harvard University Press, 1980), p. 427.

25. Edward C. Banfield, *The Unheavenly City Revisited* (Boston: Little, Brown and Company, 1974), p. 91.

26. E. Franklin Frazier, "The Impact of Urban Civilization Upon Negro Family Life," *American Sociological Review*, Vol. 2, No. 5 (October 1937), p. 615.

27. Jonathan Gill, *Harlem*, p. 284; E. Franklin Frazier, *The Negro in the United States*, revised edition (New York: The Macmillan Company, 1957), pp. 239, 257–258; Willard B. Gatewood, *Aristocrats of Color: The Black Elite, 1880–1920* (Bloomington: Indiana University Press, 1990), pp. 194–195; Stephen Birmingham, *Certain People: America's Black Elite* (Boston: Little, Brown and Company, 1977), pp. 196–197; "Sugar Hill: All Harlem Looks Up to 'Folks on the Hill'," *Ebony*, November 1946, pp. 5–11.

28. Carlo M. Cipolla, *Clocks and Culture: 1300–1700* (New York: Walker and Company, 1967), pp. 66–69.

29. As to the role of these Jewish scientists in getting President Franklin D. Roosevelt to create the Manhattan Project that produced the first atomic bomb, see Richard Rhodes, *The Making of the Atomic Bomb* (New York: Simon & Schuster, 1986), pp. 305–314. As for the scientists being Jewish and playing

major roles in that project, see Ibid., pp. 13, 106, 188–189; Silvan S. Schweber, *Einstein and Oppenheimer: The Meaning of Genius* (Cambridge, Massachusetts: Harvard University Press, 2008), p. 138; Michio Kaku, *Einstein's Cosmos: How Albert Einstein's Vision Transformed Our Understanding of Space and Time* (New York: W.W. Norton, 2004), pp. 187–188; Howard M. Sachar, *A History of the Jews in America* (New York: Alfred A. Knopf, 1992), p. 527; American Jewish Historical Society, *American Jewish Desk Reference* (New York: Random House, 1999), p. 591.

30. Fernand Braudel, *A History of Civilizations*, translated by Richard Mayne (New York: Penguin Books, 1993), p. 440.

31. W. Michael Cox and Richard Alm, "By Our Own Bootstraps: Economic Opportunity & the Dynamics of Income Distribution," *Annual Report 1995*, Federal Reserve Bank of Dallas, p. 8; "Movin' On Up," *Wall Street Journal*, November 13, 2007, p. A24. Similar patterns exist in Canada. See Niels Veldhuis, et al., "The 'Poor' Are Getting Richer," *Fraser Forum*, January/February 2013, pp. 24, 25.

32. Thomas A. Hirschl and Mark R. Rank, "The Social Dynamics of Economic Polarization: Exploring the Life Course Probabilities of Top-Level Income Attainment," Paper presented at the 2014 Annual Meetings of the Population Association of America, Boston, May 1–4, 2014, p. 13.

33. The Pew Charitable Trusts, *Pursuing the American Dream: Economic Mobility Across Generations* (Washington: Economic Mobility Project, an initiative of The Pew Charitable Trusts, 2012), p. 1. This is called "absolute mobility" in both the 2008 and the 2012 Pew studies. Ibid.; Isabel V. Sawhill, "Overview," Julia B. Isaacs, Isabel V. Sawhill and Ron Haskins, *Getting Ahead or Losing Ground: Economic Mobility in America* (Washington: Economic Mobility Project, an initiative of The Pew Charitable Trusts, 2008), p. 2.

34. The Pew Charitable Trusts, *Pursuing the American Dream*, p. 2.

35. Ibid., p. 1. This is called "relative mobility" in both studies. Ibid.; Isabel V. Sawhill, "Overview," Julia B. Isaacs, Isabel V. Sawhill and Ron Haskins, *Getting Ahead or Losing Ground*, p. 2.

36. The Pew Charitable Trusts, *Pursuing the American Dream*, p. 2.

37. Ibid., p. 28. A similar caveat appears in the 2008 study on page 105.

38. Isabel V. Sawhill, "Overview," Julia B. Isaacs, Isabel V. Sawhill and Ron Haskins, *Getting Ahead or Losing Ground*, p. 6.

39. Eligio R. Padilla and Gail E. Wyatt, "The Effects of Intelligence and Achievement Testing on Minority Group Children," *The Psychosocial Development of Minority Group Children*, edited by Gloria Johnson Powell, et al (New York: Brunner/Mazel, Publishers, 1983), p. 418.

40. Mandel Sherman and Cora B. Key, "The Intelligence of Isolated Mountain Children," *Child Development*, Vol. 3, No. 4 (December 1932), p. 283; Lester R. Wheeler, "A Comparative Study of the Intelligence of East Tennessee Mountain Children," *Journal of Educational Psychology*, Vol. XXXIII, No. 5 (May 1942), pp. 322, 324.

41. Otto Klineberg, *Race Differences* (New York: Harper & Brothers, 1935), p. 182.

42. *Griggs et al. v. Duke Power Co.*, 401 U.S. 424 (1971), at 432.

43. Heather Mac Donald, "How Gotham's Elite High Schools Escaped the Leveller's Ax," *City Journal*, Spring 1999, p. 74.

44. Jason L. Riley, *Please Stop Helping Us: How Liberals Make It Harder for Blacks to Succeed* (New York: Encounter Books, 2014), p. 49.

45. Susan Jacoby, "Elite School Battle," *Washington Post*, May 28, 1972, p. B4.

46. Dennis Saffran, "The Plot Against Merit," *City Journal*, Summer 2014, pp. 81–82.

47. Reginald G. Damerell, *Education's Smoking Gun: How Teachers Colleges Have Destroyed Education in America* (New York: Freundlich Books, 1985), p. 164.

48. Maria Newman, "Cortines Has Plan to Coach Minorities into Top Schools," *New York Times*, March 18, 1995, p. 1.

49. Fernanda Santos, "Black at Stuy," *New York Times*, February 26, 2012, Metropolitan Desk, p. 6.

50. See the title essay in my *Black Rednecks and White Liberals* (San Francisco: Encounter Books, 2005), as well as *Cracker Culture: Celtic Ways in the Old South* (Tuscaloosa: University of Alabama Press, 1988) by Grady McWhiney and *Albion's Seed: Four British Folkways in America* (New York: Oxford University Press, 1989) by David Hackett Fischer.

51. H.J. Butcher, *Human Intelligence: Its Nature and Assessment* (New York: Harper & Row, 1968), p. 252.

52. President Wm. W. Patton, "Change of Environment," *The American Missionary*, Vol. XXXVI, No. 8 (August 1882), p. 229; James D. Anderson, *The Education of Blacks in the South, 1860–1935* (Chapel Hill: University of North Carolina Press, 1988), p. 46.

53. See my *Black Rednecks and White Liberals*, pp. 38–40.

54. Henry S. Robinson, "The M Street High School, 1891–1916," *Records of the Columbia Historical Society, Washington, D.C.*, Vol. 51 (1984), p. 122.

55. See Table 4, School Code 0508/0598 [Dunbar High School] in my "Assumptions versus History in Ethnic Education," *Teachers College Record*, Volume 83, No. 1 (Fall 1981), p. 47.

56. Mary Gibson Hundley, *The Dunbar Story: 1870–1955* (New York: Vantage Press, 1965), p. 25.

57. Ibid., p. 75.

58. Ibid., p. 78. Mary Church Terrell, "History of the High School for Negroes in Washington," *Journal of Negro History*, Vol. 2, No. 3 (July 1917), p. 262.

59. Department of Defense, *Black Americans in Defense of Our Nation* (Washington: U.S. Department of Defense, 1985), p. 153.

60. Mary Church Terrell, "History of the High School for Negroes in Washington," *Journal of Negro History*, Vol. 2, No. 3 (July 1917), p. 264.

61. Louise Daniel Hutchison, *Anna J. Cooper: A Voice from the South* (Washington: The Smithsonian Institution Press, 1981), p. 62.

62. The first black federal judge was William H. Hastie, the first black general was Benjamin O. Davis, Sr., and the first black Cabinet member was Robert C. Weaver.

63. Mary Gibson Hundley, *The Dunbar Story*, p. 57.

64. Alison Stewart, *First Class: The Legacy of Dunbar, America's First Black Public High School* (Chicago: Lawrence Hill Books, 2013), pp. 91–93.

65. Jervis Anderson, "A Very Special Monument," *The New Yorker*, March 20, 1978, p. 93.

66. Ibid., p. 113.

67. See the title article in my *Black Rednecks and White Liberals*.

68. Jason L. Riley, *Please Stop Helping Us*, p. 43.

69. John U. Ogbu, *Black American Students in an Affluent Suburb: A Study of Academic Disengagement* (Mahwah, New Jersey: Lawrence Erlbaum Associates, 2003), Chapters 1, 2.

70. Ibid., p. 179.

71. Jason L. Riley, *Please Stop Helping Us*, p. 45.

72. Ibid., p. 46.

73. Ibid., p. 47.

74. See the data in my "Assumptions versus History in Ethnic Education," *Teachers College Record*, Volume 83, No. 1 (Fall 1981).

75. U.S. Census Bureau, "Table 4. Poverty Status of Families, by Type of Family, Presence of Related Children, Race, and Hispanic Origin: 1959 to 2013," downloaded on October 23, 2014:

    http://www.census.gov/hhes/www/poverty/data/historical/families.html

76. John H. Bunzel, "Affirmative-Action Admissions: How It 'Works' at UC Berkeley," *The Public Interest*, Fall 1988, pp. 124, 125.

77. Richard Sander and Stuart Taylor, Jr., *Mismatch: How Affirmative Action Hurts Students It's Intended to Help, and Why Universities Won't Admit It* (New York: Basic Books, 2012), p. 154.

78. None of the book's many tables separates black students who were admitted under the normal standards and those admitted under affirmative action standards. See William G. Bowen and Derek Bok, *The Shape of the River: Long-Term Consequences of Considering Race in College and University Admissions* (Princeton: Princeton University Press, 1998), pp. ix–xix.

79. Ibid., p. 61. See also p. 259.

80. Stephan Thernstrom and Abigail Thernstrom, *America in Black and White: One Nation, Indivisible* (New York: Simon & Schuster, 1997), p. 408.

81. William G. Bowen and Derek Bok, *The Shape of the River*, p. 60n.

82. Citations from these other empirical studies, as well as a more extended critique of *The Shape of the River*, can be found in my *Affirmative Action Around the World: An Emperical Study* (New Haven: Yale University Press, 2004), pp. 152–159.

83. Stephan Therstrom and Abigail Thernstrom, "Reflections on *The Shape of the River*," *UCLA Law Review*, Vol. 46, No. 5 (June 1999), p. 1589.

84. Mark H. Haller, *Eugenics: Hereditarian Attitudes in American Thought* (New Brunswick: Rutgers University Press, 1963), p. 11.

85. See, for example, Edward Alsworth Ross, *The Old World in the New: The Significance of Past and Present Immigration to the American People* (New York: The Century Company, 1914); Francis A. Walker, "Methods of Restricting Immigration," *Discussions in Economics and Statistics*, Volume II: *Statistics, National Growth, Social Economics*, edited by Davis R. Dewey (New York: Henry Holt and Company, 1899); Kenneth L. Roberts, *Why Europe Leaves Home* (Bobbs-Merrill Company, 1922); George Creel, "Melting Pot or Dumping Ground?" *Collier's*, September 3, 1921, pp. 9 ff.

86. Rudolph Pintner, *Intelligence Testing: Methods and Results*, new edition (New York: Henry Holt and Co., 1939), p. 453.

87. Carl C. Brigham, "Intelligence Tests of Immigrant Groups," *Psychological Review*, Vol. 37, Issue 2 (March 1930), p. 165.

88. H.J. Butcher, *Human Intelligence*, p. 252.

89. For details, compare Carl C. Brigham, *A Study of American Intelligence* (Princeton: Princeton University Press, 1923), pp. 16–19, 36–38; [Robert M. Yerkes,] National Academy of Sciences, *Psychological Examining in the United States Army* (Washington: Government Printing Office, 1921), Vol. XV, Part III, pp. 874, 875; Thomas Sowell, "Race and IQ Reconsidered," *Essays and Data on American Ethnic Groups*, edited by Thomas Sowell and Lynn D. Collins (Washington: The Urban Institute, 1978), pp. 226–227.

90. James R. Flynn, "The Mean IQ of Americans: Massive Gains 1932 to 1978," *Psychological Bulletin*, Vol. 95, No. 1 (1984), pp. 29–51; James R. Flynn, "Massive IQ Gains in 14 Nations: What IQ Tests Really Measure," *Psychological Bulletin*, Vol. 101, No. 2 (1987), pp. 171–191.

91. James R. Flynn, *Where Have All the Liberals Gone? Race, Class, and Ideals in America* (Cambridge: Cambridge University Press, 2008), pp. 72–74, 87.

92. Robert William Fogel, *The Escape from Hunger and Premature Death, 1700–2100* (Cambridge: Cambridge University Press, 2004), pp. 55–57.

93. Daniel Schwekendiek, "Height and Weight Differences Between North and South Korea," *Journal of Biosocial Science*, Vol. 41, No. 1 (January 2009), pp. 51–55. *The Economist* reported that North Koreans were "on average three

inches shorter" than South Koreans. "We Need to Talk About Kim," *The Economist*, December 31, 2011, p. 8.

94. Robert William Fogel, *The Escape from Hunger and Premature Death*, p. 41.

95. Kenneth L. Roberts, "Lest We Forget," *Saturday Evening Post*, April 28, 1923, pp. 3 ff; Kenneth L. Roberts, *Why Europe Leaves Home*; Kenneth L. Roberts, "Slow Poison," *Saturday Evening Post*, February 2, 1924, pp. 8 ff; George Creel, "Melting Pot or Dumping Ground?" *Collier's*, September 3, 1921, pp. 9 ff; George Creel, "Close the Gates!" *Collier's*, May 6, 1922, pp. 9 ff.

96. Clifford Kirkpatrick, *Intelligence and Immigration* (Baltimore: The Williams & Wilkins Company, 1926), pp. 24, 31, 34.

97. Philip E. Vernon, *Intelligence and Cultural Environment* (London: Methuen & Co., Ltd., 1970), p. 155; Lester R. Wheeler, "A Comparative Study of the Intelligence of East Tennessee Mountain Children," *Journal of Educational Psychology*, Vol. XXXIII, No. 5 (May 1942), pp. 322, 324; Hugh Gordon, *Mental and Scholastic Tests Among Retarded Children* (London: His Majesty's Stationery Office, 1923), p. 38.

98. Arthur R. Jensen, "How Much Can We Boost IQ and Scholastic Achievement?" *Harvard Educational Review*, Winter 1969, p. 95.

Chapter 5: Political Factors

1. Freeman Dyson, "The Case for Blunders," *New York Review of Books*, March 6, 2014, p. 6.

2. Karl Polanyi, *The Great Transformation: The Political and Economic Origins of Our Time* (Boston: Beacon, 1957), p. 45. For specific examples of major retrogressions in Europe in the centuries following the decline and fall of the Roman Empire, see Bryan Ward-Perkins, *The Fall of Rome and the End of Civilization* (New York: Oxford University Press, 2005), Chapters V, VI; N.J.G. Pounds, *An Historical Geography of Europe* (Cambridge: Cambridge University Press, 1990), pp. 70, 71, 86, 165, 373–374; N.J.G. Pounds, *An Historical Geography of Europe: 1800–1914* (Cambridge: Cambridge University Press, 1985), p. 146; James Campbell, "The End of Roman Britain," *The Anglo-Saxons*, edited by James Campbell (Oxford: Phaidon Press, 1982), p. 9.

3. Ellen Churchill Semple, *Influences of Geographic Environment* (New York: Henry Holt and Company, 1911), p. 523.

4. See, for example, Ibid., pp. 595, 596. Alton C. Byers, et al., "Introduction to Mountains," *Mountain Geography: Physical and Human Dimensions*, edited by Martin F. Price, et al (Berkeley: University of California Press, 2013), p. 2; James S. Gardner, et al., "People in the Mountains," Ibid., p. 276.

5. See, for example, Ellen Churchill Semple, *Influences of Geographic Environment*, pp. 237, 591, 593, 599; J.R. McNeill, *The Mountains of the Mediterranean World: An Environmental History* (New York: Cambridge University Press, 1992), p. 48.

6. Ellen Churchill Semple, *Influences of Geographic Environment*, pp. 592, 593.

7. Ibid., p. 597.

8. James S. Gardner, et al., "People in the Mountains," *Mountain Geography*, edited by Martin F. Price, et al., p. 288; Ellen Churchill Semple, *Influences of Geographic Environment*, p. 535; Fernand Braudel, *The Mediterranean and the Mediterranean World in the Age of Philip II*, translated by Siân Reynolds (New York: Harper & Row, 1972), Vol. I, pp. 41, 207.

9. Ellen Churchill Semple, *Influences of Geographic Environment*, pp. 535, 548.

10. Gordon F. McEwan, *The Incas: New Perspectives* (Santa Barbara: ABC-CLIO, 2006), p. 3; The Economist, *Pocket World in Figures: 2014 edition* (London: Profile Books, Ltd., 2013), pp. 148, 150, 222.

11. Gordon F. McEwan, *The Incas*, p. 23; Jeffrey Quilter, *The Ancient Central Andes* (New York: Routledge, 2014), p. 32; Thomas E. Weil, et al., *Area Handbook for Peru* (Washington: Government Printing Office, 1972), p. 36.

12. *The World Almanac and Book of Facts: 2014* (New York: World Almanac Books, 2014), p. 696.

13. Ellen Churchill Semple, *Influences of Geographic Environment*, p. 374.

14. Gordon F. McEwan, *The Incas*, p. 3.

15. Alan L. Kolata, *Ancient Inca* (Cambridge: Cambridge University Press, 2013), pp. 128, 129–130; Gordon F. McEwan, *The Incas*, pp. 84–85, 121–122; John H. Bodley, *Cultural Anthropology: Tribes, States, and the Global System* (Mountain View, California: Mayfield Publishing Company, 1997), pp. 215–216.

16. Ellen Churchill Semple, *Influences of Geographic Environment*, p. 419.

17. Orlando Patterson, *Slavery and Social Death: A Comparative Study* (Cambridge, Massachusetts: Harvard University Press, 1982), pp. 406–407, note 172; W. Montgomery Watt, *The Influence of Islam on Medieval Europe* (Edinburgh: Edinburgh University Press, 1972), p. 19; Bernard Lewis, *Race and Slavery in the Middle East: An Historical Enquiry* (New York: Oxford University Press, 1990), p. 11; Daniel Evans, "Slave Coast of Europe," *Slavery & Abolition*, Vol. 6, Number 1 (May 1985), p. 53, note 3.

18. Robert C. Davis, *Christian Slaves, Muslim Masters: White Slavery in the Mediterranean, the Barbary Coast, and Italy, 1500–1800* (New York: Palgrave Macmillan, 2003), p. 23.

19. Philip D. Curtin, *The Atlantic Slave Trade: A Census* (Madison: University of Wisconsin Press, 1969), pp. 72, 75, 87.

20. Jean W. Sedlar, *East Central Europe in the Middle Ages, 1000–1500* (Seattle: University of Washington Press, 1994), p. 97.

21. Ehud R. Toledano, *The Ottoman Slave Trade and Its Suppression: 1840–1890* (Princeton: Princeton University Press, 1982), pp. 18, 59, 168, 171, 188, 189.

22. R.W. Beachey, *The Slave Trade of Eastern Africa* (New York: Barnes & Noble Books, 1976), p. 182; Robert Stock, *Africa South of the Sahara: A Geographical Interpretation*, third edition (New York: The Guilford Press, 2013), pp. 179, 180; Ellen Churchill Semple, *Influences of Geographic Environment*, p. 275; Harold D. Nelson, et al., *Nigeria: A Country Study* (Washington: U.S. Government Printing Office, 1982), p. 16.

23. Martin A. Klein, "Introduction," *Breaking the Chains: Slavery, Bondage, and Emancipation in Modern Africa and Asia*, edited by Martin A. Klein (Madison: University of Wisconsin Press, 1993), p. 10; James F. Searing, *West African Slavery and Atlantic Commerce: The Senegal River Valley, 1700–1860* (Cambridge: Cambridge University Press, 1993), p. 69.

24. R.W. Beachey, *The Slave Trade of Eastern Africa*, pp. 182, 183, 189.

25. Donald L. Horowitz, *Ethnic Groups in Conflict* (Berkeley: University of California Press, 1985), p. 5.

26. Ibid., p. 76.

27. Amy Chua and Jed Rubenfeld, *The Triple Package: How Three Unlikely Traits Explain the Rise and Fall of Cultural Groups in America* (New York: The Penguin Press, 2014), p. 42.

28. Ibid., p. 43.

29. Ibid., p. 7.

30. N.J.G. Pounds, *An Historical Geography of Europe: 1800–1914*, pp. 457–458.

31. Walter Nugent, *Crossings: The Great Transatlantic Migrations, 1870–1914* (Bloomington: Indiana University Press, 1992), p. 84.

32. *Grutter v. Bollinger*, 539 U.S. 306 (2003), at 328, 329.

33. Mahathir bin Mohamad, *The Malay Dilemma* (Singapore: Asia Pacific Press, 1970), p. 25.

34. Ibid., p. 44.

35. Donald L. Horowitz, *Ethnic Groups in Conflict*, p. 226.

36. Pyong Gap Min, *Ethnic Business Enterprise: Korean Small Business in Atlanta* (New York: Center for Migration Studies, 1988), p. 104.

37. Illsoo Kim, *New Urban Immigrants: The Korean Community in New York* (Princeton: Princeton University Press, 1981), p. 114.

38. Elissa Gootman, "City to Help Curb Harassment of Asian Students at High School," *New York Times*, June 2, 2004, p. B9; Joe Williams, "New Attack at Horror HS: Top Senior Jumped at Brooklyn's Troubled Lafayette," *New York Daily News*, December 7, 2002, p. 7; Maki Becker, "Asian Students Hit in Rash of HS Attacks," *New York Daily News*, December 8, 2002, p. 7; Samuel G. Freedman, "Students and Teachers Expect a Battle in Their Visits to the Principal's Office," *New York Times*, November 22, 2006, p. B7; Kristen A. Graham and Jeff Gammage, "Two Immigrant Students Attacked at Bok," *Philadelphia Inquirer*, September 21, 2010, p. B1; Jeff Gammage and Kristen A. Graham, "Feds Find Merit in Asian Students' Claims Against Philly School," *Philadelphia Inquirer*, August 28, 2010, p. A1; Kristen A. Graham and Jeff Gammage, "Report Released on Racial Violence at S. Phila. High," *Philadelphia Inquirer*, February 24, 2010, p. A1; Kristen A. Graham, "Other Phila. Schools Handle Racial, Ethnic Tensions," *Philadelphia Inquirer*, February 4, 2010, p. A1; Kristen A. Graham and Jeff Gammage, "Attacking Immigrant Students Not New, Say Those Involved," *Philadelphia Inquirer*, December 18, 2009, p. B1; Kristen A. Graham, "Asian Students Describe Violence at South Philadelphia High," *Philadelphia Inquirer*, December 10, 2009, p. A1; Colin Flaherty, *'White Girl Bleed A Lot': The Return of Racial Violence to America and How the Media Ignore It* (Washington: WND Books, 2013), Chapter 5.

39. Myron Weiner, *Sons of the Soil: Migration and Ethnic Conflict in India* (Princeton: Princeton University Press, 1978), pp. 45–46, 102–136; Mary Fainsod Katzenstein, *Ethnicity and Equality: The Shiv Sena Party and Preferential Policies in Bombay* (Ithaca: Cornell University Press, 1979), pp. 28–29; Myron Weiner and Mary Fainsod Katzenstein, *India's Preferential Policies: Migrants, The Middle Classes, and Ethnic Equality* (Chicago: University of Chicago Press, 1981), pp. 114–115; David Marshall Lang, *The Armenians: A People in Exile* (London: George Allen and Unwin, 1981), pp. 3, 10, 37; David Lamb, *The Africans* (New York: Vintage Books, 1987), pp. 307–308; Donald L. Horowitz, *Ethnic Groups in Conflict*, pp. 46, 153, 155–156, 212–213; Donald L. Horowitz, *The Deadly Ethnic Riot* (Berkeley: University of California Press, 2001), pp. 4–5, 195, 198.

40. Larry Diamond, *Class, Ethnicity and Democracy in Nigeria: The Failure of the First Republic* (Syracuse: Syracuse University Press, 1988), p. 50.

41. Irina Livezeanu, *Cultural Politics in Greater Romania: Regionalism, Nation Building, & Ethnic Struggle, 1918–1930* (Ithaca: Cornell University Press, 1995), pp. 218–231.

42. Martin Meredith, *The First Dance of Freedom: Black Africa in the Postwar Era* (New York: Harper & Row, 1984), pp. 229–230.

43. P.T. Bauer, *Reality and Rhetoric: Studies in the Economics of Development* (London: Weidenfeld and Nicolson, 1984), p. 46.

44. Amy Chua, *World on Fire: How Exporting Free Market Democracy Breeds Ethnic Hatred and Global Instability* (New York: Doubleday, 2003), p. 50.

45. Derek Sayer, *The Coasts of Bohemia: A Czech History* (Princeton: Princeton University Press, 1998), pp. 168–169, 221–248.

46. Amy Chua, *World on Fire*, p. 4.

47. Ibid., p. 2.

48. Lord Kinross, *The Ottoman Centuries: The Rise and Fall of the Turkish Empire* (New York: William Morrow, 1977), p. 558.

49. David Marshall Lang, *The Armenians*, pp. 31, 34. A fuller account of these atrocities can be found in Ambassador Morgenthau's book *Ambassador Morgenthau's Story* (Detroit: Wayne State University Press, 2003), pp. 202–223.

50. "To Hell and Back," *The Economist*, April 5, 2014, p. 53.

51. "Devils and Enemies," *Far Eastern Economic Review*, July 7, 1994, p. 53.

52. As a Sri Lankan scholar described the situation: "In striking contrast to other parts of South Asia (including Burma), Sri Lanka in 1948 was an oasis of stability, peace and order. The transfer of power was smooth and peaceful, a reflection of the moderate tone of the dominant strand in the country's nationalist movement. More important, one saw very little of the divisions and bitterness which were tearing at the recent independence of the South Asian countries. In general, the situation in the country seemed to provide an impressive basis for a solid start in nation-building and national regeneration." K. M. de Silva, "Historical Survey," *Sri Lanka: A Survey,* ed. K. M. de Silva (Honolulu: The University Press of Hawaii, 1977), p. 84. "Sri Lanka had better prospects than most new states when independence came in 1948." Donald L. Horowitz, "A Splitting Headache," *The New Republic*, February 23, 1987, p. 33. "In general, relations among these main communities in Ceylon are cordial, unmarred by the sort of friction that exists between Hindus and Moslems in India. Except for one sad episode in 1915, racial riots have been unknown." I.D.S. Weerawardana, "Minority Problems in Ceylon," *Pacific Affairs*, Vol. 25, No. 3 (September 1, 1952), p. 279. See also Robert N. Kearney, *Communalism and Language in the Politics of Ceylon* (Durham: Duke University Press, 1967), p. 27.

53. Linda Chavez, *Out of the Barrio: Toward a New Politics of Hispanic Assimilation* (New York: Basic Books, 1991), p. 29; Rosalie Pedalino Porter, *Forked Tongue: The Politics of Bilingual Education,* second edition (New Brunswick: Transaction Publishers, 1996), pp. 33, 35.

54. Randall K.Q. Akee and Jonathan B. Taylor, *Social and Economic Change on American Indian Reservations: A Databook of the U.S. Censuses and the American Community Survey, 1990–2010* (Sarasota, Florida: Taylor Policy Group, Inc., 2014), pp. 6, 7, 16.

55. Winston S. Churchill, *A History of the English-Speaking Peoples* (London: Cassell and Company, Ltd., 1956), Vol. I, p. 31.

56. Nicholas Kristof, "Is a Hard Life Inherited?" *New York Times*, August 10, 2014, Sunday Review section, p. 1.

57. Ibid.

58. Walter E. Williams, *Race and Economics: How Much Can Be Blamed on Discrimination?* (Stanford: Hoover Institution Press, 2011), Table 3.2.

59. Nicholas Kristof, "When Whites Just Don't Get It, Part 2," *New York Times*, September 7, 2014, Sunday Review section, p. 11.

60. Stephan Thernstrom and Abigail Thernstrom, *America in Black and White: One Nation, Indivisible* (New York: Simon & Schuster, 1997), p. 238.

61. Ibid., p. 237.

62. Nicholas Eberstadt, *The Poverty of "The Poverty Rate": Measure and Mismeasure of Want in Modern America* (Washington: AEI Press, 2008), Chapter 6.

63. Robert Rector and Rachel Sheffield, "Air Conditioning, Cable TV, and an Xbox: What Is Poverty in the United States Today?" *Backgrounder*, No. 2575, Heritage Foundation, July 18, 2011, p. 10.

64. Lawrence E. Harrison, *The Pan-American Dream: Do Latin America's Cultural Values Discourage True Partnership with the United States and Canada?* (New York: Basic Books, 1997), p. 207.

65. E. Franklin Frazier, *The Negro in the United States*, revised edition (New York: The Macmillan Company, 1957), p. 166.

66. Herbert G. Gutman, *The Black Family in Slavery and Freedom, 1750–1925* (New York: Pantheon Books, 1976), pp. 455–456.

67. James P. Smith and Finis Welch, *Race Differences in Earnings: A Survey and New Evidence* (Santa Monica: Rand, 1978), p. 10.

68. Gunnar Myrdal, *An American Dilemma: The Negro Problem and Modern Democracy* (New York: Pantheon Books, 1975), Volume II, p. 950.

69. Henry Reid Hunter, *The Development of the Public Secondary Schools of Atlanta, Georgia 1845–1937* (Atlanta: Office of School System Historian, Atlanta Public Schools, 1974), pp. 51–54.

70. Stephan Thernstrom and Abigail Thernstrom, *America in Black and White*, pp. 233–234.

71. Ibid., pp. 159, 164–165.

72. Ibid., pp. 160, 162.

73. Frederick C. Luebke, *Germans in Brazil: A Comparative History of Cultural Conflict During World War I* (Baton Rouge: Louisiana State University Press, 1987), pp. 64, 66.

74. Gary B. Cohen, *The Politics of Ethnic Survival: Germans in Prague, 1861–1914*, second edition (West Lafayette: Purdue University Press, 2006), Chapters 1 and 2.

75. Lawrence J. McCaffrey, "Forging Forward and Looking Back," *The New York Irish*, edited by Ronald H. Baylor and Timothy J. Meagher (Baltimore: Johns Hopkins University Press, 1996), p. 229.

76. Stephen Steinberg, *The Ethnic Myth: Race, Ethnicity and Class in America* (Boston: Beacon Press, 1989), pp. 154, 165.

77. *The New York Irish*, edited by Ronald H. Baylor and Timothy J. Meagher, p. 562.

78. Charles Murray, *Losing Ground: American Social Policy, 1950–1980* (New York: Basic Books, 1984), pp. 116, 256.

79. Kay S. Hymowitz, "The Black Family: 40 Years of Lies," *City Journal*, Summer 2005, p. 21.

80. U.S. Bureau of the Census, *Historical Statistics of the United States: Colonial Times to 1970* (Washington: Government Printing Office, 1975), Part I, p. 135; *Economic Report of the President, 2014* (Washington: U.S. Government Printing Office, 2014), p. 380; Walter E. Williams, *Race and Economics*, pp. 42–43.

81. Jason L. Riley, *Please Stop Helping Us: How Liberals Make It Harder for Blacks to Succeed* (New York: Encounter Books, 2014), pp. 67–73.

82. See, for example, Katie DeLong, "He Thought It Was a Flash Mob: Man Caught up in Attack Outside Kroger Says He Feels Lucky He Wasn't Hurt," *Fox 6 Now* (Memphis), September 8, 2014; Therese Apel, "FBI to Assist in Allegedly Racially-Motivated West Point Beating," *The Clarion-Ledger* (Mississippi), August 27, 2014; "Family Thinks Otterbein Assault May Have Been Hate Crime," *CBS Baltimore*, August 25, 2014; Danielle Schlanger, et al., "Woman Hit in Head with Pellet Gun in Alleged Hate Crime While Walking Through Central Park," *New York Daily News*, August 23, 2014; Steve Fogarty, "North Ridgeville Police Seek 3 Males in Assault of Teenager," *Chronicle-Telegram* (Elyria, Ohio), August 14, 2014; "Indiana Man Charged in Shooting Death of Gary Police Officer," *5 NBC Chicago*, July 24, 2014; Julie Turkewitz and Jeffrey E. Singer, "Family Mourns at Site of a Fatal Beating," *New York Times*, May 13, 2014, p. A14; Mark Morales, "68-Year-Old Man Dies a Day After He Was Beaten in E. Village; Video Captured Assault as Cops Hunt Suspect," *New York Daily News*, May 11, 2014; Paris Achen, "Two Men Held in Rose Village Gun Assault," *The Columbian* (Vancouver, Washington), April 10, 2014; "White Man Beaten by Mob in Detroit After Hitting Boy with Truck: Was It a Hate Crime?" *CBS Detroit*, April 4, 2014; "Police: Man Punches People

in Face, Runs to Getaway Car," *KCCI 8 News.com* (Iowa), February 24, 2014; Ed Gallek, "Mob of Teens Attack Man in Downtown Cleveland," *19 Action News* (Cleveland, Ohio), February 11, 2014; Wayne Crenshaw, "Victim Recounts Snow Day Attack at Warner Robins High; 2 Arrests Made," *The Telegraph* (Macon, Georgia), February 5, 2014; Carlie Kollath Wells, "NOPD Makes Arrest in Connection with French Quarter Beating of Musician," *The Times-Picayune* (New Orleans), January 23, 2014; "Knock It Off," *New York Post*, December 10, 2013, p. 32; Thomas Tracy, et al., "Wild Bunch: Brooklyn Punks Pummel Couple, Scream out Slurs," *New York Daily News*, October 20, 2013, p. 13; Kaitlin Gillespie, "Police Seek Teens in Death of World War II Veteran," *The Spokesman-Review*, August 23, 2013; "Father of Teen Charged in Florida School Bus Beating Says Son Is 'Sorry'," *Fox News*, August 13, 2013; Peter Bernard, "3 Teens Charged in Pinellas School Bus Beating," *WFLA.com*, August 8, 2013; Jennifer Mann, "Man Convicted of Second-Degree Murder in St. Louis 'Knockout Game' Killing," *St. Louis Post-Dispatch*, April 10, 2013; Crimesider Staff, "Antonio Santiago Shooting: Suspects in Georgia Baby's Murder Face First Court Appearances," *CBSNews.com*, March 25, 2013; "Sauk Rapids Teen Charged as Adult in One-Punch Killing," *CBS Minnesota*, January 7, 2013; Michelle Pekarsky, "Stone Murder: Metro Squad Will Disband," *Fox 4 News Kansas City*, May 15, 2012; Laura McCallister and Betsy Webster, "Men Beat and Rob World War II Vet," *KCTV 5 News*, May 11, 2012; Michelle Washington, "A Beating at Church and Brambleton," *The Virginia Pilot*, May 1, 2012, p. B7; WKRG Staff, "Mobile Police Expect to Make Arrests in the Matthew Owens Beating Case Today," *WKRG* (Mobile-Pensacola), April 23–24, 2012; Michael Lansu, "Officials: Trayvon Case Cited in Racial Beating," *Chicago Sun-Times*, April 21, 2012, p. 2; Chad Smith, "Gainesville Beating Case Drawing National Attention," *Gainesville Sun*, April 10, 2012; Suzanne Ulbrich, "Father Searching for Answers in Son's Attack," *Daily News* (Jacksonville, North Carolina), April 7, 2012; Justin Fenton, "Viewers of Shock Video Shed Light on Baltimore Assault; Tips From Social Media Users Lead Police to Victim, Possible Suspect," *Baltimore Sun*, April 5, 2012, p. 1A; Ray Chandler, "Seneca Police Referring Assault Case to Federal Authorities," *Anderson Independent Mail* (South Carolina), March 28, 2012; Jerry Wofford, "Killing Ends 65-Year Romance," *Tulsa World*, March 20, 2012, p. A1;

Stephanie Farr, "'Geezer' Won't Let Thugs Ruin His Walks," *Philadelphia Daily News*, October 20, 2011, p. 26; "Concealing Black Hate Crimes," *Investor's Business Daily*, August 15, 2011, p. A16; Barry Paddock and John Lauinger, "Subway Gang Attack," *New York Daily News*, July 18, 2011, News, p. 3; Meg Jones, "Flynn Calls Looting, Beatings in Riverwest Barbaric," *Milwaukee Journal Sentinel*, July 6, 2011, pp. A1 ff; Joseph A. Slobodzian, "West Philly Man Pleads Guilty to 'Flash Mob' Assault," *Philadelphia Inquirer*, June 21, 2011, p. B1; Mareesa Nicosia, "Four Skidmore College Students Charged in Assault; One Charged with Felony Hate Crime," *The Saratogian*, December 22, 2010; Kristen A. Graham and Jeff Gammage, "Two Immigrant Students Attacked at Bok," *Philadelphia Inquirer*, September 21, 2010, p. B1; Jeff Gammage and Kristen A. Graham, "Feds Find Merit in Asian Students' Claims Against Philly School," *Philadelphia Inquirer*, August 28, 2010, p. A1; Alfred Lubrano, "What's Behind 'Flash Mobs'?" *Philadelphia Inquirer*, March 28, 2010, p. A1; Ian Urbina, "Mobs Are Born as Word Grows by Text Message," *New York Times*, March 25, 2010, p. A1; Kirk Mitchell, "Attacks Change Lives on All Sides," *Denver Post*, December 6, 2009, pp. A1 ff; Alan Gathright, "Black Gangs Vented Hatred for Whites in Downtown Attacks," *The DenverChannel.com*, December 5, 2009; Kirk Mitchell, "Racial Attacks Part of Trend; Gangs Videotape Knockout Punches and Sell the Videos as Entertainment, Experts Say," *Denver Post*, November 22, 2009, p. A1; Samuel G. Freedman, "Students and Teachers Expect a Battle in Their Visits to the Principal's Office," *New York Times*, November 22, 2006, p. B7; Colin Flaherty, *'White Girl Bleed A Lot'*, 2013 edition.

83. Rasmussen Reports, "More Americans View Blacks as Racist Than Whites, Hispanics," July 3, 2013; Cheryl K. Chumley, "More Americans Say Blacks More Racist Than Whites: Rasmussen Report," *Washington Times* (online), July 4, 2013; Steven Nelson, "Poll Finds Black Americans More Likely to Be Seen as Racist," *U.S. News & World Report* (online), July 3, 2013.

84. James N. Gregory, *The Southern Diaspora: How the Great Migrations of Black and White Southerners Transformed America* (Chapel Hill: University of North Carolina Press, 2005), p. 123; Isabel Wilkerson, *The Warmth of Other Suns: The Epic Story of America's Great Migration* (New York: Random House, 2010), p. 291.

85. Carl Wittke, *The Irish in America* (New York: Russell & Russell, 1970), pp. 101–102; Oscar Handlin, *Boston's Immigrants* (New York: Atheneum, 1970), pp. 169–170; Jay P. Dolan, *The Irish Americans: A History* (New York: Bloomsbury Press, 2008), pp. 118–119; Irving Howe, *World of Our Fathers* (New York: Harcourt Brace Jovanovich, 1976), pp. 229–230.

86. See, for example, David Levering Lewis, *When Harlem Was in Vogue* (New York: Penguin Books, 1997), pp. 182–183; Jervis Anderson, *This Was Harlem: A Cultural Portrait, 1900–1950* (New York: Farrar Straus Giroux, 1982), pp. 138–139.

87. Milton & Rose D. Friedman, *Two Lucky People: Memoirs* (Chicago: University of Chicago Press, 1998), p. 48.

88. Jervis Anderson, *This Was Harlem*, p. 344. As a personal note, I happened to work as a delivery boy in a grocery store near the subway station where she would have exited. Although I often worked until about midnight on Saturday nights and walked home past that subway station, I never encountered any problems there, though I weighed no more than about a hundred pounds at the time.

89. Lizette Alvarez, "Out, and Up," *New York Times*, May 31, 2009, Metropolitan section, p. 1.

90. Ibid., p. 6.

91. Walter E. Williams, *Up from The Projects: An Autobiography* (Stanford: Hoover Institution Press, 2010), pp. 6–7.

92. Ibid., p. 7.

93. Robyn Minter Smyers, "High Noon in Public Housing: The Showdown Between Due Process Rights and Good Management Practices in the War on Drugs and Crime," *The Urban Lawyer*, Summer 1998, pp. 573–574.

94. William Julius Wilson, "The Urban Underclass in Advanced Industrial Society," *The New Urban Reality*, edited by Paul E. Peterson (Washington: The Brookings Institution, 1985), p. 137.

95. Theodore Dalrymple, *Life at the Bottom: The Worldview That Makes the Underclass* (Chicago: Ivan R. Dee, 2001), p. 150.

96. Ibid., p. 164.

97. Ibid., p. 159.

98. Ibid., pp. 68–69.

99. Joyce Lee Malcolm, *Guns and Violence: The English Experience* (Cambridge, Massachusetts: Harvard University Press, 2002), p. 168.

100. Ibid., p. 209.

101. Ibid., pp. 90–91, 164–167; James Q. Wilson and Richard J. Herrnstein, *Crime and Human Nature* (New York: Simon and Schuster, 1985), pp. 409–410.

102. "A New Kind of Ghetto," *The Economist*, November 9, 2013, Special Report on Britain, p. 10.

103. Theodore Dalrymple, *Life at the Bottom*, p. 70.

104. Ibid., pp. 155–157.

105. Peter Hitchens, *The Abolition of Britain: From Winston Churchill to Princess Diana* (San Francisco: Encounter Books, 2000), Chapter 3.

106. Theodore Dalrymple, *Life at the Bottom*, pp. 155–156.

107. Michael Tanner and Charles Hughes, *The Work Versus Welfare Trade-Off: 2013* (Washington: The Cato Institute, 2013).

108. U.S. Census Bureau, "Table HINC–05. Percent Distribution of Households, by Selected Characteristics within Income Quintile and Top 5 Percent in 2010," from the *Current Population Survey*, downloaded on October 28, 2014: https://www.census.gov/hhes/www/cpstables/032011/hhinc/new05_000.htm

109. Mark Robert Rank, et al., *Chasing the American Dream: Understanding What Shapes Our Fortunes* (New York: Oxford University Press, 2014), p. 92.

110. Donald L. Horowitz, *Ethnic Groups in Conflict*, p. 180.

111. See, for example, Colin Flaherty, *'White Girl Bleed A Lot'*, 2013 edition, pp. iii, 2, 3, 5, 10, 14, 26, 28, 33, 35, 36, 91, 113, 196–197, 209.

112. Ibid., p. 113.

113. See, for example, Katie DeLong, "He Thought It Was a Flash Mob: Man Caught up in Attack Outside Kroger Says He Feels Lucky He Wasn't Hurt," *Fox 6 Now* (Memphis), September 8, 2014; Therese Apel, "FBI to Assist in Allegedly Racially-Motivated West Point Beating," *The Clarion-Ledger* (Mississippi), August 27, 2014; "Family Thinks Otterbein Assault May Have Been Hate Crime," *CBS Baltimore*, August 25, 2014; Danielle Schlanger, et al., "Woman Hit in Head with Pellet Gun in Alleged Hate Crime While Walking Through Central Park," *New York Daily News*, August 23, 2014; Steve Fogarty, "North Ridgeville Police Seek 3 Males in Assault of Teenager," *Chronicle-Telegram* (Elyria, Ohio), August 14, 2014; "Indiana Man Charged in Shooting Death of

Gary Police Officer," *5 NBC Chicago*, July 24, 2014; Julie Turkewitz and Jeffrey E. Singer, "Family Mourns at Site of a Fatal Beating," *New York Times*, May 13, 2014, p. A14; Mark Morales, "68-Year-Old Man Dies a Day After He Was Beaten in E. Village; Video Captured Assault as Cops Hunt Suspect," *New York Daily News*, May 11, 2014; Paris Achen, "Two Men Held in Rose Village Gun Assault," *The Columbian* (Vancouver, Washington), April 10, 2014; "White Man Beaten by Mob in Detroit After Hitting Boy with Truck: Was It a Hate Crime?" *CBS Detroit*, April 4, 2014; "Police: Man Punches People in Face, Runs to Getaway Car," *KCCI 8 News.com* (Iowa), February 24, 2014; Ed Gallek, "Mob of Teens Attack Man in Downtown Cleveland," *19 Action News* (Cleveland, Ohio), February 11, 2014; Wayne Crenshaw, "Victim Recounts Snow Day Attack at Warner Robins High; 2 Arrests Made," *The Telegraph* (Macon, Georgia), February 5, 2014; Carlie Kollath Wells, "NOPD Makes Arrest in Connection with French Quarter Beating of Musician," *The Times-Picayune* (New Orleans), January 23, 2014; "Knock It Off," *New York Post*, December 10, 2013, p. 32; Thomas Tracy, et al., "Wild Bunch: Brooklyn Punks Pummel Couple, Scream out Slurs," *New York Daily News*, October 20, 2013, p. 13; Kaitlin Gillespie, "Police Seek Teens in Death of World War II Veteran," *The Spokesman-Review*, August 23, 2013; "Father of Teen Charged in Florida School Bus Beating Says Son Is 'Sorry'," *Fox News*, August 13, 2013; Peter Bernard, "3 Teens Charged in Pinellas School Bus Beating," *WFLA.com*, August 8, 2013; Jennifer Mann, "Man Convicted of Second-Degree Murder in St. Louis 'Knockout Game' Killing," *St. Louis Post-Dispatch*, April 10, 2013; Crimesider Staff, "Antonio Santiago Shooting: Suspects in Georgia Baby's Murder Face First Court Appearances," *CBSNews.com*, March 25, 2013; "Sauk Rapids Teen Charged as Adult in One-Punch Killing," *CBS Minnesota*, January 7, 2013; Michelle Pekarsky, "Stone Murder: Metro Squad Will Disband," *Fox 4 News Kansas City*, May 15, 2012; Laura McCallister and Betsy Webster, "Men Beat and Rob World War II Vet," *KCTV 5 News*, May 11, 2012; Michelle Washington, "A Beating at Church and Brambleton," *The Virginia Pilot*, May 1, 2012, p. B7; WKRG Staff, "Mobile Police Expect to Make Arrests in the Matthew Owens Beating Case Today," *WKRG* (Mobile-Pensacola), April 23–24, 2012; Michael Lansu, "Officials: Trayvon Case Cited in Racial Beating," *Chicago Sun-Times*, April 21, 2012, p. 2; Chad Smith, "Gainesville Beating Case Drawing National Attention,"

Gainesville Sun, April 10, 2012; Suzanne Ulbrich, "Father Searching for Answers in Son's Attack," *Daily News* (Jacksonville, North Carolina), April 7, 2012; Justin Fenton, "Viewers of Shock Video Shed Light on Baltimore Assault; Tips From Social Media Users Lead Police to Victim, Possible Suspect," *Baltimore Sun*, April 5, 2012, p. 1A; Ray Chandler, "Seneca Police Referring Assault Case to Federal Authorities," *Anderson Independent Mail* (South Carolina), March 28, 2012; Jerry Wofford, "Killing Ends 65-Year Romance," *Tulsa World*, March 20, 2012, p. A1; Stephanie Farr, "'Geezer' Won't Let Thugs Ruin His Walks," *Philadelphia Daily News*, October 20, 2011, p. 26; "Concealing Black Hate Crimes," *Investor's Business Daily*, August 15, 2011, p. A16; Barry Paddock and John Lauinger, "Subway Gang Attack," *New York Daily News*, July 18, 2011, News, p. 3; Meg Jones, "Flynn Calls Looting, Beatings in Riverwest Barbaric," *Milwaukee Journal Sentinel*, July 6, 2011, pp. A1 ff; Joseph A. Slobodzian, "West Philly Man Pleads Guilty to 'Flash Mob' Assault," *Philadelphia Inquirer*, June 21, 2011, p. B1; Mareesa Nicosia, "Four Skidmore College Students Charged in Assault; One Charged with Felony Hate Crime," *The Saratogian*, December 22, 2010; Kristen A. Graham and Jeff Gammage, "Two Immigrant Students Attacked at Bok," *Philadelphia Inquirer*, September 21, 2010, p. B1; Jeff Gammage and Kristen A. Graham, "Feds Find Merit in Asian Students' Claims Against Philly School," *Philadelphia Inquirer*, August 28, 2010, p. A1; Alfred Lubrano, "What's Behind 'Flash Mobs'?" *Philadelphia Inquirer*, March 28, 2010, p. A1; Ian Urbina, "Mobs Are Born as Word Grows by Text Message," *New York Times*, March 25, 2010, p. A1; Kirk Mitchell, "Attacks Change Lives on All Sides," *Denver Post*, December 6, 2009, pp. A1 ff; Alan Gathright, "Black Gangs Vented Hatred for Whites in Downtown Attacks," *The DenverChannel.com*, December 5, 2009; Kirk Mitchell, "Racial Attacks Part of Trend; Gangs Videotape Knockout Punches and Sell the Videos as Entertainment, Experts Say," *Denver Post*, November 22, 2009, p. A1; Samuel G. Freedman, "Students and Teachers Expect a Battle in Their Visits to the Principal's Office," *New York Times*, November 22, 2006, p. B7; Colin Flaherty, *'White Girl Bleed A Lot'*, 2013 edition.

114. Colin Flaherty, *'White Girl Bleed A Lot'*, 2013 edition, pp. 6, 14–15, 77, 83–84, 89, 94, 109, 133, 173–174, 178–179, 202, 203, 206.
115. See, for example, Ibid., pp. i, iv, 3, 7–8, 84–85, 88, 95, 112, 192, 220.

116. "Concealing Black Hate Crimes," *Investor's Business Daily*, August 15, 2011, p. A16.

117. See, for example, "Brooklyn Rabbi: Gang of Teens Playing Disturbing Game Of 'Knock Out The Jew'," *CBS New York*, November 12, 2013; Thomas Tracy, "Jews Target of Twisted Street Game," *New York Daily News*, November 13, 2013, p. 45; "Knock It Off," *New York Post*, December 10, 2013, p. 32; Colin Flaherty, *'White Girl Bleed A Lot'*, 2013 edition, pp. 144–145, 151, 330.

118. Colin Flaherty, *'White Girl Bleed A Lot'*, 2013 edition, Chapter 2.

119. See, for example, Norman M. Naimark, *Fires of Hatred: Ethnic Cleansing in Twentieth-Century Europe* (Cambridge, Massachusetts: Harvard University Press, 2001), pp. 117–119; R.M. Douglas, *Orderly and Humane: The Expulsion of the Germans After the Second World War* (New Haven: Yale University Press, 2012), pp. 96–97; Derek Sayer, *The Coasts of Bohemia*, p. 243.

120. See William McGowan, *Only Man Is Vile: The Tragedy of Sri Lanka* (New York: Farrar, Straus and Giroux, 1992).

121. Donald L. Horowitz, *The Deadly Ethnic Riot*, pp. 19–20.

Chapter 6: Implications and Prospects

1. Alan Greenspan, *The Age of Turbulence: Adventures in a New World* (New York: Penguin Press, 2007), p. 95.

2. P.T. Bauer, *Equality, the Third World and Economic Delusion* (Cambridge, Massachusetts: Harvard University Press, 1981), p. 23.

3. Daron Acemoglu and James A. Robinson, *Why Nations Fail: The Origins of Power, Prosperity, and Poverty* (New York: Crown Business, 2012), pp. 1–2.

4. Darrel Hess, *McKnight's Physical Geography: A Landscape Appreciation*, eleventh edition (Upper Saddle River, New Jersey: Pearson Education, 2014), p. 200.

5. Daron Acemoglu and James A. Robinson, *Why Nations Fail*, p. 428.

6. "Class and the American Dream," *New York Times*, May 30, 2005, p. A14.

7. E.J. Dionne, Jr., "Political Stupidity, U.S. Style," *Washington Post*, July 29, 2010, p. A23.

8. Peter Corning, *The Fair Society: The Science of Human Nature and the Pursuit of Social Justice* (Chicago: University of Chicago Press, 2011), p. ix.

9. W. Michael Cox and Richard Alm, "By Our Own Bootstraps: Economic Opportunity & the Dynamics of Income Distribution," *Annual Report 1995*, Federal Reserve Bank of Dallas, p. 8.

10. Ibid.

11. "Movin' On Up," *Wall Street Journal*, November 13, 2007, p. A24; U.S. Department of the Treasury, "Income Mobility in the U.S. from 1996 to 2005," November 13, 2007, p. 9.

12. Niels Veldhuis, et al., "The 'Poor' Are Getting Richer," *Fraser Forum*, January/February 2013, p. 25.

13. Armine Yalnizyan, *The Rise of Canada's Richest 1%* (Ottawa: Canadian Centre for Policy Alternatives, December 2010).

14. Thomas Piketty, *Capital in the Twenty-First Century* (Cambridge, Massachusetts: Harvard University Press, 2014), p. 252.

15. Thomas A. Hirschl and Mark R. Rank, "The Social Dynamics of Economic Polarization: Exploring the Life Course Probabilities of Top-Level Income Attainment," Paper presented at the 2014 Annual Meetings of the Population Association of America, Boston, May 1–4, 2014, p. 8; Mark R. Rank, "From Rags to Riches to Rags," *New York Times*, April 20, 2014, Sunday Review, p. 9.

16. Thomas A. Hirschl and Mark R. Rank, "The Social Dynamics of Economic Polarization: Exploring the Life Course Probabilities of Top-Level Income Attainment," Paper presented at the 2014 Annual Meetings of the Population Association of America, Boston, May 1–4, 2014, p. 13.

17. Paul Krugman, "Rich Man's Recovery," *New York Times*, September 13, 2013, p. A25.

18. U.S. Department of the Treasury, "Income Mobility in the U.S. from 1996 to 2005," November 13, 2007, p. 4.

19. Thomas Piketty, *Capital in the Twenty-First Century*, pp. 253, 254.

20. Ibid., pp. 252, 301.

21. U.S. Department of the Treasury, "Income Mobility in the U.S. from 1996 to 2005," November 13, 2007, pp. 2, 4.

22. Ibid., p. 7.

23. Ibid., pp. 2, 4.

24. Ibid., p. 11.

25. Internal Revenue Service, "The 400 Individual Income Tax Returns Reporting the Highest Adjusted Gross Incomes Each Year, 1992–2000," *Statistics of Income Bulletin*, Spring 2003, Publication 1136 (Revised 6–03), p. 7.

26. Joseph A. Schumpeter, *History of Economic Analysis* (New York: Oxford University Press, 1954), p. 529.

27. Thomas Piketty, *Capital in the Twenty-First Century*, pp. 473, 507; Robert A. Wilson, "Personal Exemptions and Individual Income Tax Rates, 1913–2002," *Statistics of Income Bulletin*, Spring 2002, p. 219.

28. Eugene Robinson, "The Fight-Back Plan," *Washington Post*, September 20, 2011, p. A17.

29. Carmen DeNavas-Walt and Robert W. Cleveland, "Money Income in the United States: 2001," *Current Population Reports*, P60–218 (Washington: U.S. Bureau of the Census, 2002), p. 19.

30. U.S. Census Bureau, "Table HINC–05. Percent Distribution of Households, by Selected Characteristics within Income Quintile and Top 5 Percent in 2010," from the Current Population Survey, downloaded on October 28, 2014: https://www.census.gov/hhes/www/cpstables/032011/hhinc/new05_000.htm

31. Charles Murray, *Human Accomplishment: The Pursuit of Excellence in the Arts and Sciences, 800 B.C. to 1950* (New York: Harper Collins, 2003), p. 298.

32. Ibid., pp. 304, 305.

33. Ibid., p. 98.

34. Ibid., pp. 97–100.

35. James Corrigan, "Woods in the Mood to End His Major Drought," *Daily Telegraph* (London), August 5, 2013, pp. 16–17.

36. Charles Murray, *Human Accomplishment*, p. 102.

37. John Powers, "Kenya's Domination in Marathons Has Raised the Level of Running Excellence, and the Rest of the Field Is Still Having a Hard Time Catching Up," *Boston Globe*, April 12, 2013, p. C2.

38. Joseph White, "A 1st in 52 Years: Co-champs at the Spelling Bee," The Associated Press, May 30, 2014.

39. *Sports Illustrated Almanac 2013* (New York: Sports Illustrated Books, 2012), pp. 69, 78.

40. *The Chronicle of Higher Education: Almanac 2014–2015*, August 22, 2014, p. 45.

41. Ibid.

42. U.S. News & World Report, *America's Best Colleges*, 2010 edition (Washington: U.S. News & World Report, 2009), pp. 137, 140, 191.

43. Mohamed Suffian bin Hashim, "Problems and Issues of Higher Education Development in Malaysia," *Development of Higher Education in Southeast Asia: Problems and Issues*, edited by Yip Yat Hoong (Singapore: Regional Institute of Higher Education and Development, 1973), Table 8, pp. 70–71.

44. Previous lists of statistical disparities in outcomes have appeared in such previous books of mine as *The Vision of the Anointed: Self-Congratulation as a Basis for Social Policy* (New York: Basic Books, 1995), pp. 35–37 and *Intellectuals and Society*, second edition (New York: Basic Books, 2012), pp. 116–119. Isolated examples have appeared in *Conquests and Cultures: An International History* (New York: Basic Books, 1998), pp. 125, 210, 217; *Migrations and Cultures: A World View* (New York: Basic Books, 1996), pp. 4, 17, 31, 57, 123, 130, 135, 152, 154, 157, 176, 179, 193, 196, 211, 265, 277, 278, 289, 297, 298, 300, 320, 345–346, 353–354, 355, 358, 366, 372–373.

45. Thomas A. Hirschl and Mark R. Rank, "The Social Dynamics of Economic Polarization: Exploring the Life Course Probabilities of Top-Level Income Attainment," Paper presented at the 2014 Annual Meetings of the Population Association of America, Boston, May 1–4, 2014, p. 13.

46. Alan Reynolds, *Income and Wealth* (Westport, Connecticut: Greenwood Press, 2006), pp. 27–28.

47. John Rawls, *A Theory of Justice* (Cambridge, Massachusetts: Harvard University Press, 1971), p. 73.

48. Ibid., p. 74.

49. Ibid., pp. 79–80.

50. Ibid., pp. 75–78.

51. Ibid., pp. 79–80, 82–83.

52. Ibid., pp. 4, 302, 303.

53. James M. McPherson, *The Abolitionist Legacy: From Reconstruction to the NAACP* (Princeton: Princeton University Press, 1975), p. 198.

54. Alexis de Tocqueville, *Democracy in America*, edited by J.P. Mayer and Max Lerner (New York: Harper & Row, 1966), p. 485.

55. Edward C. Banfield, *The Moral Basis of a Backward Society* (New York: The Free Press, 1958), pp. 19, 20, 76.

56. Nicholas Eberstadt, *Russia's Peacetime Demographic Crisis: Dimensions, Causes, Implications* (Seattle: National Bureau of Asian Research, 2010), p. 259.

57. Stephan Thernstrom and Abigail Thernstrom, *America in Black and White: One Nation, Indivisible* (New York: Simon and Schuster, 1997), pp. 233–234.

58. *The World Almanac and Book of Facts: 2013* (New York: World Almanac Books, 2013), pp. 748, 770, 771, 796, 806, 818, 821, 832, 839, 846; U.S. Census Bureau, "S0201: Selected Population Profile in the United States, 2013 American Community Survey 1-Year Estimates, downloaded from the Census website on November 10, 2014:

    http://factfinder2.census.gov/faces/tableservices/jsf/pages/productview.xhtml?
    pid=ACS_13_1YR_S0201&prodType=table

59. Rupert B. Vance, *Human Geography of the South: A Study in Regional Resources and Human Adequacy* (Chapel Hill: University of North Carolina Press, 1932), p. 463.

60. See, for example, P.T. Bauer, *Equality, the Third World and Economic Delusion*, Chapters 5, 6, 7; William Easterly, *The White Man's Burden: Why the West's Efforts to Aid the Rest Have Done So Much Ill and So Little Good* (New York: Penguin Press, 2006).

61. Lawrence E. Harrison, *Underdevelopment Is a State of Mind: The Latin American Case* (Cambridge, Massachusetts: The Center for International Affairs, Harvard University, 1985), p. 103.

62. *The World Almanac and Book of Facts: 2014* (New York: World Almanac Books, 2014), pp. 750, 754.

63. Robert F. Foerster, *The Italian Emigration of Our Times* (New York: Arno Press, 1969), p. 236; Carl Solberg, *Immigration and Nationalism: Argentina and Chile, 1890–1914* (Austin: University of Texas Press, 1970), p. 38.

64. Robert F. Foerster, *The Italian Emigration of Our Times*, p. 230.

65. Ibid., p. 243.

66. Fred C. Koch, *The Volga Germans: In Russia and the Americas, from 1763 to the Present* (University Park: Pennsylvania State University Press, 1977), p. 227; Timothy J. Kloberdanz, "Plainsmen of Three Continents: Volga German Adaptation to Steppe, Prairie, and Pampa," *Ethnicity on the Great Plains,* edited by Frederick C. Luebke (Lincoln: University of Nebraska Press, 1980), pp. 66–67.

67. Carl Solberg, *Immigration and Nationalism*, p. 51.

68. Robert F. Foerster, *The Italian Emigration of Our Times*, p. 261.

69. Mark Jefferson, *Peopling the Argentine Pampa* (New York: American Geographical Society, 1926), p. 1.

70. Carl Solberg, *Immigration and Nationalism*, pp. 49–50.

71. Robert F. Foerster, *The Italian Emigration of Our Times*, pp. 254–259.

72. Carl E. Solberg, "Peopling the Prairies and the Pampas: The Impact of Immigration on Argentine and Canadian Agrarian Development, 1870–1930," *Journal of Interamerican Studies and World Affairs*, Vol. 24, No. 2 (May 1982), pp. 136, 152; Gloria Totoricagüena, *Basque Diaspora: Migration and Transnational Identity* (Reno: Center for Basque Studies, University of Nevada, 2005), pp. 171, 180. See also Lawrence E. Harrison, *The Pan-American Dream: Do Latin America's Cultural Values Discourage True Partnership with the United States and Canada?* (New York: Basic Books, 1997), p. 151.

73. Adam Giesinger, *From Catherine to Krushchev: The Story of Russia's Germans* (Winnipeg, Manitoba, Canada: Adam Giesinger, 1974), p. 229; Fred C. Koch, *The Volga Germans*, pp. 222, 224.

74. Fred C. Koch, *The Volga Germans*, pp. 226, 227.

75. "A Century of Decline," *The Economist*, February 15, 2014, p. 20.

76. Seymour Martin Lipset, *Revolution and Counterrevolution: Change and Persistence in Social Structures* (New York: Basic Books, 1968), pp. 90–91; Emilio Willems, "Brazil," *The Positive Contribution by Immigrants*, edited by Oscar Handlin (Paris: United Nations Educational, Scientific and Cultural Organization, 1955), p. 133.

77. Jean Roche, *La Colonisation Allemande et le Rio Grande do Sul* (Paris: Institut Des Hautes Études de L'Amérique Latine, 1959), pp. 388–389.

78. Gabriel Paquette, *Imperial Portugal in the Age of Atlantic Revolutions: The Luso-Brazilian World, c. 1770–1850* (Cambridge: Cambridge University Press, 2013), p. 80; Carl E. Solberg, "Peopling the Prairies and the Pampas: The Impact of Immigration on Argentine and Canadian Agrarian Development, 1870–1930," *Journal of Interamerican Studies and World Affairs*, Vol. 24, No. 2 (May 1982), pp. 131–161; Adam Giesinger, *From Catherine to Krushchev*, p. 229; Frederick C. Luebke, *Germans in the New World: Essays in the History of Immigration* (Urbana: University of Illinois Press, 1990), pp. 94, 96.

79. Warren Dean, *The Industrialization of São Paolo: 1880–1945* (Austin: University of Texas Press, 1969), p. 35.

80. Carl Solberg, *Immigration and Nationalism*, Chapter 1; George F. W. Young, "Bernardo Philippi, Initiator of German Colonization in Chile," *Hispanic American Historical Review*, Vol. 51, No. 3 (August 1971), p. 490; Fred C. Koch, *The Volga Germans*, pp. 231–233.

81. Fernand Braudel, *A History of Civilizations*, translated by Richard Mayne (New York: Penguin Books, 1993), p. 440.

82. J.F. Normano and Antonello Gerbi, *The Japanese in South America: An Introductory Survey with Special Reference to Peru* (New York: The John Day Company, 1943), pp. 38–39.

83. C. Harvey Gardiner, *The Japanese and Peru: 1873–1973* (Albuquerque: University of New Mexico Press, 1975), p. 25; J.F. Normano and Antonello Gerbi, *The Japanese in South America*, p. 70.

84. C. Harvey Gardiner, *The Japanese and Peru*, pp. 62, 64; Toraji Irie and William Himel, "History of Japanese Migration to Peru, Part II," *Hispanic American Historical Review*, Vol. 31, No. 4 (November 1951), p. 662.

85. C. Harvey Gardiner, *The Japanese and Peru*, pp. 61–62.

86. William R. Long, "New Pride for *Nikkei* in Peru," *Los Angeles Times*, April 28, 1995, p. A1.

87. Pablo Macera and Shane J. Hunt, "Peru," *Latin America: A Guide to Economic History, 1830–1930*, edited by Roberto Cortés Conde and Stanley J. Stein (Berkeley: University of California Press, 1977), p. 566.

88. C. Harvey Gardiner, *The Japanese and Peru*, p. 68; J.F. Normano and Antonello Gerbi, *The Japanese in South America*, pp. 109–110.

89. C. Harvey Gardiner, *The Japanese and Peru*, p. 68.

90. J.F. Normano and Antonello Gerbi, *The Japanese in South America*, pp. 77, 113–114.

91. Carl Solberg, *Immigration and Nationalism*, p. 63.

92. Seymour Martin Lipset, "Values, Education, and Entrepreneurship," *Elites in Latin America*, edited by Seymour Martin Lipset and Aldo Solari (New York: Oxford University Press, 1967), pp. 24–25.

93. Jaime Vicens Vives, "The Decline of Spain in the Seventeenth Century," *The Economic Decline of Empires*, edited by Carlo M. Cipolla (London: Methuen & Co., 1970), p. 127.

94. Norman R. Stewart, *Japanese Colonization in Eastern Paraguay* (Washington: National Academy of Sciences, 1967), p. 153.

95. Harry Leonard Sawatzky, *They Sought a Country: Mennonite Colonization in Mexico* (Berkeley: University of California Press, 1971), p. 365.

96. Lawrence E. Harrison, *The Pan-American Dream*, p. 83.

97. Joseph Stiglitz, "Equal Opportunity, Our National Myth," *New York Times*, February 17, 2013, Sunday Review, p. 4.

98. Jason L. Riley, *Please Stop Helping Us: How Liberals Make It Harder for Blacks to Succeed* (New York: Encounter Books, 2014), p. 49.

99. John U. Ogbu, *Black American Students in an Affluent Suburb: A Study of Academic Disengagement* (Mahwah, New Jersey: Lawrence Erlbaum Associates, 2003), pp. 23–31.

100. See, for example, Diana Furchtgott-Roth and Christine Stolba, *Women's Figures: An Illustrated Guide to the Economic Progress of Women in America* (Washington: The A.E.I. Press, 1999), Part II; Thomas Sowell, *Economic Facts and Fallacies*, second edition (New York: Basic Books, 2011), Chapter 3.

101. "The Economic Role of Women," *The Economic Report of the President, 1973* (Washington: U.S. Government Printing Office, 1973), p. 105.

102. For statistical data, see Table 1 in my *Affirmative Action Reconsidered: Was It Necessary in Academia?* (Washington: American Enterprise Institute, 1975), p. 16.

103. Donald Harman Akenson, "Diaspora, the Irish and Irish Nationalism," *The Call of the Homeland: Diaspora Nationalisms, Past and Present*, edited by Allon Gal, et al (Leiden: Brill, 2010), pp. 190–191.

104. Karyn R. Lacy, *Blue-Chip Black: Race, Class, and Status in the New Black Middle Class* (Berkeley: University of California Press, 2007), pp. 66–68, 77; Mary Pattillo-McCoy, *Black Picket Fences: Privilege and Peril Among the Black Middle Class* (Chicago: University of Chicago Press, 1999), p. 12.

105. Donald R. Snodgrass, *Inequality and Economic Development in Malaysia* (Kuala Lumpur: Oxford University Press, 1980), p. 4.

106. Amy L. Freedman, "The Effect of Government Policy and Institutions on Chinese Overseas Acculturation: The Case of Malaysia," *Modern Asian Studies*, Vol. 35, No. 2 (May 2001), p. 416.

107. Michael Ornstein, *Ethno-Racial Inequality in the City of Toronto: An Analysis of the 1996 Census*, May 2000, p. ii.

108. Charles H. Young and Helen R.Y. Reid, *The Japanese Canadians* (Toronto: University of Toronto Press, 1938), pp. 9–10, 49, 53, 58, 76, 120, 129, 130, 145, 172; Tomoko Makabe, "The Theory of the Split Labor Market: A Comparison of the Japanese Experience in Brazil and Canada," *Social Forces*, Vol. 59, No. 3 (March 1981), p. 807, note 1.

109. John A. A. Ayoade, "Ethnic Management of the 1979 Nigerian Constitution," *Canadian Review of Studies in Nationalism*, Spring 1987, p. 127.

110. Burton W. Folsom, Jr., *The Myth of the Robber Barons: A New Look at the Rise of Big Business in America*, sixth edition (Herndon, Virginia: Young America's Foundation, 2010), pp. 83–92.

111. Rob Kling, "Information Technologies and the Shifting Balance between Privacy and Social Control," *Computerization and Controversy: Value Conflicts and Social Choices*, second edition, edited by Rob Kling (New York: Academic Press, 1996), p. 617. See also Marvin Cetron and Owen Davies, *Probable Tomorrows: How Science and Technology Will Transform Our Lives in the Next Twenty Years* (New York: St. Martin's Press, 1997), p. x.

112. Richard A. Epstein, *Overdose: How Excessive Government Regulation Stifles Pharmaceutical Innovation* (New Haven: Yale University Press, 2006), p. 15.

Epilogue

1. Paul Krugman, *The Conscience of a Liberal* (New York: W.W. Norton & Company, 2007), p. 11.

2. Sally C. Pipes, *The Top Ten Myths of American Health Care: A Citizen's Guide* (San Francisco: Pacific Research Institute, 2008), p. 9.

3. A condensed, documented account of this process can be found in the essay, "The Real History of Slavery" in my *Black Rednecks and White Liberals* (San Francisco: Encounter Books, 2005).

4. Charles Murray, *Losing Ground: American Social Policy, 1950–1980* (New York: Basic Books, 1984), pp. 116, 256.

5. U.S. Census Bureau, *Historical Statistics of the United States: Colonial Times to 1957* (Washington: U.S. Government Printing Office, 1960), p. 72; U.S. Census Bureau, *Statistical Abstract of the United States: 1984* (Washington: U.S. Government Printing Office, 1983), p. 407; U.S. Bureau of Labor Statistics, *Labor Force Characteristics by Race and Ethnicity, 2013*, Report 1050 (August 2014), p. 14.

6. The years were 1953 through 1959. *Sports Illustrated Almanac 2015* (New York: Sports Illustrated Books, 2014), pp. 44–45.

7. Ibid., p. 50.

8. *The Baseball Encyclopedia*, ninth edition (New York: The Macmillan Company, 1993), pp. 770, 829, 1034–1035, 1053, 1491.

9. Ibid., pp. 776, 783, 1086, 1090, 1216, 1313, 1315.

10. Ibid., p. 2074; T. Wendel, "Joe McGinnity," The National Baseball Hall of Fame and Museum, *The Hall: A Celebration of Baseball's Greats in Stories and Images, The Complete Roster of Inductees* (New York: Little, Brown and Company, 2014), p. 22.

11. Malcolm Macfarlane, *Bing Crosby: Day by Day* (Lanham, Maryland: The Scarecrow Press, 2001), p. 358.

12. Joel Whitburn, *The Billboard Book of Top 40 Hits*, revised and expanded ninth edition (New York: Billboard Books, 2010), p. 870.

13. Robert G. Barrier, "Only the Game Was Real: The Aesthetics and Significance of Re-created Baseball Broadcasting," *Baseball/Literature/Culture: Essays, 2006–2007*, edited by Ronald E. Kates and Warren Tormey (Jefferson, North Carolina: McFarland & Company, 2008), pp. 41–42; John E. DiMeglio, "Baseball," *Encyclopedia of Southern Culture*, edited by Charles Reagan Wilson and William Ferris (Chapel Hill: University of North Carolina Press, 1989), pp. 1210–1211.

14. James S. Gardner, et al., "People in the Mountains," *Mountain Geography: Physical and Human Dimensions*, edited by Martin F. Price, et al (Berkeley: University of California Press, 2013), pp. 288–289.

15. J.R. McNeill, *The Mountains of the Mediterranean World: An Environmental History* (New York: Cambridge University Press, 1992), pp. 223, 225–227.

16. Don Funnell and Romola Parish, *Mountain Environments and Communities* (London: Routledge, 2001), p. 157.

17. Ellen Churchill Semple, *Influences of Geographic Environment* (New York: Henry Holt and Company, 1911), p. 579.

18. Don Funnell and Romola Parish, *Mountain Environments and Communities*, p. 170.

19. Arthur Hu, "Minorities Need More Support," *The Tech*, March 17, 1987, pp. 4, 6.

20. Robert A. McGuire and Philip R.P. Coelho, *Parasites, Pathogens, and Progress: Diseases and Economic Development* (Cambridge, Massachusetts: MIT Press, 2011), pp. 1–2.

21. "To Each According to His Abilities," *The Economist*, June 2, 2001, p. 39.

22. Weiying Zhang, *The Logic of the Market: An Insider's View of Chinese Economic Reform*, translated by Matthew Dale (Washington: Cato Institute, 2015), p. 126.

23. Jeffrey D. Sachs, *Common Wealth: Economics for a Crowded Planet* (New York: Penguin Press, 2008), pp. 162–163.

24. Milton & Rose Friedman, *Free to Choose: A Personal Statement* (New York: Harcourt Brace Jovanovich, 1980), p. 147.

25. David S. Landes, *The Wealth and Poverty of Nations: Why Some Are So Rich and Some So Poor* (New York: W.W. Norton & Company, 1998), pp. xvii–xviii.

26. Leon Volovici, *Nationalist Ideology and Antisemitism: The Case of Romanian Intellectuals in the 1930s*, translated by Charles Kormos (Oxford: Pergamon Press, 1991), p. 6.

27. Donald L. Horowitz, *Ethnic Groups in Conflict* (Berkeley: University of California Press, 1985), p. 117.

28. Ibid., p. 118.

29. Mary Fainsod Katzenstein, *Ethnicity and Equality: The Shiv Sena Party and Preferential Policies in Bombay* (Ithaca: Cornell University Press, 1979), pp. 137–138.

30. Donald L. Horowitz, *Ethnic Groups in Conflict*, pp. 117–118.

31. Yash Tandon, *Problems of a Displaced Minority: The New Position of East Africa's Asians* (London: Minority Rights Group, 1973), p. 15; C. Harvey Gardiner, *The Japanese and Peru: 1873–1973* (Albuquerque: University of New Mexico Press, 1975), pp. 67–68; J.F. Normano and Antonello Gerbi, *The*

Japanese in South America: An Introductory Survey with Special Reference to Peru (New York: The John Day Company, 1943), pp. 109–110.

32. Donald L. Horowitz, *Ethnic Groups in Conflict*, p. 122.
33. Ibid., pp. 113–114.

INDEX

INDEX